The Treasure of the San José

The Treasure of the San José

Death at Sea in the War of the Spanish Succession

CARLA RAHN PHILLIPS

The Johns Hopkins University Press

Baltimore

This book has been brought to publication with the generous assistance of the Program for Cultural Cooperation between Spain's Ministry of Culture and United States Universities.

The Johns Hopkins University Press
2715 North Charles Street
Baltimore, Maryland 21218-4363
www.press.jhu.edu

Library of Congress Cataloging-in-Publication Data
Phillps, Carla Rahn, 1943–
The treasure of the San José : death at sea in the War of the Spanish Succession / Carla Rahn Phillips.
p.   cm.
Includes bibliographical references and index.
ISBN-13: 978-0-8018-8580-8 (alk. paper)
ISBN-10: 0-8018-8580-9 (alk. paper)
1. San José (Galleon) 2. Spanish Succession, War of, 1701–1714—Naval operations, Spanish. 3. Spanish Succession, War of, 1701–1714—Atlantic Ocean. 4. Shipwrecks—Colombia—Barú Island. I. Title.
D282.P55 2007
940.2′526—dc22   2006025983

A catalog record for this book is available from the British Library.

CONTENTS

ACKNOWLEDGMENTS

This project began in May 1989 with an unexpected invitation to join a group of scholars and museum professionals on a trip to Colombia under the auspices of the J. Paul Getty Museum in Los Angeles. For several days we met with officials of the Colombian government in Bogotá and Cartagena to discuss the possible salvage and conservation of an early-eighteenth-century shipwreck, which the government hoped would serve as the centerpiece of a maritime museum. After returning home, I decided to pursue the history of that ship from its origins in Spain to its demise in Colombia.

Over the years since then, several individuals and institutions have supported my research and writing, and I am grateful to them all. In addition to the initial trip to Colombia, funded by the Getty Museum, several of my research trips to Spain were supported by the Graduate School and the McMillan Travel Fund at the University of Minnesota. Grants from the Graduate School allowed me to hire a succession of graduate students to aid in the location and transcription of archival documents. They included Amy Brown, JoEllen Campbell, Patricia J. Kulishek, Lawrence V. Mott, and Allyson Poska, all of whom helped to move this complicated project along faster than I could have done alone. The university and the Bush Foundation supported a sabbatical in 2000–2001 that allowed me to complete most of the research and writing for this book. And in 2003 I was able to spend five months at the John Carter Brown Library, at Brown University, as the Andrew W. Mellon Senior Fellow.

The professional staffs of archives and libraries in Spain and England helped me to make the most of my limited visits to their excellent collections. Scholars sometimes joke that the best archival catalogs have two legs. That remains true in the age of the Internet. Important archival information about the commander of the *San José*, the first Count of Casa Alegre, also came my way from Don Javier de Solís, the current holder of that title. On numerous occasions he sent me transcriptions of documents from his family's archive, as well as items I had overlooked at the Archive of the Indies and illustrations from rare books in his family's library. The documentation for this book is much richer because of his generosity.

And finally, my husband, William D. Phillips, provided unstinting support and sound advice about this project from beginning to end, in the process hearing much more about the maritime history of Spain than I suspect he really wanted to know. I cannot imagine a more ideal traveling companion on this particular scholarly voyage of discovery, or any other.

AGI, CD	Archivo General de Indias, Seville, Contaduría
AGI, CT	Archivo General de Indias, Seville, Contratación
AGI, ESC	Archivo General de Indias, Seville, Escribanía
AGI, IG	Archivo General de Indias, Seville, Indiferente General
AGI, Lima	Archivo General de Indias, Lima
AGI, Santa Fe	Archivo General de Indias, Santa Fe
AGM	Archivo General de Marina, Madrid
AGS	Archive General de Simancas, Simancas (Valladolid)
AHN, Estado	Archivo Histórico Nacional, Madrid, Estado
AHN, OM	Archivo Histórico Nacional, Madrid, Ordenes Militares
BL	British Library, London
PRO	Public Record Office, London
PRO, ADM	Public Record Office, Admiralty

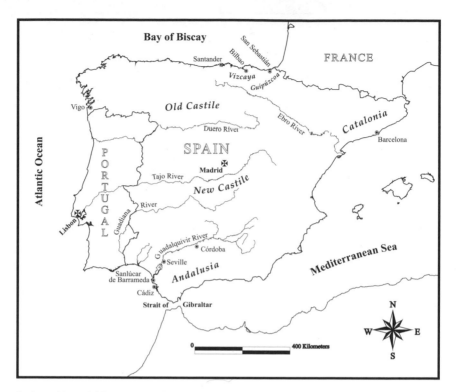

Spain and its neighbors in 1700. Lawrence V. Mott

The oceanic connections between Spain and its American empire in 1700. Lawrence V. Mott

From the Gulf of Mexico to Peru, the main area of concern for Spanish viceroys in 1700.
Lawrence V. Mott

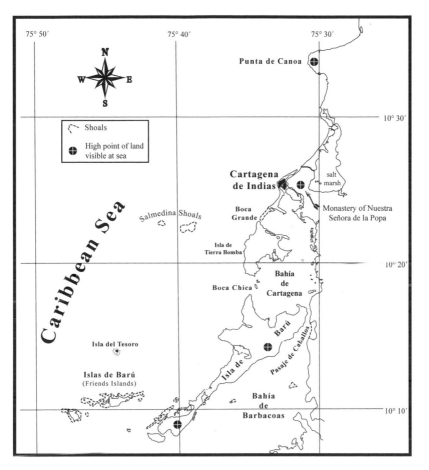

Cartagena de Indias and its immediate area. Lawrence V. Mott

The Treasure of the San José

Introduction

In his powerful tale of life and loss *Love in the Time of Cholera* the Colombian author Gabriel García Márquez refers to a famous shipwreck near Cartagena de Indias:

> Several times a year, fleets of galleons carrying the treasures of Potosí, Quito, and Veracruz gathered in the bay, and the city lived its years of glory. On Friday, June 8, 1708, at four o'clock in the afternoon, the galleon *San José* set sail for Cádiz with a cargo of precious stones and metals valued at five hundred billion *pesos* in the currency of the day; it was sunk by an English squadron at the entrance to the port, and two long centuries later it had not yet been salvaged. That treasure lying in its bed of coral, and the corpse of the commander floating sideways on the bridge, were evoked by historians as an emblem of the city drowned in memories.[1]

Stories of lost riches can exercise a powerful force on the human imagination centuries later, whether or not they are true. In this case the loss evoked by García Márquez was quite true, as were the date and the statement that the *San José* sank while confronting an English adversary. Nearly every other detail in the author's haunting passage is false, belied by the historical record. Rather than focusing on the historical record, García Márquez chose to focus on the historical memory of his countrymen. Many contemporaries on both sides of the battle believed that the *San José* carried vast quantities of gold, silver, and other treasure, destined for the Bourbon government in Madrid and for merchants and other private parties. Although parts of the battle occurred within sight of the coast, the wreck of the *San José* has not yet been found. The memory of untold riches just beyond human reach therefore substitutes for history in the collective imagination of Colombians and of others interested in sunken galleons from the heyday of the Spanish empire.

For more than two hundred years galleons provided much of the defense for the merchant fleets traveling between Spain and its American empire. Galleons also carried most of the registered treasure transported back to Spain as mercantile profit and tax revenue for the crown. In the last two centuries of the Spanish empire in the Western Hemisphere other types of ships replaced galleons in the fleets, if not in the popular imagination. The *San José* was built at the end of the seventeenth century, in other words, near the end of the age of galleons. The ship remains famous, not for its design, however, nor even for its distinguished career in Spain's transatlantic fleet system, but for the circumstances of its loss.

Gold and silver from the Indies, in addition to sustaining mercantile activities in Europe, provided revenues for the Spanish monarchy. During most of the sixteenth century about 20–30 percent of the registered bullion that crossed the Atlantic belonged to the Spanish crown, raised primarily from a tax called the "royal fifth" on gold, silver, and other treasure, plus fees for assay and coinage. Ecclesiastical taxes given to the crown by the Roman Catholic Church, penalties and condemnations for smuggling, revenue from the sale of offices, and various minor taxes also added to the royal share. Although revenue from the New World was rarely more than 20 percent of the Spanish government's income and averaged about half that, the ambitious foreign policy of Spain in Europe during the sixteenth, seventeenth, and eighteenth centuries could not have been sustained without it.

International politics formed the background to the construction of the *San José* and other warships through the four centuries that Spain's empire lasted in the Americas. International politics also formed the background to the dramatic demise of the *San José* and explains why the ship was believed to carry so vast a quantity of treasure in 1708. In 1700 the Habsburg dynasty of Spain died out, and a French Bourbon inherited the throne as Philip V (fig. 1). The War of the Spanish Succession, which began in 1701, pitted the Bourbons of France, under Louis XIV (fig. 2), and Spain against most of the rest of Europe, which feared their combined power. Although the war took place largely in Europe, it had a global aspect as well, as England and her allies tried to break into the Spanish empire. The war lasted until 1714. When the dust cleared, the Bourbon dynasty was firmly seated on both the French and Spanish thrones, but the Spanish navy had been all but destroyed and the empire had been seriously shaken. It would take the combined talents of generations of skilled bureaucrats in the eighteenth century to reestablish Spain as a naval presence and to strengthen royal control over the Spanish empire in the Americas.

Curiously, as famous as the *San José* is in certain circles—even today—it is nearly invisible in serious historiography about Spanish maritime history. Numerous general histories of the eighteenth-century navy, as well as specific scholarly works devoted to the war of succession in several languages, make little or no mention of the *San José* and its legendary treasure. There are literally millions of documents in Spanish archives, which trained and experienced scholars can easily consult. Given the thoroughness of the Spanish bureaucracy, an important royal ship such as the *San José* should have left a wide paper trail. Why have so few scholars taken the trouble to follow it, despite the popular fame of the *San José* and its cargo?

Part of the explanation may lie with bureaucratic norms that the Bourbons brought to Spain, which changed the organization of the government. Until the recent introduction of a unified search engine for Spanish archives on the Internet, it was often difficult to follow documentation in the transition from Habsburg to Bourbon times.[2] Apart from other difficulties during the war, Philip V's administration included many Frenchmen as well as Spaniards, who presumably kept records differently even when they got along with each other. The English occupation of Madrid in 1710 may also have disrupted normal record-keeping or encouraged bureaucrats to keep official records in their possession for safekeeping. Moreover, scholars have traditionally focused on either early modern or modern Spain, neglecting the crucial transition from the Habsburg period to the Bourbon. With the realization that the eighteenth century shows many continuities with earlier times and with the anniversary of the Bourbon accession, scholars have begun to rectify that neglect.

During a research trip to Spain in 1989 my husband, the historian William D. Phillips, and I spent several days looking for documentary remains of the *San José* in various archives and found all sorts of records, including the official measurement of the hull when it was built; cost accounts for materials and artillery assigned to the vessel; reports of the battle in which the *San José* sank; and accounts for the remaining treasure in the fleet, which arrived in Spain in 1712. Some of those records had been read and cited in a few scholarly and popular books and articles over the years.[3] Other documents had largely escaped scholarly notice. Since then, I have conducted additional forays into Spanish archives in search of documentation for the *San José*, its officers, and its crew, nearly all of whom perished when the ship went down. In the following chapters I use that documentation to bring the *San José* and its men back to life and restore them to their proper place in Spanish maritime history.

Regarding the ship itself, the official measurements of the hull and the controversy surrounding those measurements force us to consider a range of issues related to Spanish ship construction and naval administration. Like its European rivals, Spain did not develop its navy in isolation, but in the context of overall maritime needs for commerce, transport, and fishing. I discuss the planning and building of the *San José* in chapter 1 as an example of debates about the ideal size and configurations for Spanish warships in the late seventeenth and early eighteenth centuries.

Long before the ship was finished, the crown selected the principal officers who would command her, and the lives of those officers feature in numerous documents dealing with their careers in royal service. We can use those records to gain insight into the Spanish naval hierarchy at the end of the seventeenth century and to meet a fascinating set of characters: Don José Fernández de Santillán, the Count of Casa Alegre and commander of the *San José;* Don Miguel Agustín de Villanueva, his second in command; Don Nicolás de la Rosa, the Count of Vega Florida, who commanded the third ship in the fleet when the *San José* went down; and various other officers and bureaucrats who accompanied the fleet. Ordinary sailors, soldiers, and gunners left behind far fewer personal records, but their presence was recorded in the muster books for the voyage. Copies of those records, which included the names of the men who sailed and defended the *San José* on her final voyage, survive. These men can serve as representatives of all the mariners who went to sea in the late seventeenth and early eighteenth centuries, whose lives were shaped—and sometimes destroyed—by the same sea that sustained them.

The *San José* entered royal service in 1698 and thereafter spent several years in engagements and patrols in European waters before heading to the Indies in 1706. Meanwhile, across the Atlantic a series of threats to the Viceroyalty of Peru challenged the resources of two remarkable viceroys, one well known and the other nearly forgotten. These intertwined histories of ships and men provide the substance for another chapter.

The battle that sank the *San José* took place on the first leg of its return home as the flagship of the Tierra Firme Fleet, carrying royal revenues and other treasure from Portobelo in Panama to Cartagena de Indias in Colombia. Had all gone well, the Tierra Firme Fleet would then have sailed to Havana to meet the New Spain Fleet, coming from Veracruz, Mexico. Together they would have returned to Spain. In the event, nothing went well. In a chapter on the battle I examine the tragic chain of events that led to the sinking of the *San José* and the experiences of the rest of the fleet before, during, and after she sank. The original logbook of the *San José* presumably went down with the ship, but official inquiries into the disaster by both Spanish and English authorities allow me to reconstruct the battle in some detail. The history of the officers, men, and boys of the *San José* can also help us to understand the full human dimension of that long-forgotten battle.

The tragic loss of life on the *San José* was not the end of the story. In the aftermath of the battle several dramatic conflicts pitted officers against one another and military men against civilians and bureaucrats on both the Spanish and English sides. The character and prior histories of the men involved help us to understand how they behaved under the pressure of events. Long after the 1708 battle, the loss of the *San José* continued to influence the larger struggles over political power in Europe and control of the Spanish empire in the Americas. Centuries later the story of the *San José* and its men helps us to understand that broader context as well.

CHAPTER ONE

The Last Galleons

The *San José* was a Spanish galleon, one of the last in a distinguished line of ships that sailed for the crown as naval vessels and escorted merchant fleets back and forth across the Atlantic Ocean (fig. 3). Spain developed ships called galleons very early in the sixteenth century, taking features from full-rigged merchant ships and other sailing vessels and from Mediterranean war galleys, which could be propelled by either oars or sails. The Spanish galleon became a workhorse of Spain's transatlantic fleet system, able both to protect merchant vessels and to carry considerable loads of passengers and official cargo for the crown. The design continued to evolve until the early eighteenth century.

Typical early Spanish galleons included a beakhead below the bowsprit, clearly a feature adapted from the ramming beakhead of medieval war galleys in the Mediterranean. Over time the beakhead was shortened and eventually curled upward, serving more as a platform to work the ship and a complement to the decorative figurehead than for any military use. Other characteristic features of the galleon included a relatively low forecastle; a shallow open area, or waist, in the middle of the ship; and a half-deck, a quarter-deck, and a poop deck aft of the waist. The high structures aft and the beakhead and low structure forward gave the galleon a low-slung crescent silhouette when seen in profile. The galleon typically carried a bowsprit and three masts: a foremast and mainmast, each with at least two courses of sails, and a mizzenmast. Some galleons were fitted with a fourth mast, the bonaventure mizzen, aft of the mizzen, and the bowsprit sometimes carried a small topsail.

Venice, Flanders, England, and various other states also developed ships called galleons, though they tended to be used more exclusively for warfare than was the case in Spain. The Netherlands used ships that had many features in common with galleons, though they were called by other names.[1] In marine paintings of the seventeenth century—the heyday of the galleon—many ships with features characteristic of galleons are virtually indistinguishable. Only their flags and the titles of the paintings identify them as, for example, Spanish galleons; French galleons; English warships (sometimes called galleons); or Dutch whalers, East Indiamen, or large pinnances.[2]

Before looking at the construction of the *San José* and her sister ship, the *San Joaquín*, it is important to understand how contemporary Spaniards measured ships built for the crown and gauged their tonnage, a process called *arqueamiento*. The measure of size and capacity used for Spanish ships was the *tonelada*, equal to about 1.42 cubic meters of carrying capacity, roughly the same as the old French sea ton *(tonneau de mer)* of Bordeaux. Spanish galleons in the early seventeenth century rarely surpassed 500 toneladas. The *San José* and the *San Joaquín* would be twice that size, following general European trends toward larger warships.

The principal dimensions of a Spanish ship were expressed in terms of the *codo* (lit., elbow), which is defined here as equivalent to 22 inches, or 564 millimeters.[3] The Spanish crown paid by the tonelada for the ships it commissioned, which means that the measurement and calculation of a ship's tonnage determined what the crown would pay. Equally important, the arqueamiento verified that the builder had followed specifications in constructing a vessel.[4] The problem was how to devise a formula that would produce a reliable indication of tonnage from the measurements taken. If the formula produced a tonnage figure that was smaller or larger than the actual carrying capacity of the ship, it would not only affect how much the crown paid for the vessel but also complicate the work of officials who had to arrange for crews, cargos, and armament. In short, much was at stake in coming up with an accurate formula for calculating tonnage even as the configuration of ships changed over the years.

Spanish regulations for calculating ship tonnage ordinarily specified where to take the measures. For example, the regulations published in 1590 assumed that the decks had not yet been planked and established procedures for measuring with cords stretched from point to point inside the hull. Rejecting this approach, regulations in 1607 called for taking measurements after the lowest deck had been planked, "and not in the air as heretofore has been done."[5] When historical documents or nautical treatises provide us with some or all of the measures, it is a simple matter to calculate the ratios of length to keel, and so on, and to compare them with similar ratios for other ships, both ideal and real. First, however, we must know exactly what was meant by the measures and which set of regulations governed them.

The beam *(manga)*, defined as the widest point of the hull, was enclosed by the master ribs. At times the beam would correspond to the maximum breadth on the lowest planked deck. At other times the widest point of the hull would be located above or below the lowest deck, though its official measurement would normally be taken on the deck itself. Apart from that, the definition of the beam was straightforward, with more or less exact counterparts in all European nations. The keel *(quilla),* or spine, of the ship included only the straight portion of the timbers forming it, measured from the outside; the sloping stempost *(roda)* and sternpost *(codaste)* were not included. The definition of the keel did not change over time, and like the beam, it had more or less exact equivalents all over Europe.

The definition of length, which Spaniards called the *esloria,* was another matter. In Spanish usage the length of the ship was generally measured on the lowest planked deck, or wherever the beam was measured, from stem to stern. The length and the keel had a relationship customarily defined in two parts. The so-called *lanzamiento a proa* (overhang at the prow) was the forward extension of the lowest deck beyond the keel. The *lanzamiento a popa* (overhang at the poop) was the aft extension. Adding both lanzamientos to the keel gave the esloria on a Spanish vessel. For Spanish galleons, the forward extension was at least double the aft extension, giving the ships the pronounced forward rake mentioned above. There was no equivalent of the Spanish esloria in English usage. The English "length overall" sometimes included the distance from the fore end of the beakhead to the aft end of the stern, a considerably longer measure than the esloria. Continental nations seem to have used a measure of length closer to the Spanish than to the English usage, but any comparisons of ship lengths and the ratios of length to beam must take these varying definitions into account.

The floor *(plan)* in Spanish usage was measured at the bottom curve of the master ribs, as if the distance between them were flat. Like the other measures, the floor was best measured before the ship was finished. Once planking had been added above the bilge, it was much more difficult to gauge the floor precisely. The fifth measure, depth in the hold *(puntal),* had variable definitions over time. Some shipbuilders in the late sixteenth century seem to have used the distance between the top deck and the floor to define depth. The definition that eventually prevailed, however, included only the distance between the lowest planked deck and the floor. The 1590 regulations called for measuring the depth downward from about the point where the first deck would be placed; the 1607 rules explicitly defined the depth as the distance from the top of the lowest deck to the floor.[6] All of the later rules for Spanish ship measurement would follow this definition of depth.

Apart from the changing understanding of depth in the hold, the measures used to gauge Spanish ships remained more or less constant, although the formulas for deriving tonnage from them were revised several times. This means that historians studying the evolution of Spanish ship design from the sixteenth to the eighteenth century can confidently compare ratios of keel to beam or length to beam from one period to another. The various ratios established the proportions of a ship and therefore its carrying capacity, draft, speed, and handling qualities. Whoever built a ship, or ordered it to be built, paid close attention to its proportions because they would determine how well the finished vessel served their needs.

From very early in Spain's transatlantic trade the crown took an interest in how ships were configured and built, not only vessels commissioned for military use but also merchant ships. That was because the crown embargoed and rented private vessels in wartime, adapting them for military use. To encourage builders and shipowners to produce vessels that could serve various needs at different times, the government used positive incentives in the form of subsidies and negative incentives in the form of prohibitions on features that hindered a ship's sailing qualities or adaptability. For example, merchants and commercial shippers in the Indies trade often had outboard platforms attached to the upper deck to create additional space for carrying merchandise. These outcroppings could make a ship sluggish and hard to handle, however, so they were banned in rules for ship construction from the late sixteenth century onward.

The 1590 rules for constructing and gauging ships for Spain's Atlantic fleets underwent a series of refinements in the early seventeenth century. The crown issued revisions of the rules in 1607, 1613, and 1618, with each successive revision incorporating the results of officially sponsored debate.[7] The 1618 rules distilled two decades of debate about the ideal design for large Spanish vessels and remained in effect, with minor variations, for most of the seventeenth century. José Luis Rubio Serrano has made an exhaustive study of the official rules and their implications for a ship's carrying capacity, both its officially measured and its actual capacity.[8] The formulas used for gauging the tonnage of Spanish ships included only the hull measurements and excluded the volume of the fore- and aftcastles and other spaces above the highest full deck. On average, the volume omitted was thought to add about 20 percent to a vessel's carrying capacity.[9] When the crown commissioned a ship to be built, the rate paid per tonelada pertained only to the officially calculated tonnage. It was well understood, however, that the actual tonnage would be at least 20 percent higher.

TABLE 1

Selected Spanish ships built in the seventeenth century

Name of ship, builder, or shipyard	Type	Year	Beam in codos	Ratio: keel to beam	Ratio: length to beam	Ratio: depth to beam	Ratio: floor to beam	Toneladas calculated by 1618 rules
San Sebastián (1)	galleon	1628	15.0	2.5	3.2	0.5	0.5	342.0
Santiago (1)	galleon	1628	15.2	2.5	3.3	0.5	0.5	347.5
San Juan Baptista (1)	galleon	1628	17.0	2.5	3.1	0.5	0.5	476.6
Nuestra Señora de los Reyes (1)	galleon	1628	17.0	2.5	3.1	0.5	0.5	475.7
Nuestra Señora de Begoña (1)	galleon	1628	18.0	2.4	3.2	0.5	0.5	565.6
San Felipe (1)	galleon	1628	18.0	2.4	3.1	0.5	0.5	561.4
Nuestra Señora de la Encarnación (2)	galleon	1646	17.1	2.7	3.4	0.5	0.5	576.5
Unnamed *capitana real* (3)	galleon	1661	23.5	2.8	3.7	0.5	0.5	1,459.7
Basoanaga shipyard (4)	galleon	1668	18.5	2.9	3.6	0.4	0.5	666.4
Nuestra Señora del Pilar (5)	galleon	1668	22.5	3.1	3.9	0.5		1,377.9
Santiago (3)	galleon	1674	22.3	2.8	3.4	0.5	0.5	1,174.7
Sebastián de Roteta (3)	*capitana real*	1680	22.0	3.0	3.5	0.5	0.5	1,220.6
Simón Ruiz de Aranda (3)	*navío*	1687	16.0	3.5	0.5	0.5	0.5	519.0
María Antonia de Lezama (6)	ship	1698	18.3	3.0	3.5	0.6	0.5	835.7
San José (3)	galleon	1698	21.9	2.7	3.2	0.5	0.5	1,056.1
San Joaquín (3)	galleon	1698	22.0	2.8	3.2	0.5	0.5	1,075.1

SOURCES: (1) AGS, Guerra Antigua, leg. 3149, pt. 2; (2) AGM, MS 1311; (3) AGI, IG, leg. 2740, fols. 578r–581v; (4) AGM, Colección Vargas Ponce, XVII, doc. 262; c(5) R. C. Anderson, "Comparative Naval Architecture, 1670–1720," *Mariner's Mirror* 7 (1921): 39; (6) AGS, Guerra Antigua, leg. 3904.

This does not necessarily mean that the crown underpaid for the ships built for official use; it does mean that the tonnage mentioned for a particular ship might vary from one document to another, depending upon the context in which it was being discussed.

European warships became larger and longer in proportion to their beam from the sixteenth to the late eighteenth century, but the evolution seems to have been slower in Spain than elsewhere. There were several reasons for this. To the extent that warships became sleeker and more dedicated to a military function, they sacrificed carrying capacity and perhaps stability as well if they were heavily laden. Spanish galleons were designed and built to escort merchant fleets back and forth across the Atlantic. Because the slowest ship determined the speed of the convoy as a whole, speed was not as important to the galleons as strength and stability. Moreover, given the size of Spain's empire in the Americas, Spanish galleons such as the *San José* had to carry not only official cargo and passengers working for the crown but also arms and soldiers on the Indies run. The king's treasure remittances alone might amount to several hundred boxes of gold and silver on the homebound voyage—a considerable weight—all of which would traditionally be carried on the two principal warships accompanying the fleet.

In the late seventeenth century a vocal minority in Spanish maritime circles argued for changes in design that would yield greater speed and agility, characteristics increasingly valued in warfare. Three ships built in Spanish shipyards in the 1660s embodied those changes, including one built in the Basoanaga shipyard near San Sebastián, the capital of Guipúzcoa, in the Basque region of northeastern Spain. As table 1 demonstrates, the keel-to-beam and length-to-beam ratios of all three vessels were higher than those for many other ships of similar size.[10]

Vessels built as warships for the Spanish crown, however, rarely tested the limits of design. Although gradually growing larger and sleeker, they retained their ability to fill a variety of roles. Evolving theories of ship design and experience at sea with real vessels eventually led to minor modifications in the 1618 proportions mandated for ship construction. The crown published new ideal measurements for galleons of 500 and 700 toneladas in 1666 and for galleons of 800 toneladas in 1679.[11] Compared with the 1618 proportions, the revised proportions for large warships had much higher ratios of keel to beam and length to beam. The 800-tonelada galleon had three decks, with 2.99 codos (about 5.5 ft., or 1.7 m) between the first and second decks, counting from the lowest planked deck above the floor, and 3.25 codos (about 6 ft., or 1.8 m)

TABLE 2

Measurements from selected proposals for large warships compared with the real measurements of the *San José and the* San Joaquín

Proposed or real ship	Type	Year	Tonnage stated in source	Beam in codos	Keel in codos	Length on deck in codos	Depth in hold in codos	Width of floor in codos	Ratio: keel to beam	Ratio: length to beam	Ratio: depth to beam	Ratio: floor to beam
Spanish rules	navío	1618	821.9	20.0	49.0	63.0	9.5	10.0	2.5	3.2	0.5	0.5
Spanish rules	navío	1618	1,074.8	22.0	53.0	68.0	11.0	11.0	2.4	3.1	0.5	0.5
Spanish rules	galleon	1679	800.0	19.0	56.0	67.5	9.3	9.8	2.9	3.6	0.5	0.5
Proposal for eight galleons	galleon	1680	1,120.6	22.0	60.0	75.0	10.0	11.0	2.7	3.4	0.5	0.5
Proposal for eight galleons	galleon	1680	997.5	21.7	58.0	72.5	9.5	10.7	2.7	3.3	0.4	0.5
Proposal by Sebastián de Bernal	navío	1680	1,095.0	21.0	60.0	74.2	10.5	10.5	2.9	3.5	0.5	0.5
Proposal by Sebastián de Roteta	ship	1685	1,105.0	22.0	60.0	73.1	10.0	11.0	2.7	3.3	0.5	0.5
Proposal by Sebastián de Roteta	ship	1685	1,001.3	21.3	58.0	70.8	9.7	10.7	2.7	3.3	0.5	0.5
Rodrigo Ortiz	galleon	1685	1,071.3	20.0	65.0	77.0	10.0	10.0	3.3	3.9	0.5	0.5
San Joaquín	galleon	1698	1,071.3	22.0	62.2	71.0	10.0	10.3	2.8	3.2	0.5	0.5
San José	galleon	1698	1,066.8	21.9	60.2	71.2	10.0	10.3	2.7	3.2	0.5	0.5

SOURCES: The 1618 rules are in AGM, Caja Fuerte, 134. The other proposals are in AGI, IG, leg. 2740, fols. 327–70, 402–6, 457–60. Measurements for the two real warships are in ibid., fols. 578r–581v.

between the second and third decks.[12] All of the regulations affected ship-builders working for the Spanish crown up to the time of the *San José* and the *San Joaquín* but did not necessarily bind them. Moreover, experts and others who claimed expertise continued to argue about the ideal configurations for warships. Table 2 lists various configurations that were proposed in the 1680s.

Among the many authors of proposals for ideal ship proportions in the late seventeenth century two were especially active: Captain Rodrigo Ortiz, designated the master carpenter of the Indies fleets in Andalusia, and Captain Sebastián de Roteta y Eleyzamendi, of Seville. The latter expressed concern that many authors proposed warships considerably narrower than the ship built at Basoanaga in 1668 (see table 1), even though the ships they proposed were much larger than the Basoanaga vessel; he feared that the proposed ships would be dangerously unstable. Critics of Roteta soon joined the debate, arguing that ships should be longer and narrower than he proposed. Sebastián Ruiz de Aranda built such a ship in 1687, following proportions that seem to have been selected largely for their mathematical regularity: the keel was exactly three times the beam, and the length exactly 3.5 times the beam.[13] Overall, however, changes in Spanish designs for warships came slowly in the period leading up to the construction of the *San José* so as to avoid compromising the diverse roles those ships had to play on the Indies run.

In the seventeenth and early eighteenth centuries a great deal of confusion attended the use of terms to describe evolving warships. The 1618 rules referred to all ships listed by dimensions as *navíos*, regardless of their size; other authors also used *navío* in a generic sense to mean "ship" or "vessel." By contrast, some writers reserved the term *navío* for smaller ships and retained the traditional term *galeón* to refer to large warships. Near the end of the century, however, some writers would consciously use the term *navío* to refer to the large warships they proposed, which were narrower than traditional galleons and presumably closer to the proportions of the smaller navíos of an earlier period. As the eighteenth century advanced, Spain's dedicated warships would generally be called navíos rather than *galeones*, and the latter term would fade from use. The unpredictable use of terms that refer to warships can be quite confusing unless we keep in mind that proportions, much more than nomenclature, defined vessels such as the *San José* and the *San Joaquín*.

One of the best-known participants in the late-seventeenth-century debate about ship proportions was Antonio de Garrote, identified as a captain of sea and war *(capitán de mar y guerra)* for the crown, a native of Córdoba, and a citizen of Seville. In the introduction to his 1691 treatise Garrote faulted Spanish shipbuilding in several respects, while acknowledging that the volume and extent of Spain's maritime responsibilities made it difficult to make improvements. Garrote thought that the many defects he saw in Spanish ships could be blamed on carelessness, the limited number of shipyards, the lack of skilled shipwrights, and even the malice of those who had ordered the ships built—presumably because they wanted to save money.[14] He noted in particular the extra platforms constructed to increase cargo capacity, even on warships, which made it difficult to use the artillery properly and made the ships slow and unwieldy. Despite these criticisms, Garrote praised Spanish ships for their ability to withstand the force of the sea, which was a direct result of the strong wood, nails, and spikes used in their construction. While noting that no other nation built ships as strong as Spain's, Garrote nonetheless acknowledged that the lighter construction materials made foreign ships faster and more agile because they weighed less and required less rigging and ballast to balance the hull.

Like the authors of many other treatises, Garrote claimed that ships built to his proposed specifications would remedy all defects and still be perfect both for warfare and for trading voyages. In other words, in addition to making boastful claims, Garrote accepted without question that the best ships for Spanish needs were multipurpose vessels rather than dedicated warships.

Garrote gave precise measurements for six sizes, or orders, of vessels, the smallest suitable for dispatch ships *(pataches)* for the fleets and the larger ones suitable for heavy cargo and military uses (table 3).[15] By dealing with functions and measurements, Garrote deftly avoided the confusion regarding ambiguous terms such as *galeón* and *navío*. He provided detailed instructions for building each order of vessel so that any master river carpenter, and not just the best ones, could build them successfully. Similarly, he was careful to write the sections regarding masts, rigging, and careening so that any *contramaestre* (assistant to the ship's master) could follow his instructions with ease.

Scholars praise Garrote's treatise for its thoughtfulness and detailed discussion, and one recent author concludes that he "can be considered one of Spain's great naval shipbuilders, as well as an experienced mariner."[16] That judgment should not be accepted at face value, however. Garrote's rank as a captain of sea and war provides proof of his military experience at sea but not of his general knowledge about shipbuilding and ship design. Individuals wrote treatises for the crown on a wide variety of topics, and most of them made claims that would probably not bear close scrutiny.

Perhaps Garrote's most extravagant claim was that all six orders of ships

TABLE 3
*Proportions of Antonio Garrote's proposed warships
compared with the real proportions of the* San José *and the* San Joaquín

Proposed or real ship	Type	Year	Beam in codos	Ratio: keel to beam	Ratio: length to beam	Ratio: depth to beam
Garrote	6th order	1691	24.0	3.00	3.42	0.46
Garrote	5th order	1691	22.0	3.00	3.41	0.49
Garrote	4th order	1691	20.0	3.00	3.40	0.53
Garrote	3rd order	1691	18.0	3.00	3.39	0.56
Garrote	2nd order	1691	16.0	3.00	3.44	0.56
Garrote	1st order	1691	14.0	3.00	3.43	0.57
San Joaquín	galleon	1698	22.0	2.83	3.23	0.45
San José	galleon	1698	21.9	2.75	3.25	0.46

SOURCES: Garrote's measurements appear in a facsimile table in Manera Regueyra, "La época de Felipe V y Fernando VI," 172; measurements for the two real warships are from AGI, IG, leg. 2740, fols. 578r–581v.

that he proposed would be able to sail over the sandbar at Sanlúcar de Barrameda at any time of the year, regardless of the tidal conditions. For a century and a half before Garrote wrote, the sandbar at the mouth of the Guadalquivir River, below Sanlúcar, had tested the skill of shipbuilders and river pilots. Vessels leaving Seville, the official exit port for the Spanish empire, traditionally sailed downriver to Sanlúcar nearly empty so that they could be maneuvered through the shallow places in the river without grounding. Passengers and some of the cargo and supplies were then taken on board, but not all of them, because the sandbar at Sanlúcar still presented a formidable challenge to ships heading for the open sea. Despite Garrote's confident assertion, it is doubtful that the full range of vessels he proposed could overcome the perils of Sanlúcar at any time of year and regardless of the tides.

In fact, contemporary shipbuilders also seem to have doubted Garrote's claims. He proposed vessels that were narrower in the beam and longer in the keel than the shipbuilders of his time were producing. His proposed vessels would have sacrificed carrying capacity, and perhaps stability, in the interests of greater speed and buoyancy. That would have limited their usefulness to the merchants and military commanders who were the supposed beneficiaries of the improvements he proposed. As tables 1 and 2 demonstrate, there was a striking difference between the ratios of keel, length, and depth to beam for the larger ships proposed by Garrote and those of real ships, such as the *San José* and the *San Joaquín*, that were actually built for the crown.

The heated debate about ideal ship proportions continued to be largely theoretical at the end of the seventeenth century because almost no large ships were being built in Spain. Modern scholars attribute this inactivity to a combination of factors.[17] The crown commissioned very few ships, and when it did commission them, the delay in paying for them discouraged all but the most intrepid contractors. Private parties who might have commissioned ships also suffered from a lack of resources, especially after the drastic devaluation of the currency in 1680. As if that were not enough, nearly continual warfare at the end of the century led to enemy attacks on Spanish shipyards on the north coast.

A case in point involved Pedro de Aróztegui, a resident of San Sebastián. Aróztegui regularly dealt with the crown, building ships of various sizes for use in the Atlantic, and he was particularly active in the late 1670s. He and his financial backers also engaged in legal wrangles about payments due them from the royal treasury, though they were not unique in that regard; virtually every shipbuilder and government contractor experienced similar difficulties. In Aróztegui's case the final accounts for two galleons and a dispatch ship that he built for the crown in 1679 were not settled until 1692, and the crown did not pay those accounts until the end of 1696.[18] Despite such problems, the appeal of a new government contract must have been irresistible, given the lack of other opportunities, and that is how he came to be the builder of the *San José* and the *San Joaquín*.

Some confusion arises in considering when and where the two galleons were built. Scholars have often assumed that a ship named *San José* built at the Guipúzcoan shipyard of Aída in 1687 was the same vessel that sank near Cartagena de Indias in 1708.[19] If the vessel had really been built in 1687, it would have been twenty-one years old when it sank, an extraordinary age for a ship assigned to the difficult Atlantic crossing and subject to repeated damage from shipworms in the Caribbean. On that trajectory ships rarely lasted more than ten years in royal service.[20]

Moreover, the *San José* served as the *capitana,* or flagship, of the 1708 fleet, a role that the English would term the *admiral;* her sister ship, the *San Joaquín,* served as the *almiranta,* or vice-admiral. In Spanish usage, those positions were always given to the largest, strongest ships in a fleet. When danger threatened, as it often did, most or even all the registered treasure returning from the Indies would be carried by the capitana and the almiranta of a fleet. It would have been exceedingly rare for twenty-one-year-old ships to sail in the first two positions in a royal fleet, yet we know that the *San José* and the *San Joaquín* held those positions and between them carried nearly all the registered treasure when the *San José* sank in 1708. This seeming paradox can be explained if we discard earlier notions about where and when they were built.

The paradox stems from confusing the 1708 *San José* with an earlier vessel of the same name. Conventions for naming ships in royal service aimed to avoid just that sort of confusion. Spanish ships habitually bore religious names of one sort or another; for vessels in royal service, custom dictated that only one ship of a specific type would bear a particular name at any given time. For example, there would not be more than one galleon named *San Juan Bautista* in royal service at any time. When a ship passed out of royal service, a newly built ship incorporated into the fleet would often inherit the name of the departing vessel. If a ship of a specific type came into royal service bearing the same name as a similar ship already sailing for the crown, the newcomer would be given another name to avoid confusion. With a limited number of religious names to choose from, and the use of the same name for one ship after another, the historical record could easily become confused. For example, a ship named *Nuestra Señora del Pilar* was built in 1668 and sank in 1676 at the battle of Palermo, and another large ship with the same name served the Spanish crown in about 1690.[21] Without knowing the fate of the 1668 *Pilar* or the average life span of a large ship in royal service, one could easily confuse the two separate ships.

On the same list on which the second *Pilar* appears, there is a warship called *San Joseph (San José)*. This may have been the ship built at the Aída shipyard in 1687, or it may have been another ship altogether. The name alone cannot tell us. For positive identification, it is ideal to have the name of the ship, its full measurements and tonnage, and the name of its builder, owner, or master— or all three. Important royal ships were often identified by their name, tonnage, and builder even years after they first entered royal service.

In the case of the *San José* that sank in 1708, the archives provide a wealth of information, leaving no doubt as to her identity. One of the best pieces of corroborative evidence is her association with the *San Joaquín*. The two are known to have been sister ships, built together by Aróztegui. Official accounts provide information for both of the ships together, with hundreds of details about their construction and cost, including the fact that they were built in 1697–98 at the Mapil shipyard, in the jurisdiction of the town of Usúrbil, near San Sebastián. In other words, the *San José* was just ten years old, not twenty-one, when she sank in 1708.

Spanish shipyards were traditionally associated with the largest nearby city.

TABLE 4

Proposed measurements for the San José *and the* San Joaquín *compared with their real measures*

Proposed or real ship	Type	Year	Beam in codos	Keel in codos	Length on deck in codos	Depth in hold in codos	Width of floor in codos	Ratio: keel to beam	Ratio: length to beam	Ratio: depth to beam	Ratio: floor to beam	Toneladas given in source
Gaztañeta and Ortiz	galleon	1696	21.5	60.0	72.0	10.8	10.0	2.8	3.3	0.5	0.5	1,200.0
Echeveste brothers	galleon	1696	21.5	60.0	72.0	10.0	10.3	2.8	3.3	0.5	0.5	1,200.0
San Joaquín	galleon	1698	22.0	62.2	71.0	10.0	10.3	2.8	3.2	0.5	0.5	1,071.3
San José	galleon	1698	21.9	60.2	71.2	10.0	10.3	2.7	3.2	0.5	0.5	1,066.8

SOURCES: AGI, IG, leg. 2740, fols. 474–77, for Gaztañeta and Ortiz and the Echeveste brothers; ibid., fols. 578r–581v, for the two real warships.

For example, the Zorroza shipyard was associated with Bilbao, in Vizcaya; Co-lindres, with Santander, in Cantabria; Basoanaga, with Pasajes near San Sebastián; and Mapil, with San Sebastián itself. Originally, the men planning the construction of the *San José* and the *San Joaquín* had in mind the shipyard at Basoanaga, which lay east of San Sebastián.

Don Antonio de Gaztañeta, who held the rank of captain and the position of chief pilot of the Ocean Sea (i.e., the Atlantic), proposed the initial meas-urements for the two ships in 1696, based on measurements proposed in 1685 by Captain Rodrigo Ortiz for a slightly smaller warship and augmented by his own ideas (table 4).[22] Recently scholars have discovered that in 1688 Gaztañeta wrote an extraordinary manuscript treatise demonstrating a deep knowledge of naval architecture and ship construction, which he had developed through several decades of study and observation in Spain and elsewhere in continen-tal Europe.[23] In 1692 Gaztañeta wrote a treatise on navigation that is well known because it was published at the time.[24]

Gaztañeta's manuscript on ship construction, by contrast, was not published until 1992. Both Ortiz and Gaztañeta used the term *galeón* to refer to the war-ships they proposed. Gaztañeta's 1696 recommendations called for a beam of 21.5 codos, a keel of 60 codos, and a length on the first deck of 72 codos. Be-cause the ships were built for the crown, they had to conform substantially to official rules regarding size and configurations of warships. The crown allowed changes to those rules, however, if the designers and builders thought they could improve on the proportions.

Pedro de Aróztegui signed a contract with the crown on June 12, 1696, to build four galleons for the Indies run: the future *San José* and *San Joaquín* and two others of similar size. The contract specified that they would be built at the Basoanaga shipyard. Aróztegui agreed to complete the galleons, including lead-foil sheathing to protect the hulls against the shipworms that flourished in Caribbean waters, for a price of 46 ducados per tonelada. For the first two vessels, planned for about 1,200 toneladas each, he would receive advance pay-ments so that he could procure lumber and other supplies. When the hulls were complete, the crown was supposed to pay him the balance of the first half of the contracted price; the other half came due when the vessels were fully rigged and ready for service.[25] Once the first two ships were completed, Aróztegui would begin the other two. Gaztañeta sent the measures he proposed for the first two ships to the Council of the Indies for approval. The council then dis-patched them to the north coast, where Don Francisco de Necolalde y Zavaletta, a gentleman of the noble military order of Santiago, served the crown as the superintendent for shipbuilding in Guipúzcoa. Necolalde's main contact in Madrid was the Count of Adanero, who sat on the Junta de Guerra de Indias, a committee whose members came equally from the Council of War and the Council of the Indies, usually about eight men in all. Much of the subsequent correspondence dealing with the construction of the *San José* and the *San Joaquín* linked Necolalde on the north coast with Adanero in Madrid.[26]

Before construction could begin, all the major participants had to agree on the proportions and measurements for the first two galleons, based on the tonnage specified in Aróztegui's contract with the crown. Although Aróztegui remained the shipbuilder of record, he entrusted the actual construction to Miguel de Echeveste. Miguel and his brother Juan were both master shipwrights *(maestros de fábricas)* in Guipúzcoa. Another brother, Gerónimo de Echeveste, presumably the oldest of the three, worked as a master shipwright in Cantabria, west of Guipúzcoa and Vizcaya. At Necolalde's request, all three brothers joined him for a meeting in the central plaza of the town of Usúrbil on November 7, 1696, to go over the proposal that Gaztañeta had submitted to the Council of the Indies. After carefully examining the proposed measures and other documents, the Echevestes came up with recommendations for slight changes, all designed, in their words, to produce ships "of the greatest perfection, as well as achieving the greatest fortification and security."[27] They agreed with Gaztañeta's proposed dimensions for the beam, keel, and length, but they argued for adjustments to the depth, the width of the floor, the space between the decks, and the narrowing of the hull from the beam to the prow. On November 10, 1696, Necolalde sent the Echevestes' report of the meeting to Adanero with his favorable comments, referring to the brothers as "the only master shipwrights in Guipúzcoa who, for their intelligence and long experience, merit having a vote in this matter."[28]

Meanwhile, royal officials in Seville put together a financial package for the construction. Most of the funds would come directly from the king's share of incoming treasure shipments from the Indies. In the spring of 1697 Aróztegui received several payments to reimburse him for lumber purchased by Miguel de Echeveste for the two ships. Aróztegui's contract gave him exclusive rights to buy wood in the vicinity of the shipyard—despite the protests of local officials—until he had enough for the two vessels. Miguel de Echeveste reported at the end of March that most of the materials for the keel, the ribs, and the internal bracing for the ship had been cut during the waning moon in February or purchased. He then had it stored for seasoning before construction began. When Necolalde sent his report to Madrid two weeks later, he praised Echeveste and the rest of the shipwrights associated with the project.[29]

As Necolalde and others continued to study the proposed measurements, it became apparent that the ships would be too large for the Basoanaga shipyard. At an estimated 1,200 toneladas each, with a draft of 11.75 codos, neither the *San José* nor the *San Joaquín* could be launched from Pasajes, which, even at high tide, could handle ships no larger than 8 codos of draft.[30] Necolalde noted that the realization came as a bitter disappointment to Pasajes, which was accustomed to having the prime shipyard in Guipúzcoa. Given the decline in naval construction at the end of the seventeenth century, the construction of four warships was a prize that the authorities in Pasajes were loathe to lose. Nonetheless, there was no choice but to look for other shipyards that were both secure and suitable for the construction and launching of the larger warships that were becoming the norm. Necolalde reported to Adanero that "the shipyards of Orio, Usúrbil, and Mapil are completely satisfactory, and right now they do not have any ongoing projects, so that it makes sense to choose the best from among them."[31]

Discussion about the relative merits of Gaztañeta's proposal and the changes proposed by the Echeveste brothers continued through the first half of 1697, forming part of the ongoing debate about speed and agility versus strength and stability. A memorandum dated April 28, 1697, written in Madrid by Augustín Rodríguez Márquez for the Count of Adanero, summarized the points at issue. First of all, Rodríguez agreed with the Echevestes that the narrowing toward the prow should be 3.5 codos rather than the 4.0 codos proposed by Gaztañeta. He also agreed that the floor should be increased to 10.25 codos from the 10 proposed by Gaztañeta so that the ship would be less likely to run aground upon entering and leaving port. As Rodríguez noted, because Gaztañeta had set the beam at 21.5 codos, a wider floor was necessary to bring the measures into line with the official guidelines and to add strength without adding more planking to reinforce the hull. Rodríguez noted that such reinforcements *(embonos)* were often added to Spanish galleons, even those in royal armadas, whereas other nations used a wider floor to reduce strain on the hull. He clearly favored the latter option.[32]

Rodríguez also commented at length about other changes proposed by the Echeveste brothers. Above all, he agreed with their notion to increase the height of the gun deck to 3.5 codos (about 6.4 ft., or 1.97 m): the additional headroom would make it easier for the men to use the artillery and would also allow the smoke to clear faster after the guns were fired. He recommended that the extra room simply be subtracted from the space *(entrecubierta)* between the first deck and the second deck, or gun deck, reducing it to 2.5 codos (4.6 ft., or 1.64 m). Rodríguez noted that the entrecubierta on galleons was habitually used as dead storage space anyway, stuffed with the heaviest bales and boxes of cargo, which tended to make the ship unstable even in the mildest storms. Resigning himself to the fact that the practice was likely to continue, Rodríguez argued to reduce the capacity of the entrecubierta so that more of the heavy cargo would have to be stowed in the hold, where it belonged. A reduced entrecubierta would also discourage the addition of more gunports so close to the water line, which was inadvisable in Rodríguez's view.

Regarding Necolalde's request to move the construction site from Basoanaga, Rodríguez noted that Necolalde already had the authority to order the move and did not need approval from Madrid. He speculated that Necolalde had requested such approval merely to justify overriding the terms of Aróztegui's contract, which specified Basoanaga as the shipyard. Aróztegui had also mentioned Basoanaga in his agreement with the Echeveste brothers. Rodríguez dismissed as "ridiculous" the claim that Aróztegui and his subcontractors had exclusive rights to local wood and that no other ships could be built while the royal ships were under construction. He argued that there was plenty of wood in the vicinity for all the active shipyards. Despite such critical comments, he recommended sending Necolalde explicit orders to choose the most appropriate shipyard for the construction, to drag the wood there, and to begin the construction without further delay. That way, the ships could be finished by the coming year (1698), sail to Cádiz, and take up their assignments for the crown.

The rest of Rodríguez's memorandum concerned finances for the vessels. Aróztegui's contract specified that he was to be paid 46 ducados in silver for each tonelada. If the ships measured 1,000 toneladas each at their official gauging, that would be the equivalent of more than 1 million silver reales. By the end of April 1697 the Casa de la Contratación (House of Trade) in Seville had put aside 137,000 reals for the construction and had released 60,000 of it to Aróztegui in gold doblones, or doubloons. He had spent about half to purchase wood, in addition to acquiring wood worth more than twice that amount on credit. Rodríguez advised the king to order Aróztegui to use the remaining cash on hand to pay the master shipwrights and other workers for their labor in cutting, shaping, and sawing the wood; the creditors and suppliers could wait. With the benefit of Rodríguez's advice, the Count of Adanero wrote to Necolalde on

May 11 that, although the terms of Aróztegui's contract had specified the ship-yard of Basoanaga, the Junta de Guerra had decided that no pretext should hinder Aróztegui from fulfilling his contract; if he had to relocate elsewhere, so be it.[33]

To find a suitable substitute for Basoanaga, Necolalde and others concerned with the construction inspected all the shipyards and ports in the *ría*, or estu-ary, of Orio, west of San Sebastián. In a document dated July 13, 1697, sent from Villa Real, they reported that Mapil was the "most ideal of all, and the most advantageous for the launching." Miguel de Echeveste and Juan de Arriola agreed that Mapil was a good choice, though they favored Saria and Naza de Orio as more secure locations in which to make the final outfitting of the ships before taking them to the open ocean. That was the most dangerous time for a new vessel, when it was virtually complete but unarmed and there-fore defenseless in the case of enemy attack.[34] Despite their reservations, Mapil remained the choice.

At last the construction could begin. In the traditional manner of building large ships in most of western Europe, the two vessels rose from the keel, which served as the spine of the vessel. Miguel de Echeveste's crew of carpenters formed the keel from a series of heavy timbers, notched and fitted together to the prescribed length. Everyone involved in the design had agreed that each of the keels should be 60 codos long. In the event, however, the *San Joaquín* had a slightly longer keel than the *San José*, so that it was destined from the outset to be the slightly larger ship. The master ribs fixed to the keel defined the beam. Everyone had also agreed about the size of the beam of each vessel—21.5 codos—but there again, the actual construction altered the plans a bit. The *San José* would have a beam of 21.7 codos and the *San Joaquín* a beam of 22 codos when they were officially measured.

The carpenters shaped the other ribs in proportion to the master ribs, nar-rowing the hull toward the prow and stern. Everyone involved in the design agreed that the narrowing toward the stern *(rasel de popa)* should reduce the width of the vessel by 8 codos. They disagreed, however, about the narrowing toward the prow *(rasel de proa)*, with Gaztañeta proposing 4 codos and the Echeveste brothers holding out for 3.5. They argued that too much narrowing would weaken the ability of the prow to withstand constant battering from the waves. The carpenters must have had the final say, because both ships meas-ured just 3 codos narrower near the prow than at the beam.

With the ribs all in place and secured to the keel with the *sobrequilla* (keel-son), the carpenters could begin attaching planking to the hull. Rodrigo Ortiz had recommended specific thicknesses for the planking on warships in 1685, and officials updated his figures in 1696 for the construction of the *San José* and the *San Joaquín*. Because these were warships destined for the carrera de Indias, the Echeveste brothers recommended additional bracing in various sectors of the hull, with the thickest planks located where the hull would experience the most stress.[35] Work proceeded apace during the late summer and fall of 1697.

Many sectors of government took part in the construction of the two galleons. As we have seen, the Council of the Indies and the Junta de Guerra de Indias played key roles in approving the design and marshaling the funds to pay for the construction. As the two galleons approached completion, however, the Council of War, the government body that would approve them for the king's service, took charge. In early December the Council of War sent Necolalde a letter for the Marquis of Valladarías, the governor and captain general of Guipúzcoa, telling him to appoint two experienced inspectors for the two "navíos" that Aróztegui was building. The construction was by then at an ideal stage, because the vessels were "only half planked and not closed up," and the inspection could also take advantage of the weather, "before the winter tides came in."[36] The council may have used the word *navíos* as a generic term, because the *San José* and the *San Joaquín* were usually called galeones once they were finished—proof that these terms were far from settled at the end of the seventeenth century.

Necolalde was at the shipyard in Mapil when the letter arrived at his residence in Villa Real, and he did not forward it to Valladarías until a week or so after it arrived. He hoped to be able to attend the inspection himself so that he could make his own report and also correct any "repairable defect" that might be found during the inspection. Heading off any possible criticism of the ships, he wrote the Council of War that he doubted any such defect would be found, "because the material is without doubt the best that has come out of Cantabria in many years, and the carpenters are taking every care in reinforcing the ships and following the rules as to their measurements."[37] Necolalde dated and sent his letter from Villa Real on December 24, 1697; the Council of War in Madrid read it on January 7, 1698. By then Valladarías had already carried out his inspection, which occurred on January 2 at the Mapil shipyard.

Valladarías complained that he had not received the letter from Madrid until December 28, an oblique criticism of Necolalde, and said that he had proceeded directly to Mapil as soon as the letter reached him. Soon after arriving, he named two master shipwrights to inspect the works: Gerónimo de

Echeveste, head of the body of shipwrights in Guipúzcoa and captain of all the shipyard workers in the province, and Simón de Zelaraín, a citizen of San Sebastián. Valladarías mentioned that both men were well respected for their knowledge and experience; he did not mention that Echeveste was the brother of Miguel de Echeveste, the head builder on the project, and that both brothers had been involved in the discussions concerning the measures and configurations of the vessels. Their relationship presumably did not trouble Valladarías, and there is no question that Gerónimo Echeveste had the necessary expertise to judge the soundness of the construction.

The inspectors made a verbal report of their findings before a notary at the shipyard when they finished and afterwards traveled to San Sebastián to file the papers. Their report noted that "the quality of the materials with which the two ships [*navíos*] are worked is totally satisfactory, consisting of good green wood that was cut locally nine months earlier, and the form of their construction is in conformity with the law and of goodly line [*galibo*, or shape]." They then went on to describe the precise state of completion of the vessels, one of which was further along than the other.[38]

Valladarías confirmed to the Council of War that the inspectors had found the workmanship "entirely satisfactory, with nothing to correct." Nonetheless, he worried that some of the wood had been cut only nine months before construction began and therefore might not have been seasoned enough for shipbuilding. Necolalde also wrote a brief report to the council, noting that the inspectors had carried out their task "with great precision and diligence" and that Valladarías had made a visual inspection of his own and had seemed pleased and entirely satisfied with the work.[39] The council reviewed the reports and thanked Valladarías for his work on January 16.[40]

Necolalde wrote again to the Council of War on February 2 regarding the green wood mentioned by Valladarías. Necolalde argued that "in Cantabria, one does not see ships constructed with warehoused materials, but rather with wood that is not yet dry," and he wrote at some length defending the notion that this circumstance did not constitute a defect. To test its quality, the master carpenters had drilled out a core sample, burned it, and inspected the ashes. They judged the sample to be satisfactory, although acknowledging that "it would have been of greater satisfaction had the wood dried out longer," in other words, longer than nine months. Necolalde concluded by reiterating his judgment that the ships were being built admirably and that their like had not been seen for many years in Cantabria. His one concession to the concerns about unseasoned wood related to some planks that had been cut as recently as November 1697. Those, he conceded, should be used where they would cause the least potential harm.[41]

Work continued through the winter and spring, and in late April 1698 officials began to make plans for the official launching and gauging of the vessels. With their hulls complete enough to form a floatable shell, the two embryonic galleons were hauled into the water, probably by teams of oxen hired specially for the purpose. It is likely that well over one hundred teams were involved in each launch, given the great size of the ships. On April 14 Necolalde wrote to the Junta de Guerra de Indias in Madrid that one of the vessels had been launched and hauled downriver as far as the port of Orio. "Depending upon God's favor," the capitana and almiranta of the Armada of the Indies, as he called them, "will make their voyage to Cádiz by September of this year."[42]

Although the Mapil shipyard had been chosen for its ability to handle larger ships, the launch still proved difficult. A flurry of letters between Madrid and the north coast in late April discussed the need to remove various irrigation dams from the river so that the nearly completed vessels could be towed to the port of Pasajes, where they would be fitted with masts and rigging.[43] In Pasajes, carpenters would also work to complete the decks and interior compartments of both galleons.

Even though the vessels were still far from finished, officials in Madrid and on the north coast arranged to arm them for their first voyage. The artillery would come from warehouses in Santander, but officials in Madrid did not want to authorize their deployment until just before the vessels were ready to leave for Andalusia. In addition to their own armament, the two galleons would carry various munitions from the factory at Liérganes, near Santander, to Andalusia. In early May officials in Liérganes were not sure how much they could send, because they also had to provide Catalonia with ball, shot, and grenades. Eventually they would designate 110 *quintales* (hundredweight) to load on the two galleons.[44]

Officials gauged both ships on May 18, 1698, and recorded their measurements in documents signed in San Sebastián.[45] Spanish ships traditionally remained nameless until the official measuring took place, and the *San José* and the *San Joaquín* exemplified that custom; in earlier documents they are referred to only as the "two galleons [or navíos] that Pedro de Aróztegui is building for the crown" or, more rarely, as the capitana and the almiranta of the Indies fleet. In the documents for the May 18 arqueamiento, however, they became the *San José* and the *San Joaquín*, three-decked galleons and among the

TABLE 5

Measurements of the San José *and the* San Joaquín

(in codos of 22 in., or 564 mm)

	San Joaquín	San José
Beam	22.00	21.91
Keel	62.18	60.18
Length on deck	71.18	71.00
Depth in hold	10.00	10.00
Floor width	10.27	10.27
Ratio of keel to beam	2.83	2.75
Ratio of length to beam	3.25	3.23
Ratio of depth to beam	0.46	0.45
Ratio of floor to beam	0.47	0.47
Draft (estimated)	11.75	11.75
Toneladas calculated by 1613 rules	1,026.48	1,009.29
Toneladas calculated by 1618 rules	1,075.11	1,056.08
Toneladas given in the documentary source	1,071.25	1,066.75

SOURCE: AGI, IG, leg. 2740, fols. 578r–581v.

NOTE: The 1613 formula for ships with more than one deck was the depth times ½ the sum of the keel and length, times ½ the sum of ¾ the beam plus ½ the floor, divided by 8. For military use, the formula was altered to account for space lost to bracing and gained by packing in more men and supplies. The net change from the basic measurement was considered to be an increment of 14 percent. Although documents for the late seventeenth century mentioned the 14 percent increment, the real increment seems to have been nearly 17 percent.

In the 1618 rules, the formula changed slightly. It can be expressed most simply as beam times depth times the sum of the keel and length, divided by 32, times 1.14, times 1.03. See the detailed discussion in Rubio Serrano, *Arquitectura de las naos y galeones,* 2:40–44. Some discrepancies between the figures given in the documentary source and the figures calculated here using official formulas may have resulted from the use of decimals rather than fractions. The larger discrepancies are more likely explained by variations in the way the official formula was applied in any given case.

largest warships that had ever been built in Spain. As table 5 demonstrates, the *San Joaquín* was slightly larger than the *San José* overall. Minor variations naturally occurred in the days of hand-sawn planks and hand craftsmanship, even though the two vessels were designed to be sister ships, and all of the documentation regarding their design and measurements pertained to both vessels.

The arqueamiento of the *San José* and the *San Joaquín* calculated only the volume and presumed capacity of the enclosed hulls. We can assume that everyone involved understood that the fore- and aftcastles and other areas above the highest full deck added at least 20 percent to the officially gauged tonnage. That would explain why both ships, which were gauged at just over 1,000 toneladas each, were often mentioned in discursive records as being of 1,200 toneladas.

For the *San José,* the keel measured 60.18 codos (110.25 ft.) long "from elbow to elbow" along its straight part. The stempost curved forward and upward from the foremost point of the keel, so that the first deck extended 9 codos (16.5 ft.) farther forward than the keel in the lanzamiento a proa. The sternpost rose more sharply from the aft end of the keel, so that the first deck extended only 2 codos (3.67 ft. farther than the aft end of the keel in the lanzamiento a popa. This would have given the ship the pronounced forward rake typical of galleons, even more pronounced than galleons in the early seventeenth century. The length, or esloria, of the ship—the sum of the keel and the extensions fore and aft—measured 71.14 codos (130.42 ft.). As table 1 shows, the *San José* and the *San Joaquín* were both considerably slimmer than a half-dozen galleons built for the crown in 1628 yet more than twice their average size. Nonetheless, the *San José* and the *San Joaquín* were not as slim as many authors had recommended in the debate over ideal warships.

Both galleons were slightly less deep in the hold than warships in the early seventeenth century but had the same ratio of floor to beam as the earlier ships. Many theorists in the late seventeenth century argued for a wider floor, and the 1679 rules for an 800-tonelada warship had adopted that notion. The builders of the *San José* and the *San Joaquín* continued to follow more traditional lines, however, so as to enhance maneuverability and stability.

For the official arqueamiento, neither ship carried rigging, but a typical complement of masts and sails presumably would have included three courses of rectangular sails on both the foremast and the mainmast and a lateen sail on the mizzen. A rectangular spritsail on the bowsprit would be added to this, and both the mizzen and the bowsprit would be fitted with topsails and topgallants, as the fore- and mainmasts were. Despite slight differences in their official measures, the *San José* and the *San Joaquín* would have been virtually indistinguishable to most observers, especially from a distance, except for the different images on their sterns and the flags that distinguished the capitana from the almiranta.

A painted image or bas-relief of its namesake would have been added to the flat face of the stern above the rear corridor on each ship. San José, or St. Joseph, the earthly father of Jesus Christ, enjoyed great popularity in late-seventeenth-century Spain and its American empire. He had been Mexico's patron saint since 1555 and was named Spain's official protector in 1679.[46] As the representation of the ideal spouse and father, San José was often depicted standing alone, cradling the child Jesus in one arm and holding his emblematic flowering staff with his other hand. In Spanish religious tradition, he was often depicted in early middle age rather than as a man of advanced years, as biblical tradition presented him.

One typical image of San José, created about 1700, resides in the church inside the Hospital de los Venerables in Seville. Another typical image appears in an engraving of the stern of a 60-gun ship, drawn to accompany a treatise on shipbuilding by Antonio de Gaztañeta (fig. 4). Published in 1720, Gaztañeta's treatise was based on measures he had recommended in 1712, which in turn were the product of his decades of study and discussion about the ideal proportions for warships. As we know, in 1696 Gaztañeta had proposed the original measurements for the *San José* built by Pedro de Aróztegui. Although the engraving in Gaztañeta's treatise and that particular ship have no necessary connection, it is tempting to think that we are looking at the stern of the *San José* itself in Gaztañeta's treatise.[47] It is also tempting to think that the various detailed drawings of a 60-gun ship in Gaztañeta's treatise represent the capitana and almiranta built by Aróztegui.

The *San Joaquín* would also have carried an image on its stern, namely of San Joaquín, the father of the Virgin and therefore St. Joseph's father-in-law. Just as the biblical San Joaquín was senior to San José in familial terms but less important in religious terms, so the galleon *San Joaquín* was larger than the *San José* but subordinate in military terms. Whenever they sailed together, the *San José* would serve as the capitana and the *San Joaquín* as the almiranta, from the time they were named until the *San José* sank. Does the relative status suggested by their names signify that the *San José* was recognized as the better ship from the outset, despite being smaller? We can only guess, but the circumstances suggest that was the case.

The decoration on Spanish galleons built for the crown in the 1620s often included no more than a gilded rampant lion on the prow, some painting and gilding on the poop corridors, and the painting of the ship's namesake on the flat face of the stern. By the late seventeenth century, however, decoration on large royal ships all over Europe had become much more elaborate, as nations heaped on statuary and gilt to intimidate their rivals with magnificent displays. French ships in particular were known for their lavish ornamentation, which reflected the position of Louis XIV's France as the most powerful country in Europe and a trendsetter in many spheres of life. Although heavy carved ornamentation detracted from the sailing qualities of a ship, any country with pretensions to power and stature had to follow fashion. The *San José* and the *San Joaquín* were without doubt more ornate than their Spanish precursors in the early seventeenth century but probably not as ornate as their French contemporaries a century later.

Francisco de Necolalde's hope that the two galleons would be able to sail to Cádiz by September 1698 proved overly optimistic. One of the complicating factors was the death of Pedro de Aróztegui, the man who had signed the contract with the crown to build them. His son Pedro Francisco de Aróztegui appeared before a notary in the town of Rentería on September 13, 1698, representing himself and his siblings Pedro Joseph and Gracia, to authorize an inventory of their father's estate. The paperwork for building the *San José* and the *San Joaquín* would take some time to sort out. The final accounts bear the date May 21, 1703, four year after the ships entered royal service.[48]

Most of the masts and much of the rigging for the two galleons were purchased from Amsterdam and other ports in the Netherlands. A network of Dutch entrepreneurs who were well established in Spanish finance and commerce, together with their Spanish factors and other contacts, supplied the items. Pedro de Aróztegui had worked before with the chief supplier, Huberto de Hubrechtz. A resident of Madrid, Hubrechtz held the contract to provide the *San José* and the *San Joaquín* with masts, rigging, tar, and other naval stores, plus arms and munitions, which Spaniards generally grouped under the general heading *pertrechos* (military supplies). Hubrechtz had men working with and for him in Bilbao and elsewhere on the eastern side of the Bay of Biscay. He also held contracts for the collection of the salt tax in Galicia and Asturias in the northwest, which meant that he was well connected on Spain's north coast as a whole.[49] The business dealings between Aróztegui and Hubrechtz provide a good example of the close commercial ties that had developed between Spain and the United Netherlands in the aftermath of the Dutch war of independence from Habsburg rule. The eighty-year struggle ended successfully for the Dutch in 1648, and in the late seventeenth century the former foes joined together to combat the ambitions of their mutual enemy, Louis XIV of France.

Hubrechtz arranged for several large shipments of masts, rigging, and munitions for the *San José* and the *San Joaquín* in the early part of 1699. One large list of materials dated in Amsterdam on January 20, 1699, indicates that the items were purchased by Salomon Van de Blocquenes, on orders from Hubrechtz, and loaded on a Dutch ship, the *Golden Grape*, for the trip to Spain. Don Nicolas Van Duffel and Company, of Bilbao, served as Hubrechtz's consignment agent.[50] Van de Blocquenes meticulously recorded every mast and cable, giving their weight, length, and price. In all he bought eighty masts and spars, the largest of which were 26 palms *(palmos)* in girth and 101 feet in length. He also bought hundreds of cables and lines of varying sizes and weights, four anchors weighing from 2,690 to 3,700 pounds each, sailcloth, and a wide array of other equipment for the two galleons.

The miscellaneous items included everything from linseed oil and sewing needles to flags, gilt buttons, reserve drumskins, and enclosed lanterns for use in the powder magazine. The cargo was so extensive that not all of it would fit on the *Golden Grape*. Van de Blocquenes sent the rest of it on a second ship in mid-March. The total cost was about 47,000 florins in the currency of Amsterdam, with a 1 percent discount for prompt payment. The Dutch money translated into about 208,000 Spanish reals in new silver, which Hubrechtz claimed from the crown in Madrid. Rigging made up about 45 percent of the total, the masts 25 percent, the sailcloth 20 percent, and miscellaneous supplies the other 10 percent. Van Blocquenes earned 3 percent of the total for his fee as purchasing agent. In late May he sent another shipment from Amsterdam to Pasajes that included lead, nails, and paper, as well as gunpowder, pistols, and shot. Two more large cables for the *San José* and the *San Joaquín* were sent directly to Cádiz in early August, to await the galleons' arrival.[51]

Pedro de Aróztegui died before turning the vessels over to the crown, a task that his heirs finished for him. After taking delivery of the galleons, the crown also took over responsibility for provisioning and outfitting them for their first voyage. Huberto Hubrechtz advanced 80,000 reals to the crown for the outfitting, sending it via a letter of credit for 2,000 gold doubloons to Nicolas Van Duffel in Bilbao. From Madrid, Don Juan de Goyeneche advanced another 95,520 reals with a letter of credit for 2,388 gold doubloons sent to Don Nicolás Alanier and Company, in San Sebastián.[52] Francisco de Necolalde kept track of the purchases and cash outlays overall. He reported to the Council of War that he had "tried to procure the greatest savings and benefits in the purchase of the many items that this outfitting requires; and although in some [purchases] I have succeeded, in the foodstuffs the price has risen excessively because of the year's sterility, which has caused great scarcity in the region."[53]

Necolalde provided itemized lists of everything spent on outfitting the two galleons.[54] Under the general heading *proveeduría* (provisioning), he began with the cure of souls in the form of ornaments and supplies for the chapel on board each galleon. Thereafter he listed supplies for the cure of bodies, in the form of boxes of medicines and surgical tools. The list of kitchen supplies included a great variety of inexpensive items, including copper cauldrons and spoons for cooking, tin cups, wooden plates, spoons, mortars and pestles, grills, trivets, frying pans, knives, and various baskets, barrels, boxes, and other containers.

The food itself consisted of the standard Spanish shipboard fare of biscuit, salted meat, dried codfish, bacon and ham, oil, fava beans, garlic, salt, ground sweet peppers, and other common foodstuffs. Because Necolalde bought the items on the north coast, he supplied hard cider as well as water for drinking, rather than the wine provided for ships in southern Spain. The two galleons would also carry live animals to provide fresh meat on the voyage—not for everyone, but for officers and the sick. Such items were usually grouped together under the heading *dietas* in lists of Spanish provisions. Here they were scattered through the list, presumably added as they were purchased, even though usually identified as part of the dietas. Eight rams and eighty chickens would begin the voyage to Cádiz, though few, if any, of them would survive the journey. The ships also carried barley and maize as chicken feed, as well as four hundred eggs. Supplies for the maintenance of the ship included brushes for tar, pine planks, buckets, nails, tow, *alquitrán* (a mixture of pitch, tar, and grease), and numerous other items.

The artillery supplies merited a separate list of their own. One hundred large guns that the crown had assigned to the galleons were moved from their warehouses in Santander by a commission agent named Pedro de Aróztegui Urrutia, presumably a family member of the late shipbuilder. Necolalde arranged for loading the armaments on board the galleons just before departure. The list of munitions and related supplies bought locally occupied four manuscript pages in Necolalde's accounts. Additional munitions that Huberto Hubrechtz had purchased in the Netherlands arrived on June 22. Necolalde divided them evenly between the *San José* and the *San Joaquín*, but their cost did not form part of the outfitting budget that he controlled.

The most poignant miscellaneous expense appeared first on Necolalde's list: the dowry for an orphaned girl. María Ignacia de Lagárzazu was the daughter of Juan de Lagárzazu, a carpenter who had been killed working on the two galleons at the Mapil shipyard. Because she had been orphaned by his death, the king authorized Necolalde to give her 1,467.5 silver reals for a dowry—a significant sum, equivalent to half a year's wages for an experienced ship's carpenter.[55]

Most of the other miscellaneous expenses involved wages paid to sailors and casual laborers ("podaquines o peones") who helped to load the two galleons. Among other tasks, they conveyed and loaded the 230 boatloads of rocks that were used to ballast the ships. Sailors from many ports in the vicinity signed

TABLE 6

Costs of outfitting the San José *and the* San Joaquín *for their voyage from Pasajes to Cádiz, summer 1699*

Items entered in the accounts	Amount in silver reals
Provisions, including food and supplies	49,427.75
Artillery and munitions, plus some food and supplies	37,044.50
Miscellaneous expenses, including food and supplies	12,602.50
Provisions, etc., for the small ship *(naveta)* that accompanied the galleons	14,431.75
Total expenses	113,506.50
Total budgeted	175,520.00
Amount remaining in San Sebastián, in the crown's favor	62,013.50

SOURCE: AGI, IG, leg. 2740, fols. 649–50.

on for the voyage to Cádiz—937 in all. Necolalde arranged for the men to be brought to Pasajes in small boats and paid them 2 reals a day to buy food for the few days the ships remained in port before departure.

At the end of August 1699, when the galleons were laden, armed, provisioned, and manned, a small flotilla of launches towed them from Pasajes into open water under the direction of local pilots. The city of San Sebastián provided seven of the launches without charge. Necolalde paid for the services of twenty-one others from Pasajes and Motrico. The commander of the voyage to Cádiz was none other than Antonio de Gaztañeta, who had by then been promoted to admiral.[56] As author of the original measurements proposed for the construction of the *San José* and the *San Joaquín* in 1696, he would finally have the opportunity to see how they performed at sea.

Francisco de Necolalde filed a summary account of expenses for the outfitting, quite pleased that the provisioning had come in under budget (table 6).[57] Even so, outfitting the two galleons for their first short voyage cost more than half as much as all their masts and anchors and most of their rigging combined (208,000 reals). That was fairly typical for Spanish fleets. The initial cost of building and rigging warships paled in comparison with the cost of outfitting and provisioning them over the course of their working lives. And the salaries and wages of officers and crews increased that cost many times over.

The construction of the *San José* and the *San Joaquín* illustrates the state of Spanish shipbuilding at the end of the seventeenth century, a period of great controversy about the ideal size and shape for a warship. The proposals of experts such as Antonio Gaztañeta and others pushed the design toward larger, slimmer vessels, built for speed and agility, just as their contemporaries were doing elsewhere in Europe. Their ideas influenced the vessels that were actually built, but only to a point. Somewhat surprisingly, those with a voice in the final design of Spanish warships included not only the members of the Council of the Indies, the Council of War, and the Junta de Guerra de Indias but also shipbuilders and shipwrights, minor bureaucrats, and a variety of other interested parties. The rich extant documentation for these two galleons allows us to follow the complex process of consultation and negotiation that produced their final design and construction.

When royal officials measured and gauged the *San José* and the *San Joaquín* in May 1698, the galleons were somewhat smaller than the ideal warships many experts envisioned. Moreover, they hewed closer to traditional lines, with more space for cargo and munitions and presumably greater stability under sail than the most advanced designs could guarantee. This resulted not only from the strength of tradition but also from the proven utility of traditional designs. In the extensive correspondence and consultation regarding the *San José* and the *San Joaquín* from 1696 to the middle of 1697, government officials considered a range of contemporary ideas about the ideal warship. They settled on a design that they hoped would incorporate the best new ideas with the time-tested features that had served Spain and its imperial trade well for two centuries.

The documentation for the *San José* and the *San Joaquín* also illustrates the fragile nature of the supply lines that supported ship construction. The crown relied on a network of bureaucrats all over Spain to secure materials and labor for the construction, and they, in turn, had to cast their nets very wide to secure the supplies needed at the shipyard. A considerable amount of those supplies came from northern Europe; in the event of war, and the hostility of habitual suppliers, the seaborne lifeline of ships and fleets that held the empire together could easily be broken.

On September 23, 1700, a year after the galleons arrived in Cádiz, the crown named a captain general for the fleet that the two new galleons would lead to Tierra Firme. Nonetheless, against all hopes and expectations, that fleet would not depart for six more years. When it finally sailed, a new dynasty held power and Spain was engaged in a desperate war for the survival of the empire. In that struggle the *San José* and the *San Joaquín* would have important roles to play. In one of the many ironic twists in their history, two of the last galleons built for the Spanish Habsburgs would be among the first to defend the Bourbon succession.

CHAPTER TWO

Commanders of the Fleet

The men who would command the *San José* and the *San Joaquín* had pursued their own destinies in the decades before fate brought them together with those particular ships. We know the commander of the *San José*—and of the whole Tierra Firme Fleet of 1706—as the Count of Casa Alegre. That was his noble title and one that he spent years of effort and expense in acquiring. It is also the title by which he was known in all of the documents pertaining to the fleet. His name, however, was Don José Fernández de Santillán, which identified him with an ancient and distinguished lineage in Castile. In fact, we should understand the title of Count of Casa Alegre as an appendage to the Fernández de Santillán name, rather than the other way around.

In northern Spain there are three important medieval towns with *Santillán* in their names, and the noble family of Santillán presumably came from somewhere in that part of the peninsula. In the Middle Ages, gentlemen from the Santillán clan went south to aid in the reconquest of Spain from the Muslims. Several of them fought under the banner of King Ferdinand III in the wars in Andalusia in the thirteenth century. The clan owed its subsequent position in Spanish society to those campaigns, especially the famous reconquest of Seville by the Castilian navy in 1248. A knight named Domingo Polo de Santillán participated in that campaign and received lands from the king for his efforts. A family story relates that it was Domingo Polo de Santillán who planted the battle standard of the king of Castile on top of the Muslim minaret known later and ever since as La Giralda, the most famous and most recognizable symbol of Seville. Whether or not the story is true, it comes as no surprise, because the Santillán clan identified closely with Seville thereafter.[1]

Generation after generation, the descendants of Domingo Polo de Santillán continued to serve the crown in the wars that gradually took control of southern Spain from the Muslims. They also played a prominent role in the governance of Seville, with several members of the family serving as aldermen and members of the city council. This latter group was known in Seville simply as the *veinte y quatros* or *veinticuatros,* literally the "twenty-fours," because that was how many men served on the council. The Santillán family also made marriage alliances with other noble families to consolidate their wealth and position. From sometime in the fourteenth century the main lineage was known as the Fernández de Santillán, honoring one particularly astute marriage alliance. The clan's fortunes took a giant leap upward in the late sixteenth century, when Alonso Fernández de Santillán, the third of that name in his family, married Doña Beatriz Ponce de Leon, heiress to a valuable entailed estate.

Their elder son entered the religious life and ended up as bishop of Quito, and the family fortune therefore passed to his younger brother, Francisco Fernández de Santillán, who married and raised six children who lived to adulthood. Such a large family was both a blessing and a curse in a noble family: a blessing because that increased the odds that someone would live long enough to inherit the family fortune and perpetuate the line; a curse because all of the children had to be provided for and found suitable positions in life. Francisco Fernández de Santillán evidently had sufficient resources to place his children well. The third child, a boy named Baltasar, entered the religious life as a monk attached to the cathedral of Seville. The other five, including three girls, all married. It was somewhat unusual for a noble family in the seventeenth century to marry all of its daughters, as it was generally cheaper and more prudent to usher at least one of them into a nunnery.

Francisco's eldest son, named Alonso Fernández de Santillán like his grandfather, inherited the bulk of the family fortune and became one of the veinticuatros of Seville. He also enhanced the family fortunes by marrying Doña Francisca Ana de Quesada y Manuel, the only daughter and heiress of a noble family from Baeza. Don Alonso's lineage and his wealth paved the way for his entry into the most prestigious of the Spanish military orders, Santiago, in 1625.[2] Although the family had been noble for many generations, they had enjoyed no particular distinction within that large social group. The Spanish nobility included individuals from a broad spectrum of status and wealth. In the country as a whole something like 10 percent of the population could claim noble birth, although the percentage varied greatly from region to region. Whole provinces in the north had been ennobled for services to the crown in the Middle Ages, so that being noble in the north did not necessarily mean that a person enjoyed either wealth or high social status.

Generally speaking, the farther south one moved, the less common noble status became and the more it was a reliable marker of wealth and status.[3] That was not always the case, however. We have only to remember Cervantes's Don Quixote, a poor gentleman from a family of *hidalgos* (lit., *hijos de algo*, "sons of something or somebody") who tried to live in a genteel fashion in a small village on the plains of La Mancha. His poverty made him an object of ridicule to his neighbors long before he lost his senses, but it did not rob him of his legal distinction as a nobleman, which at base meant exemption from personal taxes.

Being a member of a military order meant that a person had ascended into the middle ranks of the Spanish nobility. Because the military orders were open to new members, they provided an important avenue of upward social mobility for hidalgo families, but only for those who could prove themselves worthy of the honor. Persons aspiring to membership in a military order had to provide proof that their families had lived nobly for generations, which meant in part that they had served the crown and that they had no taint of Jewish or Muslim ancestry. The Spanish nobility as a whole, and certainly in the uppermost ranks, often included Jewish or Muslim ancestors, but it was a shared fiction that they did not. Moreover, the highest noble families had enjoyed their status for so many generations that they were virtually unassailable. Different rules applied for the military orders, which functioned as the gatekeepers for the higher ranks. In the proofs of nobility that Don Alonso Fernández de Santillán provided for the Council of the Military Orders, he documented his unimpeachable Christian ancestry and his service to the crown, and the gatekeepers let him in. His entry into the Order of Santiago marked the successful transition of his clan from the ranks of the many into the select company of the few.

Don Alonso and his first wife, Doña Francisca Ana de Quesada, had five children who lived to adulthood. The eldest, Don Francisco Fernández de Santillán, was able to rise even higher than his father, gaining the title of first Marquis of La Motilla from King Charles II in 1670. As the firstborn son, he inherited the bulk of his parents' estate. His acquisition of a title placed him near the very top of the noble hierarchy, a distinction that the Fernández de Santillán clan had been working toward for centuries. The third son of Don Alonso and Doña Francisca, born in Seville in 1637, was Don José Fernández de Santillán, the future commander of the galleon *San José*.[4] Like his older brothers, he enjoyed full noble status, which was standard practice in continental Europe, but he could not look forward to any sizeable inheritance. As soon as he could understand anything about the way the world worked, Don José would have learned that he had to make his own way in it, though his family would do everything possible to assist him.

Don Alonso and Doña Francisca seem to have settled on a career at sea for their third son. By the time he reached thirty years of age, Don José had been promoted to captain (presumably captain of sea and war) on the almiranta of the Tierra Firme Fleet. He wrote an affectionate letter to his older brother Francisco on December 24, 1667, as soon as his ship returned to Cádiz. Many men in the fleet had died during the voyage, he reported soberly, including at least one close friend of his. The original captain on the almiranta, named Rivadeneira, had perished during the voyage from Cartagena to Portobelo on May 19, and Don José had become an "unworthy captain," as he described himself, to replace Rivadeneira.[5] His career at sea was well launched.

Don José married Doña Estefanía de Cevallos, the widow of Juan de Pontejos, a distinguished naval officer, and the couple established residence in the Sevillian parish of La Magdalena.[6] Doña Estefanía had a daughter from her first marriage, but she and Don José would have no children together. In 1669 Don José went to the Indies with the Marquis of Paradas, Don Fernando de Villegas, whose sister was married to Don José's older brother Francisco. Because the marquis was governor of Caracas, he was well placed to help his young relative by marriage to prosper in Spain's American empire. Don José served as governor and captain of war for the Maracaíbo district until 1674,[7] evidently acquiring considerable experience and wealth in the post.

In late January 1677 Don José, identified as a captain of sea and war, became a gentleman of the noble military order of Alcántara. In the dossier for his admission to the order, dozens of witnesses testified to his noble status and swore that his lineage was free from the taint of Jewish or Moorish ancestry or any punishment from the Inquisition.[8] Alcántara was not as distinguished an order as Santiago, but it meant that Don José had achieved personal distinction beyond his identity as the son of a noble family. He had also acquired wealth and knew that the best way to achieve even further distinction was to offer his personal and financial services to the king.

The Spanish crown went through considerable political and financial turmoil in the late seventeenth century. Since the death of Philip IV in 1665, the central government had lurched between incompetence and collapse. Philip's successor, Charles II, was only four when his father died, and his mother, Mariana of Austria, had no head for matters of state. Despite restraints from a regency council, she handed important posts over to a succession of favorites, infuriating the aristocracy and providing the excuse for factions at court to clamor for a greater role in policymaking. One of the factions swirled around Don Juan José of Austria, one of Philip IV's bastard sons. With the economy still in disarray and inflation rampant, Spain's possessions in Europe and abroad looked ripe for the picking, and Louis XIV of France was the first to take advantage of the situation. Married to a half-sister of Charles II, Louis claimed a string of lands in the Spanish Netherlands bordering France and launched wars in 1667–68 and 1672–78 to realize his claims. In part because of strains caused by the first war, in 1668 Spain had to make peace with Portugal, which had been in rebellion since 1640. By acknowledging Portuguese independence, the government of Charles II ended Habsburg rule in the neighboring kingdom after sixty-eight years of joint monarchy.

Although Charles II gained his majority in 1675 at the age of fourteen, he was too feeble in mind and body to govern for himself. Factional strife at court continued, and the Queen Mother entrusted the government to a minor nobleman named Don Juan de Valenzuela, which further alienated the aristocracy. Valenzuela was forced out of power in 1676, and Don Juan José of Austria was able to take hold of the reins of government the following year, acting in the name of the king. During Don Juan José's tenure in power Spain signed the Peace of Nijmegen with France in 1678, losing key bits of the Southern Netherlands to Louis XIV's aggression. When Juan José unexpectedly died in 1679, the government was nearly bankrupt, inflation ran uncontrolled, and it was not clear who might be able to govern. Though Spain was at peace, no one knew how long that peace would last.

In an attempt to deal with the financial chaos, the Duke of Medinaceli took on the job of first minister in 1680. Using as leverage his personal integrity and his undoubted prestige as one of the principal aristocrats in Spain, Medinaceli gained acceptance for a drastic plan to devalue the inflated coinage. By 1686 his measures would stabilize the currency, but in the short term prices plunged, trade froze, and shock waves undermined business confidence. In that unsettled atmosphere an ambitious nobleman such as Don José Fernández de Santillán could serve the crown financially and derive personal benefit from that service.

Beginning in 1680, Don José advanced his naval career by loaning money to the crown, each loan linked openly to a favor granted by the king. Nowadays we would label such behavior corrupt, but that assumes principles of government in a democratic republic of the twenty-first century. A seventeenth-century monarchy worked under rather different rules, which included the principle of reciprocity. Honor demanded that one reciprocate for favors done and gifts received, and such reciprocity was not considered corrupt as long as it was appropriate to the situation. In the case at hand, the king appointed Don José as captain general of an upcoming fleet to New Spain, and in gratitude for his appointment Don José loaned the crown 60,000 pesos in June 1680. The king promised to repay the money, with interest, from royal tax revenue collected in Veracruz,[9] though Don José might well have doubted that promise, given the previous decades of fiscal chaos.

There is no question that Don José had the necessary prestige to command a fleet, but he lacked experience. He had never commanded a squadron of galleons, much less an important fleet. The crown's desperation for funds, and perhaps a shortage of qualified commanders, led to a notable relaxation of standards in the appointment of fleet officers. Earlier in the century a typical captain general would have had years of service in the fleets, even if he had begun life in the aristocracy. Recognizing that Don José did not yet have the requisite experience to be a captain general, the king required as a condition of his appointment that he first serve as a *capitán de galeones,* presumably on an escort squadron for the New Spain Fleet.

Even that minimal requirement was waived in exchange for another loan, however. On March 5, 1681, Don José agreed to provide 20,000 pesos to the crown, 10,000 of them in cash, a sum urgently needed to move four galleons from Vizcaya, where they were being built, to Cádiz. The funds set aside for the ships' construction could not cover the additional cost of the move. Don José promised to provide the remaining 10,000 pesos of the loan when his ship came in, that is, upon the arrival of the New Spain Fleet, commanded by Captain General Don Gaspar de Velasco. In exchange for this financial service, the king relieved Don José of the requirement to sail as a capitán de galeones before taking up his promised post as captain general of the New Spain Fleet.

Although the king did not actually sign the document, the scribe noted that he had approved the concession, and it was duly certified in the Council of War a few days later. If all went well, Don José would pay the balance of his loan to the crown; the crown would restore to the construction fund the money used to move the galleons to Cádiz; and the rest of Don José's loan would go into the general budget. The government promised to repay Don José with interest when the next fleet arrived bringing remittances from Veracruz. This cascade of transactions involving Don José's loan and the loan itself illustrates the frantic scramble necessary to keep the Spanish government functioning, even in peacetime, in the late seventeenth century and the crucial importance of revenues brought home by the Indies fleets. In this case, most of the elements fell into place as planned. By early May 1681 the ship construction fund had been replenished and Don José had paid the 10,000-peso balance of his loan to the crown.[10] All that remained was for the crown to repay the loan with interest.

Don José had to wait several more years for a fleet to command, despite the appointment. In the meantime he continued to serve as an informal banker to the crown and to receive preferment in recompense. In January 1683 he noted that he had been appointed to command the guard squadron of the contingent of galleons that would escort merchant vessels to Tierra Firme, in the first fleet after that of Don Diego Fernández de Zaldívar. In exchange for this royal favor, he promised a whopping loan of 150,000 pesos: 50,000 in cash and the other 100,000 when he took command of the guard squadron. Don José would use 30,000 pesos from that sum to careen his flagship before the voyage and would deliver the balance of 70,000 pesos to the crown. He attached several conditions to the loan, among them that the king order the 50,000 pesos, plus 8 percent interest, repaid from the revenues brought back from Veracruz by Fernández de Zaldívar, in preference to other claims on that revenue. Furthermore, Don José wanted authorization to collect the other 100,000 pesos from the revenues his fleet would fetch from Tierra Firme. In dealing with an impecunious crown, a prudent man took as few chances as possible.

Factions at court forced the duke of Medinaceli from power in 1685, before the economy stabilized, but he had laid the groundwork for recovery. By 1686 both population and production showed signs of growth. Medinaceli's successor as first minister, the Count of Oropesa, was able to continue the momentum, reforming taxation and reducing the bureaucracy, though he made many powerful enemies in the process. Like Medinaceli, Oropesa relied on his personal wealth, status, and prestige to force his contemporaries at court to accept unpopular measures, though constant swarms of factions buzzed around the court, patronized by one or another of the courtiers vying for the king's support. Charles II's German queen, María Ana of Neuburg, played a major role in the turmoil. Despite these distractions, Oropesa was able to retain his post from 1685 to 1691. During that period, Don José Fernández de Santillán finally got a fleet to command, the New Spain Fleet of 1687.

Preparations began at the start of 1686, when Don José chose three of the four ships for his small fleet: *Nuestra Señora de las Mercedes,* which would serve as his flagship; the *San Joséph;* and the *Santa Teresa. Nuestra Señora de las Mercedes* was built in Vizcaya and measured 932 toneladas in November 1685. The crown may have been in the process of buying the *Mercedes,* as the documents say that her 932 tons "are to be paid for at the rate of 20 ducados in silver per tonelada, with interest at 8 percent a year, counting from the day that the materials are assembled for her careening." The careening was estimated to cost 60,000 *reales de plata*, plus another 30,000 in wages for the men who would load provisions and supplies onto the ship. Together, these expenses constituted about 44 percent of the ship's cost.[11] The superintendent of the shipyards in Cádiz, Antonio Castaña Redondo, had all the materials in hand by January 20, 1686, and began work on the careening shortly thereafter.

According to the documents, the *Mercedes* needed a full complement of new masts and spars, plus enclosed storage compartments for ship's biscuit, gunpowder, rigging, and mercury, as well as awnings for the poop deck. These were standard requirements, along with extra bracing members, for warships in the king's service, and their inclusion in the careening order provides additional evidence that the ship had begun life as a private vessel and had just entered royal service. In addition to extensive carpentry work and new rigging, the contract provided for enough reserve supplies for a round-trip voyage to New Spain. Though the *Mercedes'* careening was finished by the end of May 1686, it would be another year before she would leave for the Indies.

By May 1687 all the ships had been careened and outfitted, and Don José was ready to sail, but before leaving he asked the Junta de Guerra to settle a matter of precedence. As captain general of a major fleet, Don José would normally have outranked any admiral, as well as the captains general of lesser Indies fleets, but not the captain general of the Armada of the Ocean Sea (the Atlantic Fleet). The two principal Indies fleets were generally separate from the Atlantic Fleet, and under normal circumstances matters of precedence would not have arisen among them because they would not have been in the same place at the same time. The year 1687 was unusual, however. Don Francisco Navarro, who held the rank of *almirante real* of the Atlantic Fleet, had taken two ships to New Spain as captain general in 1686, delivering a load of mercury, presumably for the silver mines at Zacatecas. Instead of returning to Spain immediately, he had been ordered to stay in the area to dislodge some French ships from the Bay of Espíritu Santo. Though Spain and France were officially at peace, Louis XIV seemed to be preparing for a war aimed at Spanish territories in Europe and America, and the Spanish crown could take no chances. As a consequence, Navarro was still in Veracruz, and it was likely that he and Fernández de Santillán would be required to combine their fleets and sail home together. The point in question was who would command the combined fleet?

The Count of La Calzada, president of the House of Trade, referred the matter to the Junta de Guerra de Indias in Don José's name, and the Junta members carefully examined their options in May 1687. Navarro had many years of service at sea and held the rank of almirante in the Atlantic Fleet. Though Don José had yet to undertake his first major command, he held the rank of captain general, the top rank in the Spanish military establishment. Both Navarro and Fernández de Santillán currently served as captains general of their fleets, but Navarro's Atlantic Fleet outranked Don José's New Spain Fleet, and the 1674 rules assigned precedence on the basis of the rank of the fleets, not their commanders.[12] The Junta de Guerra de Indias therefore advised the king in early June to appoint Navarro captain general of any joint fleet, though each man would retain control of the ships in his command. Given the prickly nature of many noblemen, Don José cannot have been happy with the decision, but at least the Junta de Guerra had settled the matter. He prepared to sail, with sealed orders for Navarro and a letter to the governor of Veracruz telling him who would take precedence should the two fleets be in that city at the same time.[13]

War crept closer, even as the fleet waited to load two ships with 300 quintales of mercury from the mines at Almadén for silver refining in New Spain. The Marquis of Los Vélez noted anxiously on June 20 that six French ships had arrived in the Bay of Cádiz and wrote that Fernández de Santillán should leave for New Spain with all haste. The Count of La Calzada was in Cádiz monitoring the departure plans for the House of Trade and the crown. During the last week in June a stiff east wind blew without letup for six days, preventing the ships from leaving port, but the wind suddenly died down at 11:00 PM on the twenty-ninth. On July 1, 1687, Calzada reported with relief and pleasure that the fleet of twenty-three ships had left port the previous day. He went down to the harbor before dawn and noted that Don José's capitana and the almiranta had already raised anchor and set sail.

The other ships were slower to respond to the changing weather, but all of them were ready to leave by 11:00 AM. By the time they caught up with the capitana and the almiranta, anchored three leagues away, off Rota, it was too late to make much additional progress that day. Nonetheless, Calzada was pleased to report that the fleet had left before the end of June, which was noteworthy.[14] Following common practice for the New Spain Fleet, nearly half of the ships in Fernández de Santillán's fleet were bound for separate destinations in and around the Caribbean, including Havana, Caracas, Campeche, Tabasco, Santo Domingo, Florida, Cumaná, Cartagena, Maracaíbo, and Trinidad—the last four ports being technically in Tierra Firme rather than New Spain. Fernández de Santillán reported later that the two ships bound for Havana and Cartagena ran into pirates once they separated from the fleet. When the Spanish ships put up a fight, however, the pirates lost interest in the pursuit. Contrary to popular legends, few pirate crews had the stomach or the ammunition for long battles. They preferred to concentrate on vessels that surrendered after no more than token resistance.[15]

The main contingent of twelve merchant ships, plus the capitana and the almiranta, arrived off the coast of Veracruz in the second week of September after an uneventful voyage, but a strong north wind and swelling seas hindered their passage through the dangerous shallow channel that led into port. Don José's second in command, the almirante Don Guillén de Ribera, wrote on September 21 describing a mishap that had befallen one of the merchant ships. As the fleet battled its way toward the port, the *Jesús Nazareno* ran aground at the mouth of the channel, putting it in grave danger of breaking up. Ribera said that he and some of his men had gone aboard to bring her to safe mooring, noting that his general would provide a more detailed report. General Fernández de Santillán confirmed Ribera's account, reporting that the *Jesús Nazareno* had suffered a broken keel in the mishap and that her mainmast had to be cut down to stabilize the vessel. Only then could Ribera and the men in launches from the escort vessels guide the damaged ship to safety.

Officials in Veracruz wrote that the quick and effective actions of those in charge of the fleet had saved the vessel. By ten o'clock in the morning it was safely moored with the others on the rings affixed to the wall of the castle. All the reports of the incident suggest that, despite his inexperience at sea, Don José knew how to command and had the good sense to delegate responsibility to experienced subordinates. They, in turn, presumably trusted him to report favorably on their actions and thus to advance their careers.

The safe arrival of the fleet was a source of great pride (and perhaps relief) for Don José, considering that it was his first major command. Five days after mooring the fleet he wrote a letter to the king and sent it, along with his diary of the voyage, on a ship licensed to bring slaves to New Spain. The Count of La Monclova, viceroy of New Spain, had delayed the ship's departure in anticipation of the fleet's arrival. It arrived in Cádiz on January 21, 1688, and Fernández de Santillán's letter and diary reached Madrid six days later, much to the delight of the king and his ministers. Fernández de Santillán's cover letter noted in self-congratulatory and convoluted terms that the "zeal with which I tried to fulfill the obligation Your Majesty imposed in confiding this fleet to me, was equal to the force with which I dedicated myself, so that Your Majesty would be served by my affection and anxiety until I can place myself at Your Majesty's feet."[16]

Don José's diary seems to have been misplaced sometime after it reached the king. A very polite note from the secretary of the Junta de Guerra de Indias to the Marquis of Los Vélez in late February mentioned that the diary had not made its way back to the files. He asked whether, by chance, the king or the marquis still had it.[17] With documents traveling back and forth between the Indies and Spain and between Madrid and ports in the south, it is no wonder that papers occasionally went astray. Nonetheless, the loss of Don José's diary for the 1687 fleet is a great pity. It would doubtless give us further insight into his thoughts about commanding a fleet and perhaps a clearer idea of his effectiveness at the task.

Don José's sense of his own importance was not at issue. He clashed with Don Francisco Navarro shortly after his arrival in Veracruz. In what seems to have been a deliberate provocation, Don José continued to fly the pennants of the capitana and the almiranta on the two principal ships in his fleet, even though he should have relinquished command and precedence to Navarro upon arrival. After five or six days he removed the capitana's pennant and flew the almiranta's pennant on his flagship, but only in response to a direct order from Navarro. Moreover, he took offense when Navarro sent an adjutant to advise him of his duty, an act that Don José considered out of keeping "with the obligations of my lineage and those of the posts with which Your Majesty has seen fit to honor me."[18] That is where the matter stayed as the combined fleet wintered over in Veracruz.

In loading the ships for home, all three top naval officials—Navarro, Fernández de Santillán, and Guillén de Ribera—had strict orders to ensure that all the gold and silver was duly registered. The king's orders exposed the government's frustration that contraband shipments of treasure had proven nearly impossible to stop, despite strict inspections of arriving fleets. The only hope of increasing royal revenue from the Indies lay in extraordinary diligence on the part of fleet commanders and masters of silver. Francisco de Quijano Ceballos and Joséph de Jáuregui y Olea, the masters of silver on Fernández de Santillán's two principal ships, logged in each component of the king's treasure as it came aboard.

When they had finished, however, Don José again tested Navarro's patience by hoisting the pennants of the capitana and the almiranta on his two principal ships. In response Navarro fined Fernández de Santillán the large sum of 5,000 pesos: 4,000 for the capitana's pennant and 1,000 for the almiranta's. With eight reals in a peso, the 5,000-peso fine was equivalent to 40,000 reals. To put the fine in context, the captain general of a large Indies fleet earned an annual salary of 4,000 silver ducados, or 44,000 reals. Fernández de Santillán would later claim that Navarro's hostile response made him feel "so lacking in recourse and so orphaned" that he brought the matter to Viceroy Monclova. He cannot have been pleased when Monclova and his Finance Committee sided with Navarro, authorizing Fernández de Santillán to fly a pennant appropriate only to almiranta status. Don José said that once Monclova issued his order, he had followed it "blindly, and with [the almiranta's pennant] still flying I made my voyage [back to Spain]." Ribera's ship also carried an almiranta's pennant; he was in the awkward position of serving as second in command in both the combined fleet, under Navarro, and also the New Spain contingent, under Fernández de Santillán, whom Ribera called "my general."

The *flota y azogues*, as the combined merchant fleet and returning mercury contingent was styled, left Veracruz at the end of June 1688 and reached Havana a month later. They stayed in Havana only two weeks, from July 28 to August 12, just long enough to top off their supplies and load additional royal revenue. Then the nineteen ships sailed for Spain. According to Fernández de Santillán, they sighted Bermuda on September 17 and the island of Corvo, in the Azores, on October 10. The tension between Navarro and Fernández de Santillán festered for the duration of the voyage. Both men sent dispatches ashore when they sighted the Spanish coast on October 26, alerting officials in Andalusia that they would soon arrive in port. Despite the quarrel, the seventy-six-day voyage had been happy and uneventful, which both men deemed a great blessing.

As part of his preparations to land, Don José ordered the masters of silver on his capitana and almiranta to prepare final tallies of the remittances they carried for the crown. According to the accounts dated at sea on October 27, 1688, each ship carried just over 208,805 pesos from the royal treasury in Veracruz, following standard procedures to divide the funds evenly between the capitana and the almiranta. In Havana, an additional 16,565 pesos came aboard the capitana, so that it carried nearly 225,400 pesos for the crown when it arrived in Cádiz. Fernández de Santillán estimated that the fleet as a whole carried between 10 million and 12 million pesos in registered funds. In other words, the royal share was probably no more than about 4 percent; the rest belonged to merchants and other private parties.

On November 6, 1688, Don José wrote his report to the king from aboard his flagship about five leagues offshore. The ebullient letter noted his "great jubilation" at having arrived safely "with this fleet composed of nineteen ships," neatly glossing over the fact that Don Francisco Navarro served as the combined fleet's commander. The pretext for Don José's letter was to give an account of all the ships in the fleet, but his main purpose was simply to crow about his success. Two of the ships that he had shepherded to New Spain on the outbound voyage had remained in the Indies to join the Armada de Barlovento, the on-again, off-again squadron that provided local defense in the Caribbean. Another two ships would arrive in Spain later, and a vessel owned by Captain Diego Rosales had been declared unfit to make the return voyage. Of the other ships in the return fleet, one had been built in Campeche and another in Havana, and Don José noted that he had admitted two others to the fleet in Havana, again blurring the distinction between Navarro and himself. He closed his letter by saying that the only thing lacking to make his joy complete was the news that the king considered himself well served by the zeal and application with which Don José had carried out his orders. He dispatched Don Francisco del Castillo to shore with the letter, and it seems to have reached Madrid six days later. By then the fleet had come into port. The Count of La Calzada saw it offshore at 9:00 AM on November 8 and joyfully reported the news to Madrid.

A few weeks later, the long-simmering dispute between Navarro and Fernández de Santillán spilled over onto the House of Trade, and by extension the Council of the Indies, dumped there by the contending parties. Navarro complained about the various breaches of protocol on Fernández de Santillán's part, from the moment of his arrival in Veracruz. Navarro also accused Fernández de Santillán of unjustified delay in forwarding the king's sealed orders to him for the return voyage; of abusing his authority in commandeering ballast from various merchant ships and failing to keep them informed; of failing to hand over his registers to officials in Veracruz; and of issuing a pass to the Marquis of La Laguna to inspect Navarro's flagship without Navarro's knowledge or permission. Together, the accusations against Fernández de Santillán sketch a portrait of deliberate provocation that seems to have been calculated to irritate Navarro beyond endurance. Whether Don José's actions qualified as insubordination remained an open question.

Don José responded to the charges with feigned surprise, claiming that he had followed his orders and the standing procedures for Indies fleets to the letter. Noting that he had a natural aversion to this sort of complaint, Don José said he had assumed that Navarro, like himself, would have discredited stories unworthy of his attention. Though he disliked bothering the busy committee with such matters, he nonetheless felt the need to respond to Navarro's complaints. With this opening paragraph, Don José claimed the moral high ground and hinted that Navarro lacked the breeding to behave in a proper manner. Then he answered the charges: he had flown the offending pennants only after Viceroy Monclova had confirmed that the king's revenue should be carried on Fernández de Santillán's principal ships. Fernández de Santillán acknowledged that Navarro's contingent would lead the fleet home and defend the treasure, but surely his treasure ships had to be distinguished in some way from the merchant vessels.

According to Don José, the other charges Navarro had brought against him barely merited response. Although he had taken the trouble to advise Navarro about the return route, Navarro had barely acknowledged his missive. Nonetheless, he had forwarded the king's sealed orders to Navarro when the viceroy told him to do so. He had treated the merchant ships according to regulations, which gave warships the right to claim precedence in loading ballast. Finally, because he had supplied the powder for Navarro's flagship at his own expense, it was natural for him to issue Laguna a pass to visit that vessel; Navarro must have known about it, as he had convened several meetings of the fleet officers before they left Veracruz. In closing, Fernández de Santillán said that he had shown great forbearance in the face of Navarro's insubstantial complaints, which he attributed to a rigid nature, but he feared that Navarro would continue to attack him. Perhaps, Fernández de Santillán suggested, the king should transfer his right to be captain general of a future fleet to the next person in line, which would also relieve him of a great financial burden.

The letter is a fine example of Don José's skills at political manipulation and self-promotion, or what today is often called "spin." Passed over for the joint command, he had taken his disappointment and frustration out on Navarro and prodded him into an intemperate response. Had Navarro matched Fernández de Santillán in political skills, he might have tried to flatter and cajole Don José into a willing acceptance of his subordinate role. There is no way of knowing whether such a tactic would have worked, however. The voyage across the Atlantic was long enough for Fernández de Santillán to stew over insults real and imagined, especially after waiting so long for command and spending so much of his own money in the process. He could not openly blame the king or the Council of the Indies, but he could blame Navarro for having the poor grace to be in Veracruz when their fleets met. His response to

Navarro's exasperated complaints at his insubordination can be read as an indirect rebuke to the council for taking away his command halfway through the voyage. It can also be read as an indirect threat to a government habitually strapped for cash. If the king wished to rescind the agreement to give Don José a proper command in acknowledgment of his financial services, he would be pleased to obey.

The charges against Don José formed part of the general inspection of the returning fleet by officials from the House of Trade.[19] Their inquiry lasted from 1687 to 1689, rather longer than usual, in part because of a complaint from the gunpowder merchants of Seville. Don Juan de Alvarado, who held a contract for supplying gunpowder in Spain, had traveled to New Spain with Don José's fleet. Upon arriving in Veracruz, he accused local merchants of smuggling gunpowder into New Spain on Don José's fleet rather than buying it from him. He filed papers to that effect once he returned to Spain. The situation and the accusation were typical of the Indies market in the late seventeenth century. With the disruptions caused by warfare in Europe and the erratic schedule of fleets crossing the Atlantic, merchants in the Indies routinely engaged in contraband to avoid paying taxes and to assure their supplies of a wide range of goods. The merchants holding official contracts and monopolies to supply the Indies market could do little except complain after the fact.

The other charges filed against fleet officers included routine breaches of procedures, such as failure to carry out the requisite number of inspections, failure to prevent the desertion of eighteen soldiers and a gunner from the infantry regiments, and irregularities in provisioning in Veracruz. Don Alonso del Castillo, judge of the royal *audiencia* of the House of Trade, conducted the official inquiry and handed down his sentences and schedule of fines in May 1689. Typical fines ranged from 100 to 600 silver pesos for each of the officers charged. The audiencia fined one of the infantry captains and the almirante Don Guillén de Ribera for carrying a total of four black slaves in their service without proper licenses; they also fined the almirante for carrying three priests and a Dominican friar on the return voyage without proper passenger licenses. The Council of the Indies reviewed the sentences at the start of the new year and confirmed all but a few of them.

The charges against Don José Fernández de Santillán took longer to sort out. Judge del Castillo reviewed the evidence and testimony carefully and issued his sentence on December 23, 1689, absolving Don José of insubordination and revoking the fine of 5,000 pesos; he also dismissed the other charges. Judge del Castillo seems to have followed a strict interpretation of the rules:

Don José had never disobeyed an order; he had simply dragged his feet until the order came. He had also taken full advantage of the ambiguities in the standing fleet instructions and in his prerogatives as commander of the New Spain Fleet.

There is no hint that Don José used his social status or wealth to influence the outcome, though Judge del Castillo may have been related to Don Francisco del Castillo, whom Fernández de Santillán sent ashore with his letter to the king before arriving in Cádiz. In any case, in mid-March 1690 the king's legal expert on the Council of the Indies reviewed all the paperwork and likewise found no merit in the complaint about Don José's offending pennants. He noted, however, that if Navarro chose to submit evidence about the other complaints, the council would try to determine "who caused the dispute and the merits of each side." Navarro may have lost his taste for the fight by then; I have found no record that he submitted any additional material. The Council of the Indies issued the definitive sentence in mid-July 1690, confirming del Castillo's judgment that Don José should be absolved of all blame and all fines. The victory must have been doubly sweet. By a decree of April 23, 1690, the king had already granted him command of a second fleet of galleons to the Indies.[20]

Owing to the unsettled times, however, Don José would have to wait another sixteen years for that voyage to take place. France declared war on Spain once again in 1688, aiming to add more territory from the Spanish Netherlands to the northern buffer around Paris. The conflict would drag on until 1697, consuming resources and disrupting trade. The crown tried to send fleets to the Indies as regularly as possible, both to project an image of control in the New World and to discourage incursions from the French and other interlopers bringing contraband goods. Merchants in Seville, on the other hand, often opposed the dispatch of fleets in wartime because of stagnating sales in the Indies. They preferred to restrict the flow of goods into markets in New Spain and Peru in order to keep prices as high as possible. The crown prevailed regarding the New Spain fleets, dispatching twenty-five fleets between 1650 and 1700 at regular intervals, despite the merchants' reluctance to commit ships and merchandise to the saturated markets. After Don José's return in 1688, another six fleets would sail for New Spain before the end of the century.

The situation was far different on the route to Tierra Firme, the northern fringe of the vast Viceroyalty of Peru. Only sixteen fleets sailed for Tierra Firme in the second half of the seventeenth century, twelve of them before

1678, and only four in the twenty-two years between 1678 and 1700. The negotiations surrounding the last Tierra Firme Fleet of the century illustrate the issues involved.[21] The crown planned a fleet for 1693 and informed the merchant *consulado* in Seville late in 1692, but the merchants had other ideas. After a series of meetings, they decided unanimously not to designate ships for the proposed fleet, citing several compelling reasons. First of all, they still did not know how well the goods sent with the Marquis of Vado's fleet in 1690 were selling. They had also received news of increasing piracy in the area. Moreover, because the king was issuing licenses to single ships bound for Tierra Firme, the merchants knew that the value of goods on the official fleet would decline, along with the value of the king's revenue from the fleet. In a clever twist, the merchants crafted their reluctance to prepare a fleet as a way to preserve royal revenues.

While the Council of the Indies in Madrid considered the merchants' reply, the merchants gained time, though not much. In a letter dated January 27 the council wrote that the merchants' arguments were "insubstantial" and told them that "the most opportune thing would be—without reply or any further delay—to propose a list of ships and tonnages for the fleet."[22] Faced with a direct order, the merchant consulado obeyed and proposed a total of 4,000 toneladas—the same as on the last two fleets—but the merchants also repeated their objections to sending a fleet at all in the current circumstances. In the end, they got their way. The next Tierra Firme Fleet would not sail until 1695, under the command of Don Diego Fernández de Zaldívar, whose fleet to New Spain in 1683 had preceded Don José Fernández de Santillán's first Indies command. Like Don José, Don Diego used naval service to rise in social status. Upon his return, he served on the king's Council of War and was named the first Count of Saucedilla in 1689.[23] Saucedilla's 1695 fleet would be the last one sent to Tierra Firme in the seventeenth century,[24] in fact the last one sent before Don José's ill-fated command in 1706, with the *San José* as his flagship.

During his long wait for that command, Don José's fortunes continued to rise, even as Spain experienced enormous changes in its political orientation. The French war ended in 1697, and Charles II, Spain's last Habsburg monarch, died childless in 1700. His will left the Spanish kingdom and Spain's overseas empire to a French Bourbon prince, Philip of Anjou, one of Louis XIV's grandsons (see figs. 1 and 2). In other words, by a stroke of his pen the dying Charles II reversed two centuries of Spanish foreign policy and brought the Bourbon dynasty to Spain a mere three years after the most recent war against France ended. The fluid circumstances provided rich opportunities for men such as Don José Fernández de Santillán who were willing to defend the new dynasty against its enemies.

The war that broke out in 1701 over the Bourbon succession further disrupted plans for the next Tierra Firme Fleet, although officials in Madrid and Cádiz kept planning and preparing for its imminent departure. In the spring of 1702 the *San José* and the *San Joaquín* underwent a full careening in Cádiz, supervised by Fernández de Santillán and budgeted by the crown at 23 ducados per tonelada. Some of the most experienced master shipwrights and caulkers in Andalusia worked on the two galleons, including Francisco Antonio Garrote, identified as superintendent of the work crews (*superintendente de las maestranzas*); Rodrigo Ortiz, identified as chief master carpenter; and Francisco Díaz de Ágreda, identified as chief master caulker. Ortiz may have been the same man who devised the 1685 proportions for warships that informed the design of the *San José* and the *San Joaquín*.[25] It is not clear what relationship Garrote may have had to the Antonio Garrote who wrote a famous treatise on ship design in 1691, but it is plausible that they were related.

During the careening, Fernández de Santillán corresponded regularly with Domingo López Calo de Mondragón, secretary of the Council of the Indies in Madrid, regarding the progress of the work. Although Fernández de Santillán wrote in April warning that the materials cost more than he had anticipated, the final careening came in under budget, averaging less than 18.5 ducados per tonelada rather than the 23 ducados budgeted. In all, the crown paid 213,900 reales to refit the *San Joaquín* and 216,428 reales to refit the *San José*.[26]

The work ended just in time. Early in July 1702 Fernández de Santillán heard news from Paris that the Dutch and English fleets were both ready to sail and that they were likely headed toward Spain. England aimed to capture Cádiz so as to have a base for operations in the Mediterranean for the anti-Bourbon coalition.[27] Spanish witnesses saw the combined fleets, under the command of Admiral Sir George Rooke, off the coast of Cádiz at the end of August and estimated their number at 180–200 vessels, 70 of them warships.[28] Although the number of ships may have been exaggerated, the threat they posed was quite real. The loss of Cádiz to the enemy would deal a significant blow to the Bourbon cause. Officials from the House of Trade worked with naval officers and bureaucrats in Cádiz and Madrid to supply munitions and rations to the Spanish and French warships defending Cádiz Bay. A rough archival sketch shows the small Spanish fleet—five warships and a dispatch boat—behind the barrier of chains and pontoons deployed to block the far end of the bay. The fleet's capitana, the *San José,* with Don José Fernández de Santillán in command, was in the lead, followed by the almiranta, the *San Joaquín.* Eight French galleys rode in line perpendicular to the barrier and parallel to the Spanish ships (fig. 5).[29]

The Anglo-Dutch fleet sailed into the broad mouth of the bay near the town of Rota, across from the city of Cádiz on a fortified peninsula. Four thousand soldiers led by the duke of Ormonde disembarked, captured Rota, and threatened the vulnerable neighboring towns as well. The invaders demanded that the residents abandon their Bourbon king and swear allegiance to the Habsburg archduke Charles. If they did not, they faced "blade, fire, and blood."[30]

Despite the invaders' superior numbers, the city of Cádiz was well protected by fortified walls, and the bay as a whole had several well-located forts and gun batteries, which were effective deterrents as long as they could be kept manned and supplied with munitions. José Fernández de Santillán was in charge of coordinating the defenses. Ordinarily the city of Cádiz would have been responsible for supplying the forts and batteries, but in the circumstances Don José assumed that responsibility himself. He reported on September 10 that the enemy forces "continue aiming firebombs at the castle of Matagorda, [but] up to the hour [at which I am writing] this letter they have not undertaken any assault. And thus, [with the castle at Matagorda] as well as [the castle] at Puntal, the batteries and fortifications and ships supplied with the provisions, armaments, and other preparations that a matter of such importance requires, the enemy, as far as I can tell, cannot accomplish anything here."[31]

Admiral Rooke soon accepted that reality. A week later Don José reported that the enemy had withdrawn its troops from Matagorda after suffering heavy casualties in a series of futile assaults during which the attacking troops were fired upon by the defenders of the castle as well as by Don José's galleons.[32] By September 26 the invading fleet had withdrawn after another failed attempt to take the town of Puerto de Santa María. Cádiz would not be captured, and Fernández de Santillán could claim credit for its successful defense. Don Francisco de San Millán y Ceballos, a judge with the House of Trade, assisted in arranging the city's defenses and wrote a powerful endorsement of Don José's efforts. "[T]hat [the enemy] retired with the loss of many men was due to the zeal and care of General Don José Fernández de Santillán, and of his Sergeant Major Don José del Castillo,"[33] who had deployed the Spanish ships and French galleys so as to provide protective firepower for both Puntal and Matagorda.

At the same time as the enemy assault on Cádiz, the New Spain Fleet approached the Spanish coast, escorted by fifteen French warships and carrying funds vital to the Bourbon war effort. Warned of the enemy presence, the fleet headed instead for Galicia and on September 23 entered the port of Vigo, where its officers hoped to find safety. Unfortunately, an English resident of Vigo got word to the Anglo-Dutch fleet as it sailed northward from Cádiz. The enemy fleet attacked the Hispano-French fleet at anchor in Vigo on October 23, capturing considerable silver, destroying many Spanish and French ships, and thus redeeming its failure in Cádiz (fig. 6).

Concerted efforts by French and Spanish officers and bureaucrats kept the king's treasure out of enemy hands, however. They unloaded both public and private treasure before the enemy fleet arrived and in the process precluded the smuggling that often occurred when Indies fleets arrived in Cádiz or Seville. The king also confiscated silver owned by English and Dutch merchants in Spain in reprisal for the attack. According to Henry Kamen, "The result was that Philip received the largest sum in history ever obtained in any one year from America by any Spanish king."[34] In all, the king garnered more than 13.6 million silver pesos from the 1702 New Spain Fleet, although 2 million of that was borrowed from merchants in Seville. The ships destroyed by the English could not easily be replaced, but otherwise the attack on Vigo was not nearly as damaging to the Bourbon cause as has been portrayed.[35]

After the Anglo-Dutch fleet gave up its attempt to conquer Cádiz, Don José Fernández de Santillán deployed his vessels at safe moorings in Cádiz Bay and maintained a watchful defense. His main concern was to keep the squadron manned at optimal levels to respond to any new attack, but without incurring the unnecessary expense of a full crew. Although the city of Cádiz was supposed to provision the ships as long as they remained in the bay, Don José had to nag city officials periodically, with the full support of the Council of the Indies in Madrid, about the quality and quantity of the biscuit and other food provided for his men. He also pressed officials in Madrid to provide funds to pay their wages, though with only sporadic success.[36]

During the summer of 1703 Don José arranged another careening for the *San José,* the *San Joaquín,* and the rest of the squadron—five galleons and one dispatch boat in all—supervised by Pedro Fernández Navarrete, the *almirante general* of the squadron. To maintain vigilance and assist in the careening, Don José was authorized to employ 150 soldiers and 300 sailors. The former earned 1 silver real per day, and the latter earned 3 *reales de vellón.* The sailors worked far harder than the soldiers in the careening, but they had to accept their pay in inferior copper vellón coinage. The total cost for the soldiers and sailors reached 23,625 silver reals per month, paid by an official of the House of Trade.

Don José aimed to finish the careening and depart for Tierra Firme in September, but at the end of August news reached Cádiz that an Anglo-Dutch fleet of 130 vessels had just sailed through the Strait of Gibraltar. It was not clear where the fleet was headed, but it was a formidable force, with forty-six large warships, each mounting eighty to ninety guns; ten frigates, each with thirty to fifty guns; sixty-four other warships of diverse sorts; and a complement of smaller vessels to provide medical and logistical support. Faced with this stunning news, Don José scrambled to re-careen, outfit, and arm his ships for the voyage to Tierra Firme despite a shortage of powder, shot, and diverse supplies throughout Andalusia.[37]

Within a week, careening began on the five galleons, although Fernández Navarrete found serious defects in the *San José*'s masts as the work proceeded, which slowed progress. By the end of the third week in September Don José had determined that nearly 660 quintales of gunpowder was needed for the three principal galleons and their dispatch ship. Six good-sized merchant ships and two smaller boats were embargoed as reinforcements, bringing the total to thirteen vessels. Through October the ships were outfitted, armed, and supplied. Don José and his almirante, Pedro Fernández Navarrete, signed on 1,684 crewmen, 324 of them for the *San José*, though they were not paid the customary advance on their wages owing to a lack of funds.

Money finally arrived from Seville in early November of 1703, financing the purchase of more supplies and provisions, as well as wages for the men. On November 5 five French warships arrived in Cádiz to serve with the fleet, and in mid-November the owners of the merchant vessels were told to prepare their ships for departure. The vessels took on more supplies and provisions in December, and it began to look as if the Tierra Firme Fleet was finally ready to depart.

On January 25, 1704, in part for his service in the defense of Cádiz, King Philip V granted the title of Count of Casa Alegre to Don José Fernández de Santillán y Quesada, gentleman of the Order of Alcántara.[38] For the rest of his life, official documents would commonly refer to him only as the Count of Casa Alegre. His first official voyage with the new title was to have been the imminent trip to Tierra Firme, already delayed for several years. Fate had something else in mind, however. The Spanish crown evidently decided that the voyage was too risky, given fears that the anti-Bourbon alliance would make another attempt on Cádiz. So Casa Alegre was ordered to remain in port.

In the summer of 1704 Admiral George Rooke again sailed toward the Mediterranean, carrying orders to renew the attack on Cádiz.[39] Instead he convened a meeting of his principal officers on July 17 to debate the matter before proceeding. Because the fleet did not carry an army large enough to support the naval attack, a new assault on Cádiz was likely to fail. So Rooke and his officers decided to turn on a new and unexpected target: Gibraltar, which was lightly defended (fig. 7). They succeeded in taking it, but no one seemed to know whether they could hold it or even whether it was worth holding. As the modern historian John Hattendorf reports, "When news of the success of this operation reached London, the lord high treasurer remarked in a letter to Richard Hill in Savoy, 'Our last news from Sir George Rooke gave an account that he had possessed himself of Gibraltar, which I suppose you hear sooner than we; I know not how far it is tenable, or can be of use to us; those at Lisbon will be the best judges and directors of that matter.'"[40]

The English authorities eventually decided that Gibraltar was indeed worth holding since it was the only base that they were likely to take near the strait. France and Spain were determined to regain Gibraltar, not only for its strategic value but also for its symbolic importance as Spanish territory. Gibraltar was one of the Pillars of Hercules in ancient legend, flanking the entrance to the Mediterranean Sea. The Spanish monarchy traced its roots back to Hercules in mythic times, and the Bourbons as well as the Habsburgs could claim those roots as their own. The Bourbon allies assembled a large fleet to challenge the English possession of Gibraltar, bringing together contingents from both the Atlantic and the Mediterranean so as to equal the size of the Anglo-Dutch fleet. The battle of Málaga in August 1704 left heavy casualties on both sides and no clear victor, but England still held Gibraltar.[41] In October the Bourbon alliance made another attempt to dislodge the English in a combined land and sea assault led by the Baron de Pointis. That assault failed as well.

In February 1705 the baron made another attempt at Gibraltar, and this time the Count of Casa Alegre was ordered to join him with the *San José*, the *San Joaquín*, and the other three ships from his contingent at Cádiz, all well supplied.[42] That assault also failed, and there the matter rested. After the unsuccessful attempt to recapture Gibraltar, Casa Alegre served periodically on the king's Council of War and the Committee on Fleets, gaining bureaucratic experience to add to his practical experience at sea. He would command the long-delayed Tierra Firme Fleet when it finally departed on March 10, 1706, with the *San José* as his capitana.[43]

Given Casa Alegre's limited experience on the Indies run, he had good luck in the choice of his second in command. Don Miguel Agustín de Villanueva, the man ultimately chosen as almirante general of the 1706 fleet, had served the crown on land and sea for nearly thirty-five years, much of the time on the

Indies run, and he well deserved his appointment. Nonetheless, it took years of effort and expense to obtain it. His career provides ample evidence that noblemen of good family still spent their lives in royal service at the end of the Habsburg period.

Villanueva was baptized in Cádiz on December 5, 1656, the son of Don Antonio Augustín de Villanueva and Doña Inés Calvo, both of whom had come from small towns in Andalusia. His father, a member of the prestigious Order of Santiago, served the crown as a lieutenant general of artillery, and Don Miguel had been named to the Order of Santiago by the king when he was still a captain.[44] The family seems to have risen to the nobility no earlier than the seventeenth century, however. The documents do not include the honorific *Don* with the name of either of his grandfathers, though both of his grandmothers bear the honorific *Doña*.[45] Whether or not his family tree had deep roots in the nobility, Villanueva could still benefit from his father's service to the crown and his affiliation with the Order of Santiago.

Villanueva entered royal service in 1672 as a simple soldier in the garrison at Cádiz, where he served for nearly three years. From there he transferred to the guard squadron of the Armada of the Indies, based in Cádiz, the infantry division whose troops sailed on the galleons that defended the Indies fleets. He served as a soldier in the guard squadron for another three years. In many ways we can consider those six years as Villanueva's apprenticeship in royal service, preparing him for higher command, but his climb up the scale of merit in the military hierarchy proved to be slow and laborious. He would spend seven and a half years as a soldier with the Spanish infantry destined for Araya, in Venezuela, most of that time on inactive duty. His only break came when he served for two months as a captain, which suggests that he temporarily replaced a superior officer.

The lagoon at Araya was a prime location for the collection of sea salt, much prized in Europe for preserving fish and meat for storage. During the seventeenth century the Dutch made repeated incursions into Araya not only for salt but to establish a staging area for introducing contraband goods into the Spanish colonies. The Dutch capture of the island of Curaçao in 1634 gave them a permanent base that threatened all of Spanish shipping traffic to and from Tierra Firme.[46] By placing a garrison at Araya and periodically dispatching a galleon to the island of Margarita, off the Venezuelan coast, the Spanish government tried to limit the Dutch threat, but available resources rarely equaled the need for them.

During his time in the guard squadron for the Indies fleet, Villanueva made three round-trip voyages to Tierra Firme. On the last voyage, in the 1684 fleet commanded by Don Gonzalo Chacón, Villanueva volunteered to serve on a ship named *La Estrella,* which was part of a contingent going to the Isthmus of Darién. He participated in a force that relieved the city of Portobelo, under French attack at the time, and also dislodged the French from two strongholds in the vicinity. In January 1684 the king appointed Villanueva to the post of captain of sea and war for the next galleon that would be dispatched to the island of Margarita, traditionally called the *patache de la Margarita* (Margarita dispatch ship).[47] Whatever the terminology, the government sent only two galleons to Margarita in the second half of the seventeenth century, one in 1688 and one in 1695. Villanueva's appointment remained honorific and unpaid until and unless the patache sailed, but it nonetheless marked his ascent up the ladder of military command. In the meantime he continued to serve in the guard squadron.

When another war with the French erupted in 1688, Villanueva transferred to the Armada del Mar Océano, the Atlantic Fleet, as a captain of sea and war, with a salary of 40 escudos a month.[48] Contingents of the Atlantic Fleet often served in the Mediterranean as well, and during the six years that Villanueva sailed with the fleet, he served in both venues on five voyages and one land-based campaign. His service began in 1688, when the fleet sailed on its usual duty out into the Atlantic beyond Cape St. Vincent to escort the incoming Indies fleets into port. From there the Atlantic Fleet relieved a besieged Spanish garrison at Oran, on the North African coast. Villanueva's most notable campaign occurred in 1689, when he volunteered to accompany ships sailing to relieve Larache, a key Spanish stronghold on the Atlantic coast of North Africa. With permission from his general in the Atlantic Fleet, the Count of Aguilar, he remained for the entire Larache campaign. Because of Villanueva's distinguished service and notable bravery in that campaign, the king sponsored his membership in the Order of Santiago.

In 1691 Villanueva served with the Atlantic Fleet in transporting soldiers from Málaga for the army of Catalonia and convoying loads of ship timber for new naval construction. That same year the fleet carried Moorish captives from Larache to an exchange of prisoners; searched for the French fleet that was bombarding the Mediterranean coast of Spain; and carried out its regular duties of escorting and defending the incoming Tierra Firme Fleet. The following year Villanueva again sailed with a relief force to Oran and thereafter rejoined the Atlantic Fleet in Barcelona. For nearly all of 1693 the fleet remained in the Mediterranean, patrolling against the French. Villanueva's division was garrisoned in Gibraltar in 1694 and then joined the army of Catalonia for a land campaign that recaptured the castle and town of Hostellrich, north of Barcelona, from the French. Based on Villanueva's two decades of military service, a long list of distinguished commanders testified not only to his personal merit and valor but also to his intelligence and expertise in every aspect of land and naval warfare, including sailing techniques at sea and fortifications and siege warfare on land.

Villanueva added another paragraph to his résumé in August 1695, when he was appointed superintendent of ship construction for a new royal galleon named the *Santíssima Trinidad*. To carry out his duties, he moved to Colindres, on the Cantabrian coast, where the ship was being built, and remained there for three years. In the process of overseeing the construction, Villanueva added expertise in shipbuilding and outfitting to his other qualifications. By all accounts, he carried out his duties to the complete satisfaction of the naval bureaucracy, including the committee charged with fleet preparations.

After his term as superintendent ended in August 1698, the Council of War asked Villanueva for documentation of his long and exemplary service to the crown and used it to compile an official service record that was printed in Madrid on October 21, 1699, the first step toward appointing him to higher command. But the governmental machine stalled during King Charles II's final agony and death, and Villanueva was not assigned a galleon to command as the patache de la Margarita until 1701, under the new Bourbon king. He then set about repairing and careening that galleon, called *Nuestra Señora de Begoña*, at his own expense, but his run of bad luck continued. When war broke out over the Bourbon succession, the government requisitioned the *Begoña* out from under him, so that Admiral Don Francisco Antonio Garrote could take a much-needed supply of mercury to New Spain for the silver mines. Although Villanueva claimed equal distinction with Garrote and offered to take the mercury himself, the crown ordered Garrote to sail away with the refurbished *Begoña*.[49] Villanueva petitioned for reimbursement of the money he had spent on her careening, but it was not forthcoming from either Garrote or the crown.

Villanueva accepted the king's decision, of course, but that did not stop him from petitioning for his just rewards and the promised command. He already had years invested in the process, not to mention considerable sums of money, of which he reminded the king in his petition, starting with his thirty-two years of continuous service to the crown. Besides careening the *Begoña*, Villanueva had loaned the crown 25,000 pesos to help underwrite the pataches de la Margarita that had been dispatched in 1688 and 1695. The crown reimbursed him only after he had reduced the sum by 6,000 pesos plus interest. Though Villanueva had yet to receive the commission promised him since 1684, the new Bourbon king expected him to provide a second loan to underwrite the fleets in 1701. He had little choice but to comply.

Villanueva's efforts on behalf of two dynasties—and his patience—began to bear fruit after 1703, with preparations for the Tierra Firme Fleet under Don José Fernández de Santillán. By September of that year he had received his commission as captain of sea and war of the patache de la Margarita, but the crown had yet to assign him a ship. Unless and until he sailed, Villanueva had no hope of recouping his loans and paying his creditors. Setting his sights rather high, Villanueva petitioned to use "one of the two ships made in Cantabria as capitana and almiranta" of Don José's fleet, in other words, either the *San José* or the *San Joaquín.* If that could not be arranged, he wanted the almiranta real *Santíssima Trinidad,* whose construction he had overseen. The *Santíssima Trinidad* was in very good shape and ready to sail. Villanueva claimed that she also drew less water than either of the two new ships, so that she would be more agile and adaptable for a number of assignments.

The members of the Council of War were inclined to reject Villanueva's request, in large part because the two new galleons had been purposely built as the capitana and almiranta of the next fleet. To use one of them or the almiranta real of the Atlantic Fleet as the patache de la Margarita would have been inappropriate, and they were also too large and expensive to outfit for such a voyage.[50] Villanueva argued that the patache de la Margarita had to be one of the strongest and best-armed galleons in the guard squadron because it sailed alone and often had to anchor in exposed bays, open to enemy fire. His reasoning failed to persuade the councilors. Moreover, as Don Manuel García de Bustamente noted, although Villanueva was a good man, he was not yet good enough to be assigned one of the two new galleons.

As 1703 turned to 1704 and the fleet still had not sailed, Villanueva asked to be named commanding officer of the next mercury ships to depart so that he could recoup his expenses. The king agreed, but only, it seems, after Villanueva repeated his request "with the proper requisites," presumably another loan. The War Committee designated Villanueva captain of sea and war of the patache de la Margarita on February 4, 1704. To complicate matters, the *Begoña,* which Villanueva had careened at his own expense, had returned to Spain, so he asked to use her in the mercury contingent. Instead the crown designated her as capitana of another proposed fleet to the Indies, much to Villanueva's shock and dismay. At that point he was 80,000 pesos in debt, and his creditors showed little inclination to wait any longer for their money. Desperate, he wrote an impassioned letter to the king by way of various councilors. He had the letter printed and must have distributed it widely.

In his plea Villanueva repeated the litany of his long years of service to the crown and his wide experience and expertise on land and sea. He also reminded the king of his frustration since 1684 in failing to be assigned a ship to fulfill his commission as commanding officer of the patache de la Margarita. On top of everything, he complained, to send the *Begoña* to the Indies with someone else in command would cause him great financial damage and public humiliation. Having consumed his patrimony in service to the crown, deep in debt, bereft of employment, assets, and credit, and having no other recourse, he would be completely destroyed unless he received command of the *Begoña* in the regular fleet. Nonetheless, Villanueva tried to cover all contingencies. As a second choice, he asked to be assigned the royal galleon *Nuestra Señora del Sagrario*, which he would outfit for whichever voyage would best serve the king, that is, as the patache de la Margarita with the Indies fleet or with the mercury contingent.

Three events in 1704 changed Villanueva's luck for the better. First, he was officially inscribed in the Order of Santiago on April 17, 1704, for his services to the crown.[51] In further recognition of Villanueva's services the king also nominated Villanueva's first cousin Don Antonio Augustín, named for Villanueva's father, to the order.[52] Then the outgoing Indies fleets were delayed yet again, largely because merchants in Seville balked at the risk, with a huge Anglo-Dutch fleet in the vicinity. Although the delay aggravated Villanueva's financial situation, it lent added force to his claims for preferment. And last, Don Pedro Ignacio de Zulueta died in Cádiz at midnight on August 1, 1704. Zulueta was almirante, or second in command, of the delayed fleet to Tierra Firme, and until his death he had been careening the *San Joaquín* as his almiranta. Villanueva saw his chance and leaped at it. In another printed petition, filled with the familiar elements of pride in his long service, experience, and expertise, plus desperation at his current plight, he asked to be named Zulueta's replacement. Besides that, he wanted to retain his designations as captain of sea and war of the patache de la Margarita and chief commanding officer of the mercury contingent. Villanueva received everything he requested. The king appointed him to replace Zulueta as almirante on the proposed fleet, with a salary of 2,000 ducados a year, paid in silver. He also retained his other two posts, with salaries and the right to collect fees as head of the mercury contingent. With that, and the promise of reimbursement from the crown for his careening expenses, Villanueva could finally see his way clear to financial health.

On September 1, 1704, the king ordered Villanueva to report to Cádiz to continue the careening. No sooner had he taken up his post than he became embroiled in legal proceedings with Zulueta's son Fernando about reimbursement of the money his father had spent on supplies and careening for the *San Joaquín* since November 1701. Fernando de Zulueta also noted that some of the iron and other supplies for the *San Joaquín* in fact belonged to him, since the crown had not reimbursed his father for them. He wanted either to be paid or to have the supplies returned to him. Although his claim was technically against the crown, he preferred to be paid by Villanueva in exchange for transferring the claim to him. Villanueva had learned how to manipulate bureaucratic requirements during his long wait for preferment. He stalled, insisting on full documentation of the expenses. In a letter of September 24, 1704, he also balked at paying certain charges. For example, he argued that some of the compartments built by Zulueta would have to be rebuilt to meet the ship's military needs and that the fine painted decoration ordered by Almirante Zulueta was both unnecessary and unauthorized under navy regulations.

Fernando de Zulueta begged the crown to require payment from Villanueva, which it did in early December, but Villanueva continued to drag his feet, quibbling over one point or another. In early January 1705 Villanueva asked the general of the fleet, the Count of Casa Alegre, to write on his behalf to Don Domingo López Calo de Mondragón, on the War Committee, explaining why he had not settled accounts with Zulueta. Casa Alegre agreed, writing from aboard the *San José*, but the language of his letter was correct rather than supportive. He stated simply that Villanueva had not complied with the royal order because he had been participating with Casa Alegre in the campaign to recapture Gibraltar from the English. He promised to help sort things out as soon as they went ashore in Cádiz. By the end of January Villanueva had returned the disputed iron to Fernando de Zulueta, on Casa Alegre's direct order. He had also offered to make reparation for various other items supplied to the ship by Fernando's father, Almirante Zulueta.

Villanueva's dispute with the Zuluetas may have alienated some of the men on the *San Joaquín* who owed their jobs to the deceased almirante and may have transferred their loyalty to his heir. In any case, very soon after Villanueva took up his post in Cádiz, he asked for permission to replace two of the officers appointed by Zulueta. The positions at stake were those of the contramaestre and the contramaestre's assistant, the *guardián*, who had responsibility for keeping order among the apprentices and pages and commanding the ship's boat and its crew. These were not high officials, but their competence and loyalty were crucial to the smooth functioning of the ship. It is not clear what set Villanueva against them, but he argued that Andrés Fajardo, the contramaestre, and Juan Andrés Martínez, the guardián, were not fit to serve on a ship as important as the second vessel in a fleet of galleons. Martínez, in particular, was "totally unworthy of a post in royal service, and his only merit lay in having been a servant of Don Sebastián Xijón, the captain of sea and war on the *San José*, who introduced him to Zulueta." Despite their having contracts to serve in the posts, other men were more qualified, Villanueva argued, and he wanted to replace Fajardo and Martínez with men of his own choosing.

Even if Villanueva's assault on their character was true, the contracts with Fajardo and Martínez had been approved by General Casa Alegre, the Council of War, and the king. According to Spanish law, a naval commander had the right to nominate his subordinates, and he also had the right to remove officers from their posts, but only for just cause. Villanueva knew that the law did not support his request and admitted as much by citing the discussion of a commander's prerogatives from the standard manual of naval practice, Joseph de Veitia Linage's *Norte de la contratación*, of 1672.[53] It did not help his case that Veitia had served on the Council of War.

Moreover, Fajardo and Martínez fought back, hiring Don Francisco Rivera to represent them. The documents that Rivera filed noted that the men had been duly appointed and had deposited the necessary bonds (*fianzas*) to guarantee good service before taking up their posts. According to the brief summaries of their careers that Rivera included, Fajardo had served at sea for fifteen years, first as a gunner, then as a contramaestre and guardián in the guard squadron of the Indies fleets. He had made two voyages to New Spain. Martínez had served for twenty-three years, in the Barlovento fleet that periodically patrolled around the Caribbean and in the Atlantic Fleet, ascending from page to guardián. He also had worked on various careenings. Nothing in their career summaries countered Villanueva's claim that they lacked distinction, but that did not give him the right to oust them from their posts without cause. The Junta de Guerra de Indias and the Council of the Indies decided in favor of Fajardo and Martínez at the end of October 1704, and General Casa Alegre passed the news along to Villanueva in early November.

The latter was not willing to let the matter rest, however. Other issues may have been in play besides the competence of Fajardo and Martínez. Their loyalty to Zulueta and his heir may have led them to quarrel with Villanueva when he refused to reimburse the Zulueta family for the careening. Or Villa-nueva may have expected to collect fees from any men he appointed. The men already occupying posts on the *San Joaquín* may already have paid Zulueta a fee for the privilege of being nominated. If so, and if they were not disposed to pay Villanueva as well, he would have preferred to appoint others. Villa-nueva's petition says nothing about this, only that the men had been chosen because of their connections and that there were better men available.

These days, collecting fees for official appointments is considered corrupt, on the assumption that merit alone should lead to appointment. In Villanueva's time, by contrast, merit defined the pool of qualified applicants, but it was still standard practice to expect that the individual chosen for a post would pay a sort of entry fee, unless he had already earned the gratitude of the person doing the choosing. Just as the government expected Casa Alegre and Villanueva to advance the cost of careening the ships assigned to them, so it expected Villa-nueva to collect fees for many of the official functions he performed. Nonethe-less, when he asked to replace men already assigned by his precursor, he had to find just cause for his complaint to be taken seriously. An argument solely on the grounds of his prerogatives in office was not acceptable.

The controversy continued through the winter and early spring of 1705, as the ships were being careened in Cádiz. General Casa Alegre served as a con-duit for the paperwork that flowed back and forth between Villanueva in Cádiz and the bureaucracy in Madrid, but he did not take sides, as he had approved the initial appointments of the two men Villanueva wanted to oust. As work continued on the *San Joaquín* in Cádiz, relations between Villanueva and the two men went from bad to worse. In a letter to Madrid on March 15, 1705, Villanueva acknowledged his lack of legal grounds to replace Fajardo and Martínez but argued that "it would be excessively rigorous to oblige me to do everything myself in ceaseless toil, without being able to turn my back [on them] without worrying about what would happen."

To make matters worse, Roque de Fuentes, the pilot on the *San Joaquín*, also weighed in against Villanueva. In a complaint to Domingo López Calo de Mon-dragón dated February 8, 1705, Fuentes said that Villanueva had intruded into his sphere of competence as pilot on the sortie to Gibraltar, preventing him from doing his job.[54] According to standing orders in Veitia Linage's *Norte de la contratación*, the general of the fleet (in consultation with the principal pilot) defined the overall course and the points of reference that the fleet should ob-serve. He then communicated that information to his almirante, who told the captain of sea and war, who then told the pilot. It was the pilot on the almiranta, in this case Fuentes, who was supposed to decide how best to carry out the general's orders and to issue the commands for maneuvering the ship. Despite his lack of experience in navigation, Villanueva had taken on the pilot's role in the Gibraltar action, Fuentes charged, "trying to deal with unforeseen events and emergencies in the context of some book or paper, which he tried to substitute for knowledge outside his profession." Had his "notable absurdities" and "invincible dictates" on that voyage not been challenged, Fuentes argued, great harm would have resulted.

In addition to an obvious personal conflict, the clash between Villanueva and Fuentes illustrated the ongoing friction between theoretical and practical knowledge. While in other circumstances that friction might have limited consequences, at sea it could mean the difference between life and death for everyone on board. Fuentes expressed undisguised contempt for the "book learning" Villanueva tried to substitute for experience. He also took offense because Villanueva did not seem to respect his intelligence or skill simply because he lacked formal education.

Fuentes had twenty-four years' service as a licensed pilot on the Indies route. He took great pride that no ship piloted by him had ever suffered damage, loss, or mishap, a record that he credited to his care and zeal. Because of his reputation, in 1698 the Count of La Monclova, as viceroy of Peru, had named him to head an expedition of infantry, gunners, and sailors recruited from Veracruz to sail in relief of Spanish forces in the Philippine Islands. By summarizing his career, Fuentes hoped to prove that there was no reason to question his competence, and he resented Villanueva's intrusion into his sphere of competence. Had anything gone wrong because of faulty sailing directions, Fuentes knew that he, as the pilot, would have been blamed. He asked López Calo de Mondragón to remedy the situation in a manner that best served the interests of the crown.

López Calo could not allow the conflict between Fuentes and Villanueva to fester; Spain was at war, and the *San Joaquín* was one of its most important warships. After consulting the War Committee, he asked Don Pedro Fernández Navarrete, second in command, or almirante general, of the Atlantic Fleet, to use his "skill and prudence . . . experience and zeal" to reconcile Villanueva and "this pilot." López Calo told Fernández Navarrete that if he could not persuade them to forget their differences and work together, he should recommend a course of action to the War Committee, bearing in mind that each man should be retained in royal service and that experience should be preferred over theory in maneuvering ships at sea.

In dealing with the stubborn Villanueva and his prickly pilot, Fernández Navarrete justified his reputation for probity. First he talked to each man individually and decided that the cause of their discord had little or no substance. Then, as he reported on March 15, he called them together at his lodgings in Cádiz and succeeded in getting them to reconcile their differences, leaving Fuentes satisfied that Villanueva valued his intelligence and experience.

That same day, however, Villanueva wrote to the War Committee denying any wrongdoing in the matter. He reminded the committee members that in preparing to serve as a captain of sea and war he had instructed himself in the duties of a pilot. He had no doubt that he could order all the ship's maneuvers himself, but for the inconvenience of doing so. Perhaps echoing an argument that Fernández Navarrete had made, Villanueva acknowledged that "the choice of this subject [Fuentes] merited approval because of the scarcity that we suffer of this quality of officers, and that for the same reason it was doubtful that another more appropriate could be found if he were gone."

Nonetheless, Villanueva could not refrain from noting that standard practice in the Atlantic Fleet was very different from what one learned in voyages to the Indies—Fuentes's area of expertise—where superior officers rarely did more than warn the pilot about obvious dangers to the ship. During wartime in European waters, by contrast, there was no reason to set a course of action simply "to please the pilot's whim." Instead, Villanueva maintained, he had tried to make sure that the almiranta avoided the capitana's experience in coming into the bay at Gibraltar. In other words, Villanueva admitted that he had second-guessed the pilot during the Gibraltar sortie, but he argued that such intervention was fully consonant with his role as captain of sea and war and that the ship had fared better because of it. Though Fernández Navarrete had forced Villanueva to make peace with his pilot, he could not force him to admit any wrongdoing in the dispute. Moreover, despite his reconciliation with the pilot, Villanueva took advantage of his March 15 letter to reiterate his request to remove the contramaestre and guardián from the *San Joaquín*, as we have seen.

The history of Don Miguel Agustín de Villanueva reveals a man who was headstrong, proud, stubborn, and tenacious in claiming what he thought was rightfully his. He had no qualms about alienating valuable subordinates and trying the patience of superior officers and bureaucrats from Cádiz to Madrid. But he also brought decades of experience in naval matters to his position. Casa Alegre was fortunate to have him as his second in command.

Casa Alegre's third in command was Don Nicolás de la Rosa y Suárez, who held the rank of *capitán de navío*. In Spanish usage, the third vessel in an armada carried the infantry company *(tercio)*. Its commander, in this case Nicolás de la Rosa, was known as the *gobernador*, and the vessel was known as the *gobierno*. Like Casa Alegre and Villanueva, de la Rosa came from a distinguished lineage and had served the crown on sea and land for many years in the wars of the late seventeenth century.[55] From 1689, when he was still a teenager, to 1695, he had fought in Italy, North Africa, and Catalonia, as well as serving in the *presidio* at Gibraltar. His superior officers would later testify to his distinguished service in each of those venues. In 1696 he had sailed to the Indies and back as the gobernador of the infantry company in the fleet, the same post he would hold under Casa Alegre.

An incident in Cartagena de Indias during that voyage revealed much about the character of Don Nicolás and provides a fascinating glimpse into military life in one of the key ports in Spanish America.[56] With the fleet moored in the protected bay of Cartagena, Don Nicolás, then twenty-three years old, got into a fight in town with one of the infantry captains in his command, Don Luis de Guillén, on April 13. Officials in the fleet soon appeared and arrested Guillén, but he escaped and took refuge in a nearby convent. The officials immediately began an investigation into the altercation, seeking out the other party, de la Rosa, in the rooming house where he lived. They found him in an upstairs room, dressed and standing up, "with a white cloth sling supporting his right arm." Don Francisco Pérez Montalban, judge advocate for the royal councils and auditor general of the armada, took testimony from Don Nicolás, who swore by God and the sign of the cross to tell the truth. A notary recorded the testimony.

To paraphrase Don Nicolás, at 5:30 that afternoon, as he was going down the street by the Convent of Santo Domingo, he saw Guillén in the doorway of a house across from the convent. Guillén called out what de la Rosa considered to be an insulting "question," after which both men drew their swords and briefly fought. A number of people witnessed the altercation, including Don Leonardo de Lara, almirante of the fleet, who promptly detained Guillén. Don Nicolás left the scene and went home with a slight wound in one arm, but he said "he did not know who gave it to him."

The master surgeon Don Gaspar de Olivera testified that the wound he treated was rather more serious than Don Nicolás admitted. Then, with Guillén holed up in the convent and the victim refusing to name his attacker, the auditor placed de la Rosa under house arrest, with a penalty of 500 ducados if he ventured outside. The next day (April 14) the auditor and his notary went to a residential building that Guillén was known to frequent on the street called Santo Domingo, near the convent. Inside they found a male Negro, whom they described as a recent arrival *(bozal).*[57] He identified himself as Manuel de Congo, a slave of Don Juan Antonio Trelles, a gentleman of the Order of Santiago who had arrived with the armada and had lodgings in the building in question.

At the auditor's order, Manuel de Congo gave testimony, swearing by God and the sign of the cross to tell the truth. He said that the previous afternoon he had been upstairs alone in the kitchen of his master's lodgings, because his master had gone out. Hearing voices in the doorway of the building, he went downstairs. He saw two men whose names he did not know with their swords drawn, but he had previously seen one of them in the building. There were many other people there whom he did not know. At that, he went back up to his kitchen and saw nothing else. He did not sign his testimony, saying that he did not know how.

The investigators then went to a house on the corner of the Plazuela de Santo Domingo, where Juan de Pineda was staying. A twenty-six-year-old resident of Seville, Pineda had also arrived on the armada. Asked about the fight, he testified that he had been in the cloister of the convent the previous afternoon "at about five, more or less." Hearing the sound of swordplay, he had gone outside to look and found a sizeable crowd gathered, of whom he recognized no one but the almirante of the armada, Don Leonardo de Lara. He heard people say that there was an altercation between "the captain of the almiranta and a Captain Guillén," and he saw the almirante arrive with two other gentlemen who grabbed a man said to be Guillén. As Guillén and the sergeant major of the armada walked past the door of the convent's church, Guillén bolted and ran inside. Pineda said he knew nothing more and that he did not know how to sign his name.

It is not clear what happened next. Given Don Nicolás's reluctance to name his attacker and his dismissal of the wound as slight, it would appear that he wished to keep the dispute out of official channels. We might guess that some disagreement at sea had poisoned relations between Guillén and Don Nicolás and that Guillén had decided to settle the matter on land. The public nature of his challenge to Don Nicolás suggests that he welcomed an audience, though he did not accept being arrested after he wounded the object of his anger. Like so many simmering disputes among shipmates, the fight between Don Nicolás and Guillén may have settled things, so that the authorities were left with no one to punish. In any case, Don Nicolás seems to have suffered no lasting effects from the wound, except perhaps to his pride.

On the return trip to Spain the ship in which Don Nicolás sailed wrecked seven leagues from Havana. As the captain of sea and war on that voyage, he worked tirelessly to salvage the artillery and the treasure remittances for the king and for private parties, as well as supervising the burning of the wreck to make sure that enemy forces could not derive any benefit from it. The gobernador of the vessel, *maestre de campo* Don Diego de Córdoba Laso de la Vega, later wrote that de la Rosa had carried out his duties so "zealously . . . and in such difficult circumstances . . . that it caused him to become ill enough to be administered the last rites, without hope for his life."[58] Against the odds, he survived and returned to Spain to recuperate. His later career would continue to strike the same notes of pride, bravery, dedication, and self-assurance that he demonstrated on his voyage to the Indies in 1696, at the age of twenty-three.

Ten years later, on February 9, 1706, Philip V conceded the title Count of Vega Florida to Don Nicolás de la Rosa y Suárez, who then held the rank of capitán de navío. The title was associated with the land previously known as the viscountcy of Santa Rosa.[59] Following common practice, after obtaining the status of a titled noble, Don Nicolás would be referred to as the Count of Vega Florida or by his functional title on a particular voyage. In 1706 he would sail as the gobernador of the Tierra Firme Fleet, third in the chain of command behind Casa Alegre as captain general and Villanueva as almirante. The success or failure of the Tierra Firme Fleet and all the men, treasure, and goods carried in that fleet would depend on their skill.

CHAPTER THREE

The Men of the San José

Along with the posts of the three fleet officers, other key appointments in the 1706 Tierra Firme Fleet included the captains of sea and war for the *San José* and the *San Joaquín*. The war complicated the crown's search for appropriate candidates for several reasons. Merchants in Seville were reluctant to send goods to the Indies while hostilities continued. As a consequence, the fleet system to Tierra Firme broke down altogether, and the Portobelo fairs, which the fleets provisioned, ceased as well. With no revenue coming in from Tierra Firme and no fairs in Portobelo, the revenue stream that helped to fund the fleets dried up. As a result, in Madrid the crown had to shift money from one pot to another to pay for the most pressing need of the moment. And in Spanish ports the crown regularly asked naval officers to advance the money to careen and provision the ships on which they hoped to sail. Despite wartime needs for qualified officers, the paucity of ships crossing the Atlantic meant that the careers of many qualified naval men were put on hold as they waited for assignment. Unassigned and therefore unpaid, they lacked the funds to advance to the crown. All of these circumstances made the search for a captain of sea and war for the *San José* difficult, especially since the post would carry a salary of only 40 escudos per month.[1]

Don Diego Asencio de Vicuña, generally referred to as Vicuña, seems to have been the first man officially assigned to the post. When he was taken prisoner in 1704, the king rewarded him *in absentia* with a promotion to second in command (almirante general) of the Armada of the Ocean Sea, pending his release. Over the summer of 1704 the king and the government in Madrid searched for a replacement for Vicuña, entrusting the search to the Marquis of El Carpio. His success or failure would depend on the willingness of qualified men to advance money to the crown for the war effort, with the promise of reimbursement from tax revenues. We have already seen that process at work in the careers of Casa Alegre, Villanueva, and Vega Florida.

All too often, the crown delayed the promised reimbursement for years, faced with more pressing needs. For example, Don Pedro Joséph de Urdiales advanced the crown 78,000 pesos in 1698, upon his appointment as captain of sea and war and *almirante de galeones,* with a promise of repayment from the tax revenues of Panama. When that proved impossible, the crown shifted the debt to Veracruz and then, in 1703, to Quito. With stories like that floating around, by the summer of 1704 no one was willing to loan the crown money for a low-paying office such as captain of sea and war. As a consequence, the Council of War and the War Committee met on September 21 and recommended that the appointment be made in the "regular way"—solely on the basis of merit. The king agreed and asked to be informed as soon as possible about the man selected and "the merits and experience that he brought to a post of that importance."

Acting on the recommendation of the War Committee, the Council of War chose eight men for a short list in February 1705, "bearing in mind that they have been put forth as candidates because the secretary had no information on any others that might have been suitable." Don Melendo Suárez de Miranda headed the list by virtue of seniority; as of 1699 he had served the crown for forty-one years, rising through the ranks to captain of sea and war. Suárez does not seem to have been on active service after 1699, but he had not yet received the pension promised by the crown. The council may have included his name more as a matter of courtesy to an old soldier than because he was a viable candidate for the post.

Don Pedro García de Asarta, seventh on the list of eight, had been in the Armada of the Ocean Sea for more than twenty-two years by 1705. For most of his career he had served in the infantry companies of the guard squadron for the Indies fleets, rising in rank from ordinary soldier to sergeant and finally to lieutenant of sea and war. He had also served in the fort at Gibraltar and in various garrisons in North Africa. Most recently he had served as lieutenant of sea and war on the galleon *Nuestra Señora del Carmen.* Returning from a voyage to Buenos Aires with the Armada of the Ocean Sea, García de Asarta had been taken prisoner in Portugal.

The other finalists each had a record of about twenty years' service to the crown, but not necessarily the Spanish crown. Don Juan de Monsegur, born in lower Navarre, had commanded ships for Louis XIV of France for twenty years. He had only entered Spanish service in 1701 with the accession of Philip V. The king appointed him to the rank of captain of sea and war in 1702, after which he served with distinction in various campaigns. The king also recommended another Frenchman, Don Joséph de Roche, though no service record appeared with his nomination. As a backup, the king designated Roche as one of the noblemen known as *caballeros entretenidos,* who sailed on royal warships at the king's expense. In that position Roche would collect a stipend of 50 escudos per month, 10 escudos more than he could earn as captain of sea and war. Despite the king's endorsement, the council's War Committee ranked him sixth on their list of eight.

The captain of grenadiers Don Joséph Canales completed the list. The spelling of his Christian name illustrates the French influence that had begun to affect Spanish fashions. Canales had served the crown for more than fifteen years, nearly all under the captain of sea and war Don Diego Asencio de Vicuña. In his latest campaign, Canales had served with distinction in the battle of Vigo against the English in 1704. With the pending appointment of Vicuña as almirante general of the Armada of the Ocean Sea, Canales pursued his own promotion to captain of sea and war.

Of the other four men on the council's list, three had already served in that capacity: Marcos García de Urdiales, Don Rodrigo Pardo Calderón, and Don Nicolás Zelaya. Unfortunately, the secretary of the council noted that their service records were not included. They had been sent to the Marquis of El Carpio in July 1704, when he headed the selection process, but by February 1705 they still had not been returned. Without those records, the council had only a sketchy idea of each man's qualifications for the job, so the secretary wrote to Carpio requesting that the papers be returned right away if he still had them. The papers were not forthcoming, perhaps because Carpio could not find then, perhaps because he did not want to find them. He had been in charge of the selection process during the summer of 1702 but had been sidestepped thereafter. He could have had any number of professional and personal reasons not to cooperate.

It turns out that Carpio's inaction and the fate of the missing papers were irrelevant. Don Sebastián de Xijón was already installed as captain of sea and war on the capitana *San José,* and later documents reveal that he had held the post since 1702.[2] Moreover, Don Pedro García de Asarta and Don Joséph Canis de Alzamora had received the equivalent posts on the *San Joaquín* and the *Almudena,* respectively. How and when these appointments occurred is not clear, but the senior officers on the long-delayed Indies voyage may have appointed the men on their own, with the tacit approval of at least some members of the bureaucracy in Madrid.

One clue that this happened is a paper trail laid on September 26, 1705. In the morning the king made an urgent request for a precise abstract of the terms and conditions under which the general, almirante, and other senior officers on the upcoming fleet had been appointed. He wanted the abstract by four o'clock that afternoon. Don Joséph de Grimaldo, the king's secretary for matters related to war and the Indies, relayed the order to Don Domingo López Calo de Mondragón, on the Council of War, who sent it to the Duke of Atrisco. That afternoon the duke sent his reply through the bureaucratic hierarchy, via his secretary. He had not received the king's order until half past two, he wrote, which was little before four o'clock and had left him insufficient time to provide what the king requested. Instead, he simply supplied the decrees by which the general, almirante, and gobernador had been appointed in the fleet. He excused himself from supplying anything about the appointments of Captains Xijón, García de Asarta, and Canis de Alzamora "because the paperwork contained nothing out of the ordinary" and the appointments had been conferred "fairly and openly."[3]

What are we to make of this? From the urgency of the king's request we can infer that he was upset; he may have just found out about the appointments. Was he alone in the dark, or were some members of the Council of War also ignorant of the appointments? Because the king wanted to know the precise terms and conditions under which the Count of Casa Alegre and his subordinates had been appointed, we can infer that he thought someone or some organ of government had overstretched its authority. And the Duke of Atrisco? His motives for failing to comply with the king's urgent request are harder to discern. Perhaps he was allied to the fleet officers in some way. Perhaps he was reluctant to back the Bourbon king wholeheartedly, especially when doing so meant that Frenchmen might be appointed to sensitive offices in the fleet. The least likely scenario is that Atrisco simply had no time to comply. His pointed refusal to provide information about the three captains of sea and war suggests that he had no intention of complying.

There the matter rested. Xijón, García de Asarta, and Canis de Alzamora kept their posts. Although García de Asarta was seventh on the Council of War's short list of eight for captain of sea and war on the *San José*, he had had a long and distinguished career and presumably had some claim to compensation because of his imprisonment by the Portuguese. With Xijón already in place on the *San José*, however, García de Asarta had been appointed to the *San Joaquín*. Canis, originally assigned to the *Almudena*, was reassigned to the gobierno *Santa Cruz* before the fleet sailed, when the *Almudena* was dropped from the roster as unfit.

We cannot say that the three men were unqualified for their posts. We can infer, however, that there was something irregular about the way they were appointed, a process that may have sidestepped the Council of War and the king. The Duke of Atrisco died without returning the files on the appointments to the Council of War. In subsequent years the crown asked his widow several times to try to find them among his papers. They asked her again with great urgency in December 1708, when the government first learned about the loss of the *San José* and was trying to come to grips with the human and financial costs of that disaster. Judging from the strange case of the senior appointments in Casa Alegre's fleet, Philip V would also have to come to grips with his own bureaucracy before he could reign in fact as well as in name.

As for the minor officers and crew of the San José, in the perennial irony of written records, we know the least about the most. The hundreds of men who served aboard the *San José*, and died when she sank, left little trace in the records. What can we learn about their lives from the minimal records that survive them? The best sources by far are the documents regarding their service on the *San José;* officials kept careful notations about the service records of all on board.[4] Most of the men and boys earned wages calculated by the month; the amounts had been set by ordinances in 1633 and had not changed in the interim.[5]

Though the men earned wages by the month, their service records followed the more irregular rhythm of periodic musters rather than a monthly roll call. At intervals, the officers would call together everyone on board in the presence of a notary, who recorded the name of each man who appeared at the muster, noting the information in a *libro de muestras,* a book designated specifically for that purpose. The wages owed to each man or boy at the end of the voyage depended upon the record in the muster books, at least one copy of which was kept elsewhere than on the *San José.*[6]

Because it was wartime, the *San José* carried a large contingent of fighting men. Taken together, the soldiers and artillerymen accounted for more than half the men on board. The ships of the Armada de la Guardia had carried infantry contingents since the late sixteenth century. When companies of soldiers were attached to the navy more or less permanently, their officers often learned to be skilled at sea as well as on land. That distinction earned them the title captain of sea and war, and collectively they displaced ordinary infantry captains at sea from the early seventeenth century on. Despite the presence of captains of sea and war on board, however, the relationship between soldiers and sailors remained difficult; their jobs were too different, and their mutual distrust too strong.[7]

The infantry company that sailed on the *San José* in March 1706 included nine officers, thirty-eight musketeers, and seventy-two soldiers, fifteen of whom earned bonus pay for their skills and prior service.[8] The company also included three drummers and a standard-bearer. The flagship of a war fleet often carried a piper and occasionally some flageolet players as well, though these were not mentioned in the crew list for the *San José*. It may seem odd that a fighting force would devote so much of its manpower to unarmed support personnel, but the drummers, pipers, and flageolet players served an important function. The flageolet, a long end-blown flute, in particular could cut through the noise of roaring sea and cannonade alike, helping to animate and encourage the men during battle. The *San José*'s company had to make do with only three drummers. Perhaps the nearly continual warfare in the late seventeenth century had used up the available supply of pipers and flageolet players, along with so many other skilled personnel.[9]

The head of the infantry company on the *San José* was Don Sebastián de Xijón, who had been appointed to the post of captain of sea and war in March 1702, when the fleet was originally scheduled to leave. He earned 41 silver escudos a month, the equivalent of 410 reals, a considerable salary with responsibilities to match. Through repeated delays he remained in the post, serving the crown as he was needed. When the fleet finally sailed in March 1706, he left behind his wife and son. At that point he had collected only about half of the salary he had earned since 1702; royal officials carefully kept records of the amount he was owed, but the actual payment would have to wait until the crown was less strapped for cash.

The rest of Don Sebastián's officers were not recruited until just before the fleet sailed. Don Francisco Nieba (or Nieva) served as his lieutenant *(alférez)* of sea and war, earning 15 escudos a month; and Antonio Rodríguez de la Mota served as his sergeant, earning 8. Pedro de la Palma as head squadron leader (9 escudos a month) supervised the four men who led the squadrons on board, each of them earning 7 escudos a month.[10] Wages roughly corresponded to the responsibilities each man held, and all of them appeared at their first muster on March 10, 1706, as the *San José* got under way. Perhaps surprisingly, the three drummers in the company earned 6 escudos a month, less than the squadron leaders but as much as the best paid among the fighting men. Their relatively exalted position can also be explained in terms of their responsibilities. Drummers had to be visible and audible during battle as well as at more ceremonial times and to set an example of courage and steadfastness under fire, armed with no more than a drum. The government obviously thought that was worth 6 escudos a month.

The thirty-eight musketeers formed the elite corps of the infantry company. They earned their 6 escudos a month by being able to handle the heavy muskets that were traditionally assigned to the largest and strongest men on board. In the early sixteenth century other specialized soldiers, such as harquebusiers, halberdiers, and pikemen, also figured in the ranks of the infantry, but their jobs were eliminated at least a century before the *San José* set sail.[11] The musketeers alone remained. Their number included five men who carried the honorific *Don* before their names. Although that distinction was sometimes bestowed for reasons other than birth, in the context of official muster lists we can assume that it carried its traditional meaning: the five men were of noble birth. That should not surprise us. Military service in royal armies had been an acceptable occupation for the Spanish nobility since medieval times and indeed provided the justification for the noble class in the first place. Nobles in military service played a crucial role in the reconquest of the Iberian Peninsula from the Muslims, and later still in the conquest of Spain's overseas empire.

In the early eighteenth century as before, Spanish noblemen from families at the low end of the financial ranks of the nobility, and the sons of distinguished families who were not the first born, often chose military service to make their way in the world. In fact, military service was one of the classic careers open to talent, especially in a country such as Spain, which ruled lands elsewhere in Europe and often had to defend them from its rivals. In short, the army continued to be a crucial element in the preservation of the Spanish empire, and service in the army was a noble profession, so it is not surprising to find noblemen among the musketeers.

Men who were born into the nobility also served as simple soldiers. The 133 soldiers on the *San José* included 14 who bore the honorific *Don* before their names. Two of them were among the 16 who were entitled to a bonus for their military skills and prior experience *(soldados aventajados)*. The soldiers with bonus pay earned 5 escudos a month, whereas the rest of the soldiery and the company standard-bearer earned only 3. Noblemen who proved themselves in battle could hope to rise to command in fairly short order; ordinary soldiers could rise in the ranks as well, though very rarely to an exalted place in the hierarchy. Whatever their rank or status, all the men in the infantry company received an advance of one month's pay when they enlisted for the 1706 fleet.

Some spent it in debauchery; others left it behind with their families. In better times the men might have received advances of three to six months' pay. In fact, when General Casa Alegre issued a recruitment call for the fleet in July 1704, he promised the men four months' wages in advance.[12] That they received only one month's pay in advance in 1706 testifies to the government's worsening financial situation.

The artillery corps on the *San José* occupied a position somewhere between soldiers and sailors. Although they were technically part of the ship's crew, their main responsibility was to maintain and use the ship's complement of artillery. The noise, smoke, and heat from the big guns during battle transformed the gun decks into a semblance of hell, especially in summer. Add to that the unfortunate propensity of artillery pieces to explode from time to time, and it is clear that the gunners on the *San José* earned their 6 ducados a month. That was slightly more than the wages assigned to a musketeer (6 escudos) because a ducado was worth slightly more than an escudo.[13] When the *San José* sailed in March 1706 there were seventy-nine gunners on board, plus a master gunner (*condestable*), his assistant, and a gunsmith, all under the immediate authority of a captain of artillery—a total of eighty-three men. In 1629–33 the Spanish crown had calculated that a flagship should carry one infantryman for every 3.8 toneladas, and the calculation may have included the gunners along with the infantry because of their related functions.[14] The *San José* was officially listed as measuring 1,066.75 toneladas when it was launched. If we add the 83 gunners to the 122 infantrymen who sailed with the ship in March 1706, we get a total of 205 men, that is, one man for every 5.2 tons or so, considerably less than the guidelines early in the previous century.

The social profile of the artillery corps differed from that of the soldiery, despite their similar functions in handling gunnery. Diego Gil Delgado held the post of captain of artillery on the *San José* from the moment she sailed in 1706. Unlike the infantry's captain of sea and war, Don Sebastián de Xijón, Gil Delgado had not been hired prior to the voyage, nor did he compare in rank and salary. He earned only 10 ducados a month, less than a quarter of Don Sebastián's pay. Overall, the hierarchy of command and the pay scale were much more compressed in the artillery corps than in the infantry. Ordinary gunners earned 6 ducados a month, and the master gunner and his assistant both earned 8 ducados, leaving little distance or distinction between them and their captain. Moreover, not a single nobleman figured among the gunners on the *San José*, which presumably reflected the traditional prejudice favoring the army over the navy in Spain. Nonetheless, the artillery corps as a whole occupied positions several rungs up the status hierarchy from the ordinary sailors and soldiers on board, both in pay and in prestige.

Because the *San José* served as the capitana of the Tierra Firme Fleet, she carried a hierarchy of officials that extended upward in pay and status from the ordinary run of officials in charge of lesser-ranked ships.[15] At the top of that hierarchy stood the captain general, Don José Fernández de Santillán, the Count of Casa Alegre. As we already know, he had been assigned to the *San José* in 1702, at an annual salary of 4,000 ducados. That worked out to 3,667 reals a month, far and away the highest salary in the fleet, as befitted his position. Don Jose's second in command, Don Miguel Agustín de Villanueva, earned just half that amount for his service in the fleet on the *San Joaquín.*

Interestingly enough, both men's salaries were less in nominal terms than their counterparts had earned in the early 1630s. In between lay decades of unrelenting military expenditures for wars, rebellions, and general defense, paid out against a background of economic recession and monetary upheaval. The government's drastic deflation of the coinage in 1680 had aimed to control inflation, as noted above, and the effort had succeeded by 1686, but at the cost of considerable pain to Spaniards up and down the social scale. For naval officers, the deflation was another element depressing their salaries in nominal terms. In the real terms of purchasing power, however, their salaries were probably about the same in 1700 as they had been in 1630.

The captain general presided over a group of officials on the *San José* who had responsibilities in the fleet but little to do with the actual running of the ship. First among them in prestige and wages was the physician, Don Juan Silva Manzano, who earned 660 reals a month. By contrast, the chief surgeon on the *San José*, Fray Clementi Cazón, earned only 200. Fray Clementi was a member of the religious order of St. John of God, which was often associated with the medical profession, taking on the physical tasks of caring for the sick that were disdained by university-trained physicians such as Doctor Silva. The apothecary, Juan Bautista de Castro, earned 80 reals a month. These three men provided for the medical needs of the nearly six hundred men on board the *San José*, though they could rely on additional hands when the need arose.

Don Juan Andrés Hordas (or Ordaz) occupied the next rung on the status hierarchy of nonmariners, serving as general overseer of the fleet, a position he had purchased from the crown in 1701. His duties involved looking out for the interests of the crown and the House of Trade. The office paid 250,000 maravedis a year, or about 613 reals a month, but it was expected that he would collect additional fees in the course of his duties. The royal scrivener, or notary, for the fleet, Diego Luque Obregón, also sailed on the *San José*. Although he fulfilled a crucial function by certifying official records, he earned only 88 reals a month, the same as a master gunner. Wages did not correlate precisely with social status, however. Don Juan Félix Carlos de Ulloa earned 88 reals a month as the *alguacil real* (royal bailiff), though his name would indicate that he held noble status. Don Manuel Crisóstomo de León earned the same wages in the post of gentleman of the standard, and he too would seem to have been a nobleman. Don Joséph de Belmori, who held an advanced university degree, sailed on the *San José* as chief chaplain for the fleet. Ordinary chaplains on warships generally earned no more than a gunner—66 reals a month—but Don Joséph earned twice that amount and undoubtedly commanded respect not only for his job but also because of his education and social position.

The officials in charge of sailing and maintaining the ship had a hierarchy of wages and status of their own. The chief pilot, Captain Benito Alonso Barroso, clearly occupied first place in that hierarchy.[16] By his own account, Barroso had spent fifty years in military service at sea by 1705, most recently serving in the unsuccessful attempt to recapture Gibraltar in February 1705. Earlier he had served as captain of sea and war in the Armada de Barlovento in the Caribbean, and then as the chief pilot in the same fleet. Back in Cádiz after the failed assault on Gibraltar, Barroso received an endorsement from the Count of Casa Alegre.[17] He was listed as chief pilot on the *San José* when it left Cádiz in March 1706. Like the captain general and his second in command, pilots generally earned a salary calculated by the voyage or year rather than the month. Captain Barroso signed on at 750 ducados for a round-trip voyage, which would normally have lasted between six and eight months. At a salary of 1,500 ducados a year, a chief pilot would earn 1,375 reals a month, an impressive salary indeed, only slightly less than the almirante of the fleet. The pilot's assistant, Juan López Mundo, earned half that amount.

Next in the hierarchy of wages and status came the ship's master of rigging and rations, Juan Joséph Moreno, who had been associated with the *San José* since at least 1703. Before that he had made several other trips to Tierra Firme, most recently in 1691–92, 1694–95, and 1698.[18] Because the *San José* was an important warship and the capitana of the fleet, the naval hierarchy formed a thick upper layer of authority above that of the master. In earlier times and on merchant vessels or lesser navy vessels, the ship's master would have had more authority than Moreno exercised. On the *San José* he was responsible for all the equipment permanently attached to the ship, as well as all the supplies and victuals that came on board for each voyage. In a certain sense he was also responsible for all the men on board, but more as an innkeeper than as a commander.[19] Juan Joséph Moreno earned the equivalent of 250 reals a month. His assistant, the contramaestre Joséph Sánchez Quintos, earned just over half that amount.

The *dispensero* (dispenser or steward) had responsibility for distributing food rations during the voyage, and the exercise of his duties could be a cause of enormous contention if supplies ran low. Cristóbal Simón de Vilches occupied that position on the *San José*, earning wages of 66 reals a month. The skilled craftsmen who served as carpenters, coopers, and caulkers on Spanish warships were listed along with the other minor officials and traditionally rose from the ranks of simple sailors. The *San José* carried a chief carpenter and his assistant, a chief cooper and his assistant, and two caulkers when she sailed in 1706. The chiefs earned 110 reals a month, and the assistants and caulkers earned 66 reals, the same as a gunner or the dispenser.

Perhaps surprisingly, the chief diver *(buzo mayor)* on the *San José*, known simply as Juan Pedro, earned almost as much as the master, some 220 reals a month. Because the *San José* headed a fleet sailing into a war zone, Juan Pedro's high wages can best be considered as hazard pay. Technically, a diver only needed to be sailor who knew how to swim, but in practice he needed to be daring and courageous far beyond the norm. According to descriptions written in the sixteenth century, during a battle the diver worked inside the hold with the carpenters and caulkers, patching any holes made by enemy fire. After the battle ended, the diver went into the water to repair the damage from the outside, nailing lead sheet and tarred canvas over the holes.[20] The safety of the ship and everyone on board depended on his work. That was no more true in 1706 than it had been in previous times, but the diver on the *San José* earned 3.3 times the wages of his counterpart in 1633.[21] Given the hazards of the job, experienced divers presumably became scarce enough in the course of the late-seventeenth-century wars to command a premium wage in 1706.

The remainder of the ship's company, properly speaking, were the 168 sailors, apprentices, and pages who handled the daily tasks involved in maneuvering the ship. With their 25 officers, there would have been one mariner for every 5.5 tons of capacity on the *San José*. That was more than the guidelines for 1629–33 had specified, which was one sailor for every 6.25 tons. Individual ships and fleets varied considerably in the number of men they carried, however; much depended on how many men were available when a fleet was ready to sail. Given that variability, many scholars avoid the notion of manning ratios altogether.[22] Such numbers, however flawed, can suggest various useful things about a ship, however, not the least being how cramped the accommodations were. With a high manning ratio of sailors, plus the contingents of soldiers and bureaucrats for the fleet, the *San José* was cramped indeed, adding to the difficulties the sailors faced in maneuvering the ship.

Sixty-six of the San José's 168 seamen earned 44 reals a month as ordinary sailors, but we know very little about them except their names and dates of service. Like gunners, sailors tended to be between twenty and forty years of age, old enough to know the ropes and still young enough to handle them.[23] From their names alone it is impossible to tell how many of them might have been foreigners, because the recordkeepers tended to Hispanicize all the names. Foreigners had made up as much as 20 percent of some Spanish crews in the sixteenth century.[24] Thereafter the government continued to welcome and even to recruit foreign sailors to serve in the navy as long as they were Catholics. Because the war over the Bourbon succession in Spain pitted several Catholic powers against Spain and France, the sources of foreign Catholics were arguably fewer in that war than in others.

There were rather more apprentices on the *San José* than we might expect: 83, or nearly half of the working crewmen.[25] Apprentices traditionally were between seventeen and twenty years of age, some with seafaring experience and others who had never been near a ship before signing on. The ones who were quick to learn and anxious to advance might be promoted to the rank of sailor fairly quickly. Others would stay at the rank of apprentice for years, earning only 1,000 maravedis, or about 29 reals, a month. The youngest crew members on the *San José* were the nineteen pages, who could be as young as eight or as old as eighteen. Thirteen of them came directly from the Colegio Seminario de San Telmo in Seville, which had been established in 1569 to train boys—mostly orphans—for the sea. Judging from the proportion of pages from the *colegio* on the *San José*, the program was succeeding in its mission.

All of the ship's company who sailed with the *San José* in March 1706 had received a signing bonus when they enlisted. For the artillery corps and sailors of all ranks the bonus was two months' pay, a considerable incentive to a poor family and twice the rate paid to soldiers. The difference may have reflected the habitual scarcity of sailors for the Spanish fleets, which may have been particularly acute at the beginning of the eighteenth century. Not only had Spain been at war almost continuously for decades but the population had not grown much since the demographic slump in the early 1600s. The scarcity of sailors seems to have been one reason why so few fleets sailed to Tierra Firme in the late seventeenth century.

The wage scales for men in Spanish war fleets between the 1630s and the early eighteenth century provide some striking comparisons and contrasts. The pay for many sorts of jobs, such as gunners and all ranks of sailors, stayed the same, and we have seen a similar pattern for some of the officers on board. The monthly wages of soldiers even declined between the 1630s and the early eighteenth century, from 40 reals a month to 30. The economic and monetary upheavals of the seventeenth century may have left the purchasing power of those wages nearly the same or even a bit higher by the early eighteenth century, so the wages may not reflect a lower standard of living for the men. That circumstance makes the change in nominal wages for pilots and a few other specialties even more striking. The salary scale established in 1633 listed a chief pilot's salary as 250 reals a month, but the chief pilot on the *San José* earned five and a half times that amount in 1706. Similarly, the salary of an assistant pilot was more than three times as much in 1706 than it had been in 1633. The inescapable inference to draw from these figures is that qualified pilots were exceedingly scarce as the eighteenth century opened, despite government efforts to train more of them. Similarly, a diver in 1706 could earn more than three times the nominal wages of his counterpart in the 1630s, presumably reflecting a scarcity of men with a diver's crucial skills.

With the men signed on, General Casa Alegre made final preparations for the departure of the Tierra Firme Fleet. His nephew Don Diego Fernández de Santillán did the same for the New Spain Fleet under his command. The artillery and other munitions carried by the *San José* had been loaded on board in December 1705, carefully recorded by Juan Joséph Moreno, the master of rations on the *San José*. The ship had carried a full complement of artillery for the expedition to Gibraltar in 1704, but thereafter the guns and munitions were warehoused in Cádiz. Now that the fleet was nearly ready to depart for Tierra Firme, the artillery came on board again. Moreno logged in sixty-four pieces of bronze artillery in all—sixty-two guns and two mortars—plus other munitions and gunnery supplies. In addition, the *San José* would carry sixty-nine pieces of iron artillery in the hold as ballast, "considered necessary for its navigation."[26] General Casa Alegre had made sure that the *San José* was properly adorned as the capitana of an important fleet. For the expedition to Gibraltar, Moreno mentioned

a new awning of crimson damask for the skiff [*falua*] of said general with seven curtains, [and for the] seat and back of the poop benches . . . and one small standard of said damask painted and gilded on both sides with the royal arms and those of the said general, decorated with silk fringe, braids, and buttons of the same; the tassels and cords of the standard all of crimson silk; the curtains of the greatest expense with their bronze rings; and another awning of green oilcloth to cover the said one of damask, lined with fine linen [*holandilla*].[27]

Almirante Villanueva had complained about the excessive decoration that his precursor added to the *San Joaquín,* as we have seen.[28] We can only guess what he thought about his general's skiff.

The New Spain Fleet and the Tierra Firme Fleet would leave Cádiz together on March 10, 1706. Together, both fleets included only twenty-six ships, including the merchant vessels that were designed to revive the Portobelo fairs. As the officers and men on the *San José* began their voyage to the Indies, they were a diverse lot in status, wealth, age, and experience. Circumstances would nonetheless bring nearly all of them together in the same tragic fate.

CHAPTER FOUR

A Tale of Two Viceroys, One Captain General, and a World at War

The first Spanish fleet to Tierra Firme in the eighteenth century existed on paper for several years before it shaped up in reality. In the meantime, most of the ships assigned to that fleet remained moored in Cádiz, and its officers earned no salaries until circumstances cleared the way for their departure. The war in Europe controlled those circumstances, even as its effects reached halfway around the world. In the Viceroyalty of Peru the colonial administration and ordinary citizens alike had to deal with those effects on their own for the most part, complicated by the change in Spain's ruling dynasty from Habsburg to Bourbon.

Today Peru is a well-defined state in northwestern South America with nearly half a million square miles of territory. To understand the Spanish world in the early eighteenth century, however, we have to blot that image from our minds. In 1700 the Viceroyalty of Peru covered nearly the whole of South America, from Panama and the northern coast of South America to the Atlantic coast in the southeast and the Pacific coast in the west. It was an area of about 9.5 million square miles, including thousands of miles of coastline. The only part of the continent not included under the viceroy's purview was Brazil, a colony of Portugal. About 5.5 million people lived in Peru in 1700, scattered throughout the vast territory, with concentrations in the urban areas.

To provide a semblance of manageability to the viceroyalty, various regions had been defined, more or less geographically, each under the authority of a high court, or *audiencia*. The judges of each audiencia, called *oidores* (lit., auditors, hearers), and their subordinate officials oversaw the administration of justice and worked closely with governors, who held civil jurisdiction, and captains general, who held military jurisdiction. Often one person held the posts of both governor and captain general in a given district, the better to coordinate various spheres of administration, but they were technically separate posts. Each of the audiencias included a number of smaller jurisdictions, down to the basic unit of the municipality.

At the end of the seventeenth century the Audiencia of Lima included the viceregal capital of Lima, with its port at Callao; the Audiencia of Panama included the city of Panama on the Pacific coast of the isthmus of the same name and Portobelo on the Caribbean coast; the strategic city of Cartagena de Indias, on the Caribbean coast of Tierra Firme, came under the Audiencia of Santa Fe de Bogotá. The Audiencia of Chile, on the Pacific coast, included the city of Santiago, and the city of Buenos Aires came under the Audiencia of Charcas, on the south Atlantic coast.

The viceroy sat at the apex of the bureaucratic structure as the king's representative, coordinating the activities of all the administrative spheres in Peru's vast territory. Although technically outranking every other public official in his jurisdiction, the viceroy in fact had to coordinate rather than mandate. Merely keeping track of what went on in the viceroyalty as a whole, let alone controlling it, was a full-time job. Without the cooperation of officials at every level of the bureaucracy, he could accomplish nothing.

Since the time of Pizarro and Atahualpa, during the conquest of Peru in the 1530s, the Viceroyalty of Peru had been one of the two most important assignments in Spain's American empire, the other being New Spain (Mexico), in North America. After extraordinarily rich deposits of silver were discovered in the 1540s at Potosí, in the Andean highlands, Peru replaced Mexico as Spain's major American source of private profits and tax revenues; it retained that position for the rest of the sixteenth century and into the seventeenth (fig. 8). An economic depression hit Peru in the seventeenth century, however, caused in part by local developments such as population decline and agricultural distress and in part by a trade depression originating in Europe early in the century. Detailed research by a number of scholars has shown that official mining output in the Viceroyalty of Peru rose to a peak in about 1610 and thereafter declined for at least the remainder of the century.[1] New Spain also experienced an economic contraction in the same period, but it was shorter and milder than the depression in Peru.[2]

By 1700 New Spain was unquestionably the more dynamic part of the American empire, with its capital at Mexico City boasting a population of perhaps one hundred thousand souls. Unimpressed, the citizens of Lima continued to pride themselves on their wealth and importance. Known for their good humor, wit, a relaxed attitude toward moral strictures, and a fondness for fine food, music, dance, and other ingredients of a pleasant life, they also knew how to withstand tragedy, suffering through earthquakes at regular intervals.[3] Lima's official name was Ciudad de los Reyes (City of the Kings), for its reputed founding by a cohort of seventy men on January 6, 1536, the Day of the Magi-Kings, or Epiphany, in the Christian religious calendar. By 1700 the city had grown to more than 37,200 inhabitants. Along with public officials and private citizens, the census included residents of religious establishments and even the sick in hospitals, as well as servants, free blacks, and slaves. Nonetheless, we should assume that the count missed some of the population for one reason or another, as such counts usually do (fig. 9).[4]

At the top of Lima's social scale, the merchant community displayed its wealth in elegant dress and other finery, plus a lavish lifestyle and exemplary contributions to the political, social, religious, and cultural life of the city. For the official entry of the Duke of La Palata as viceroy in 1682 the merchants temporarily paved two major streets near the viceregal palace with bars of solid silver, each over a foot long, four or five inches wide, and two or three inches thick. Later visitors to Lima continued to relate this tale as proof of the viceroyalty's wealth.[5] The Duke of La Palata tapped into the merchant community's resources when he built strong and elegant fortifications around the city, traditionally dated 1685 (fig. 10). Unfortunately, just two years later, on October 20, 1687, a powerful earthquake devastated Lima, killing hundreds of people and damaging virtually every public building in the city, plus countless private homes. For lack of funds the extensive damage had not been completely repaired by 1700, but Europeans both inside and outside Spain continued to think of Peru as a dreamlike land of fabulous riches.

Successive viceroys of Peru had to deal with reality rather than dreams. As they grappled with economic difficulties in the late seventeenth and early eighteenth centuries, they also had to cope with the American implications of European rivalries. Although the French king Louis XIV had multiple family connections to the Spanish Habsburgs through his great-grandfather Philip II, his mother, Anne of Austria, and his first wife, María Teresa, the rivalry and enmity between France and Spain continued with a vengeance in Louis's reign. The French king had designs on Spanish-held territory between France and the United Netherlands. To thwart those designs, Spain fought France in 1667–68, 1672–78, and 1688–97, joined each time by an array of other countries. Only a few decades after the end of their war of independence from Habsburg rule, the United Netherlands allied with Spain against their common French enemy. So did England, although Spain and England had often been at odds in the previous two centuries. They and other allies helped Spain to fend off Louis XIV's grandest ambitions, though he still managed to collect a string of territories at Spain's expense.

European alliances had ambiguous implications in the Americas, where an array of countries had long viewed Spanish colonies with hungry eyes, despite their common front against French aggression. During the sixteenth and seventeenth centuries Spain tried to prevent any and all rivals from establishing themselves in the Americas. Moreover, even as Spain lost dominance in Europe in the seventeenth century, the Spanish Habsburgs continued to demand that all goods bound for the colonies be taxed and registered with the House of Trade in Seville.

Despite Spanish efforts, merchandise from England, the Netherlands, and France accounted for the majority of legal trade with the colonies through most of the seventeenth century, and their merchants also engaged in a lively contraband trade outside the official registry. Moreover, corsairs from England, the Netherlands, and France preyed on Spanish settlements, merchant fleets, and one another in what scholars often dub the "golden age of piracy." Spain's American colonies viewed the pirates as an infestation and would continue to suffer from their depredations well into the eighteenth century.[6] Thereafter Spain's colonial rivals would build important plantation economies in the Americas, concentrated on islands in the Caribbean and specializing in sugar production. With their own colonies at risk, they would work harder to keep the pirates in check.

Spain and its rivals alike often found pirates and other corsairs useful as auxiliaries in wartime, however, when they transformed themselves into licensed privateers sailing against enemies defined by their sponsors. In theory, at least, during the wars against Louis XIV the privateers sponsored by Spain's allies should have been aiding Spain, but the situation was more complicated than that. Dutch and English privateers attacked French settlements in the Americas, to be sure, but always with an eye to their own advantage and that of their sponsors. Everyone in Europe knew by then that the Spanish Habsburg king was likely to die without an heir. When that happened, the whole of the Spanish empire would be up for grabs.

And indeed it was, with the system of political alliances thrown into disarray as well. When the French Bourbon Philippe d'Anjou became Philip V of Spain, backed by his grandfather Louis XIV, most of the rest of Europe formed an alliance against his accession. Fear of Bourbon aggression was only part of their motivation. They also found common interest in the prospect of dividing up the Spanish empire among themselves. Had the Spanish crown gone to one of the candidates from the Germanies, the accession would not have thwarted their ambitions. Spain would have been unable to defend the integrity of the empire against them. With the protective power of Bourbon France in the background, however, Spain had a chance to keep its empire intact. In short, the survival of the Spanish empire depended upon French aid and goodwill after 1700, a turn of events that went far beyond irony, after two centuries of struggle between the two countries.

In 1701 Louis XIV made plans to send a fleet under Admiral Jean-Baptiste Ducasse to the Americas to aid in the defense of the Spanish empire. Ducasse had begun his career as a French colonial planter and sometime pirate, but he had become a colonial official, naval commander, and sometime hero under Louis XIV. Hearing rumors about the French fleet but not knowing where it was bound, the English sent word to their colonies as far north as Virginia to arm themselves.[7] Meanwhile, Philip V of Spain ordered his viceroys in the Indies to extend every courtesy to French vessels stopping in local ports, especially those dispatched to aid in the war effort. He further told them to treat the officers and men on those vessels as allies and friends and to allow them to sell enough goods in Spanish colonial ports to cover the costs of their resupply and repair. This contradicted one of the viceroy's standard duties, namely, to keep foreigners out of local markets in order to maintain the Spanish monopoly and ensure the profitability of official fleets coming from Spain.

These sudden shifts in policy from Madrid must have been confusing to Spanish bureaucrats steeped in the anti-French hostility of the late seventeenth century, especially those who had been in service for a while. Nonetheless, the war effort, and therefore the survival of the empire, depended on their cooperation. The viceroy of Peru in 1700, Melchor Portocarrero, Count of La Monclova, had served the crown for a very long while indeed. He knew how to follow orders, even from an unknown and untested Bourbon king, as his ancestry demanded. It may have helped that he first learned of Charles II's death in a letter from the queen, countersigned by Cardinal Portocarrero, the king's confessor.[8] Whether or not the two men were closely related, to share a surname was to share a lineage.

The lineage in question had ancient and distinguished origins in the northwestern Spanish kingdom of Asturias. An ancestor of the viceroy's who had traveled south in the Middle Ages to fight in the reconquest of Portugal from the Muslims had been rewarded with a place called Puerto Carrero, where he built a house to establish his possession. His descendants took the name of the town as their surname and kept it ever after, though the family itself remained Spanish, not Portuguese. Of the seven main branches of the Portocarrero lineage, the viceroy came from the seventh, which later established roots in Andalusia as the counts of Palma del Río and also were known as the lords of La Monclova. They intermarried with other noble lineages in Andalusia and rose in power and prestige in the course of the seventeenth century, acquiring an extended set of surnames to advertise their antecedents.

The third Lord of La Monclova, Don Antonio Portocarrero de Guzmán y de la Vega Enríquez, became a gentleman of the military order of Santiago, confirming his status in the highest ranks of the middling nobility. The Habsburg king Philip III raised him into the titled nobility as the first Count of La Monclova in the early seventeenth century. His wife, Doña María de Rojas Manrique de Lara, came from a noble family with roots in Madrid and Valladolid and ties to the royal court, which may have aided his career. Don Antonio served as *mayordomo* (head of the household) of Queen Isabel, the French Bourbon consort of Philip IV, and of Balthasar Carlos, their short-lived heir, the charming prince whom Velázquez often painted. Two sons of the first Count of La Monclova succeeded to the title: Gaspar Portocarrero Manrique, who died a bachelor, and his brother Melchor Portocarrero Laso de la Vega, who would serve as the viceroy of Mexico and later of Peru.

Born about 1620 in Madrid, Melchor Portocarrero was raised to be a soldier, a traditional career for the second son of a Spanish noble family. He distinguished himself in engagements against France during the Thirty Years' War and lost an arm at the Battle of the Downs in 1639. Though his lineage and family connections in the royal court may have helped his subsequent career, Don Melchor demonstrated sufficient military talent on his own to be appointed to the king's Council of War, an honor that few former soldiers achieved, no matter how distinguished their lineage. He also held the post of quartermaster general of the infantry and cavalry of Spain *(comisario general de la infantería y caballería de España)*.[9]

As he advanced in his military career, Melchor Portocarrero also moved up in the ranks of the nobility, gaining admittance to the Order of Alcántara in 1681. With the crown strapped for cash to fight against French aggression, appointment to office in the empire often required a "pecuniary service" to the crown, as well as appropriate qualifications. Even viceroyalties were essentially for sale in the late seventeenth century—to the right people. Successful applicants assumed that they would recoup their investment in the Indies by collecting fees from those they appointed to office and for performing various services required by their position. In the late 1680s, however, all the potential bidders for viceroyalties in America dropped out. Historians generally ignore the causes for this sudden lack of interest in high office, but it seems clear that monied circles near the court realized that the offices were no longer lucrative, given the recent history of economic difficulties in both Mexico and Peru and warfare's periodic disruptions of Atlantic trade.

In this situation, the crown turned to candidates such as Melchor Portocarrero, who were qualified for the available jobs but unable to provide a "pecuniary service." Lewis Hanke called him "one of the most honest administrators that had been sent to America, . . . a man who had nothing more to offer than his loyalty to the crown, his skills as a military man, and his probity as an administrator."[10] In April 1686 King Charles II named Portocarrero viceroy of New Spain, one of the two most important posts in the Spanish Indies, and he sailed across the Atlantic with his wife, Doña Antonia Jiménez de Urrea, and family. The assignment carried more than its usual importance in those years. War with France once again seemed imminent, and French and English pirates and interlopers had established a permanent presence in the Caribbean from bases on various islands. No sooner had Portocarrero arrived in Veracruz than he dispatched two well-armed brigantines to search for signs of the French around the Gulf of Mexico. Then he moved inland to establish himself in the capital, Mexico City.

In the next several months Portocarrero learned of the capture of several Englishmen who had been cutting valuable timber around the Términos Lagoon, near the Mexican coast. They were part of a much larger work party sent from Jamaica, making it unlikely that the viceroy could drive them out with the limited forces he had available. He had better news regarding the French. The brigantines found only one site where they had tried to establish themselves—the bay of San Bernardino in Texas—and they had evidently been killed by local Indians. The Spanish expedition found only ruined ships and a half-built fort at the site. The viceroy established a chain of military encampments along the Gulf coast to thwart any further attempts by the French to gain a foothold there. The first encampment, later named Monclova in his honor, was made up of 270 armed men and 150 families, a considerable presence.

The viceroy also immediately expelled all unlicensed foreign priests from the territory, an unmistakable sign that politics trumped religion in the viceroy's understanding of his mandate. Don Melchor made a lasting impression on the population of New Spain.[11] Because of the prosthesis that replaced the arm he had lost at the Battle of the Downs, he was known popularly as "Brazo de Plata" (Silver Arm), the colorful nickname that often identifies him in Mexican history. More important, he had water piped from Chapultepec Hill at his own expense to supply a fountain in the heart of Mexico City known as the Salto de Agua (Water's Leap).

Scarcely two years after he arrived in New Spain, however, Portocarrero received orders to become viceroy of Peru. He left Acapulco in May 1689, having waited a year for appropriate transport to take him to Lima's port of Callao.[12] The French military engineer Amedée-François Frézier would describe Callao in 1713 as "built on a low flat point of land, on the edge of the sea," two leagues (six miles) from Lima.[13] Although the crown had built fortifications and substantial public buildings and warehouses in Callao, the town remained vulnerable to earthquakes and the tidal waves that often followed them (fig. 11). Callao reportedly lost five hundred of its two thousand inhabitants during the earthquake of 1687.[14] Effects from that quake were still evident in Lima when Portocarrero arrived, and he would struggle for the whole of his nearly twenty years in office to find funds to repair the damage. When his brother died a bachelor in 1693, Don Melchor succeeded him as the third Count of La Monclova, the name by which he is generally known in both Mexico and Peru. Throughout his long years in Lima, Monclova had to deal with defending the coastlines of the viceroyalty from attacks by pirates and attempts by foreign interlopers to establish regular bases in the territory claimed by Spain.

The Pacific coast of northwestern South America, facing what the Spaniards called the Mar del Sur (Southern Sea), was so remote from Europe, and the route so dangerous, that foreign ships rarely found their way there until the late sixteenth century. Thereafter, foreign merchant vessels, pirates, and privateers showed up in the Southern Sea with some regularity, though not in great numbers. In general, about one hundred local ships, merchants of all sizes, were in the Southern Sea at any given time through much of the seventeenth century and into the eighteenth. Pirates cut their numbers from time to time, but they bounced back, with merchants building ships to replace the ones they lost. In an ill omen of things to come, however, the English pirate Bartholomew Sharpe captured a set of maps and charts off the coast of Peru in 1680. The 165 maps provided sketches and directions for virtually every port and town on the Pacific coast of New Spain and Peru—information that Spain was loathe to see fall into the hands of its European rivals. The English chartmaker William Hacke created a manuscript atlas from those charts in 1685.[15]

Once the sailing directions from Europe into the Southern Sea became widely known, the threat to Spanish trade and settlements in Peru increased many times over.

In 1695 foreign pirates operating off the Pacific coast of the viceroyalty posed a threat to the seventy-two merchant ships in the vicinity. To protect them, Viceroy Monclova wanted to bring the Armada of the Southern Sea to full strength, which meant maintaining several ships and about one thousand men, but he was hard pressed to fund the effort. The following year, fears of an imminent French attack increased the need for defense. Fortuitously, because of revenue generated by the Portobelo fair in 1696, Viceroy Monclova was able to arm a squadron with 1,238 men, including soldiers and sailors of all ranks. In years without a fair, he often had to rely on donations from the merchant communities in Peru when danger threatened.[16]

As one historian has noted, Monclova's regular resources would have been insufficient even to administer a city, let alone the vast Viceroyalty of Peru.[17] That was one of the most potent reasons why the Spanish empire had to be governed more by consensus than by fiat.[18] Rather than unquestioningly enforcing the decrees of an absolute monarch in Spain, viceroys such as Monclova had to calibrate their exercise of authority very carefully and choose their battles more carefully still. If Monclova alienated members of the mercantile elite in Lima, he could hardly rely on their generosity to supplement the overextended resources of his administration.

Personally, Monclova earned respect in both Mexico and Peru for his bravery, honesty, piety, probity, and evenhandedness. He had no tolerance for anyone who openly tried to buy official favor and nothing but contempt for those who defied the royal will. He also knew how to recognize reality, which often tested every virtue he possessed.

The prohibition on contraband had often been contravened in practice in the Viceroyalty of Peru, and the chaotic situation in the late seventeenth century rendered the ban all but impossible to enforce. Things got worse as the century, and the life of Spain's last Habsburg king, came to a close.[19] No official fleet from Europe reached Tierra Firme after 1696, and goods from New Spain were technically contraband and therefore illicit. Nonetheless, contraband entered Peruvian markets, and local colonists came to rely on the contraband trade as their main source for European and Asian goods. Some local merchants in Lima became deeply implicated in the illicit trade. Viceroy Monclova may not have known exactly who was involved, but he did know that without the willing cooperation of the merchant community and its periodic contributions he had no hope of defending the viceroyalty.

Part of Monclova's high reputation among the elite in Peru seems to owe to his willingness to let the merchant community police itself, perhaps in the hope that his personal example would inspire them to do the right thing. He lacked official resources to enforce their obedience, in any case, and recognized that he needed their private resources to govern at all. Consequently, Monclova was, in Lewis Hanke's words, "neither a frenetic nor an aggressive administrator, which satisfied many."[20] It is fair to assume that although he failed to enforce the ban on contraband and left the most powerful families in Lima in control of local trade, he still believed he was serving the crown's best interests. As long as the Tierra Firme Fleet failed to bring duly registered goods to the Portobelo fairs for transfer to Peru, there was no serious conflict of interest in Monclova's approach.

The situation changed after 1700 with the new dynasty and the outbreak of war over the Bourbon succession in Spain. From 1701 on, English and Dutch enemy vessels, French allied vessels, and corsairs from various states all arrived in the waters bordering the Viceroyalty of Peru—the Caribbean, the Atlantic, and the Southern Sea. Their arrival created a dilemma for viceregal authorities. In the Atlantic and the Caribbean the Bourbon allies organized fleets and squadrons from Europe to meet the challenge posed by their enemies. In the remote Southern Sea, however, the viceroy had to face the challenge largely without aid from Europe. He ordered a census in 1700 to gauge the size of the pool from which he might recruit a militia, but he faced great difficulties in finding the money to pay them.

Once the war started, Monclova learned to his dismay that both Spain and France were counting on treasure from Peru to finance the war. That meant he was asked to send substantial resources to Europe just when he needed them to defend the viceroyalty. Moreover, the merchants in Seville wanted assurances that illicit trade would be stamped out in Peru before they would risk their money in preparing a fleet to Tierra Firme. As a result Monclova received urgent orders to prevent outsiders, including Spain's French allies, from illicitly trading in the viceroyalty, at the same time that he needed French help to defend merchant shipping in the vast territory under his jurisdiction. Two hundred forty-one merchant vessels departed from Callao in the period 1701–4, with 78 in 1701 and 53–55 in each of the other years. Some of the ships were surely counted more than once, as this was not a census of shipping but a record of port traffic. Nearly all of the ships were local or were at least listed as such.[21]

Viceroy Monclova worried even more about the safety of those ships when he heard news about additional corsairs in the area. In a letter to the king in October 1704 he reported that two small English ships had entered the Southern Sea via the Strait of Magellan in February.[22] The larger of the two, the *St. George,* carried twenty-six iron cannons, each designed for ammunition of six- to nine-pound caliber, and just over one hundred men. The captain of the *St. George* was William Dampier, a name that Monclova did not seem to know; otherwise the arrival would have preoccupied him even more, because Dampier was one of the most famous English corsairs of the period. He began his career sailing off Newfoundland and working on a Jamaican plantation and in the Caribbean logwood trade before becoming a pirate and privateer.

Before his death in 1715—ironically, in poverty—Dampier raided ships and ports from the Caribbean to China, in addition to exploring the South Pacific for the English Admiralty. His detailed journals and observations of exotic peoples and places earned him a place in the history of scientific exploration, as well as a fearsome reputation as a predator. Thomas Stradling—spelled "Estraclin" in Spanish documents—captained the other English privateer that entered the Southern Sea at the turn of the century. His ship, referred to in Spanish documents as the "Simport galera," was considerably smaller than Dampier's vessel, with sixty men and sixteen guns of four-pound caliber each. Both ships carried corsairing patents from Queen Anne of England.

Not far behind the English ships were three much larger French vessels, the *St. Joseph,* the *Baron de Bertel,* and the *Sancti Espiritus,* each about 300 toneladas and each carrying from twenty-four to thirty-two guns of four- to eight-pound caliber. Together, the three ships carried 321 men. Four years earlier Monclova would have viewed the French fleet as an invasion force, as indeed it would have been. In 1704 the French ships were his allies against the English, and he would be glad to see them. The three ships scattered during a storm, and the *St. Joseph,* the smallest of the three, with seventy-six men and twenty-four small cannons, reached the Juan Fernández Islands, off the coast of Chile near the latitude of Santiago, on March 11. Since the days of Magellan, ships that made it through the strait—or later, around Cape Horn—had often missed those remote islands as they searched for winds and currents to carry them farther west. As the eighteenth century wore on, the islands would become a regular stopping-off point on the way from Cape Horn to the East Indies, but they were rarely visited in 1704.

At Juan Fernández the French encountered the two English ships rigged for combat. Captain Joseph Vermont Trublet, of the *St. Joseph,* and his men fought the English for four hours on March 12, but the agile privateers escaped without sustaining any serious damage. Presumably during the confusion of their flight, they left behind several men. The French later captured most of them, but one man—Alexander Selkirk—remained on the remote island until he was rescued by Woodes Rogers, another English privateer, in 1709. Selkirk's story would long ago have faded from historical memory but for a curious collision of history and fiction: his tale of survival captured the imagination of the popular English writer Daniel Defoe, who immortalized Selkirk's ordeal in a fictional retelling called *The Adventures of Robinson Crusoe.*

After routing the English, Captain Vermont, as the Spanish documents call him, sailed north to Callao, arriving on March 29. In a letter to the viceroy he said that he had left the French port of St. Malo in August 1703 with privateering patents from the Count of Toulouse, admiral of France, to seek out English vessels and engage them in battle. Of the four ships in his small fleet, the largest sailed to Portobelo, and the other three sailed into the Southern Sea, responding to news that England had armed three corsairs for that destination. On the way from France they had stopped in the Spanish Canary Islands and the Portuguese Madeiras for supplies. A Spanish passenger on the *St. Joseph* carried the letter to Viceroy Monclova, in which Captain Vermont also asked permission to buy supplies in Callao and seek help for his wounded men.

As soon as Monclova received Captain Vermont's letter, he called together a war committee *(junta de guerra)* comprising officials of the royal audiencia in Lima and local military commanders. After conferring about the matter and hearing testimony from the Spanish passenger, they agreed that Monclova should order medical assistance for the wounded French sailors and make arrangements for the refitting and resupply of the *St. Joseph* in Callao. Monclova praised the valor and zeal of Captain Vermont and his men and gratefully acknowledged the service they had provided in warning him of the English plans in time to call up auxiliary defense forces. In a decision that would set an important precedent, Monclova—with the junta's approval—allowed the ship to sell the cloth and other merchandise it carried in order to pay for needed supplies.

By royal decree in 1701 King Philip V had explicitly authorized French ships in transit to sell goods in the Indies to pay for supplies, but Monclova still felt the need to monitor such sales as strictly as possible in order to mollify local merchants. He noted that the Lima market was "denuded of clothing" for sale because the regular merchant fleets from Spain to Portobelo had been delayed by the war. The French goods sold were taxed at the regular rates, and representatives from the Audiencia of Lima and other royal officials went down to Callao "to see that the clothing was marketed for the use and succor of the public good, not allowing the most powerful to control the items that ought to go to relieve the poor." As much as possible, in other words, Monclova presented the "illicit commerce" as a public service and even an act of charity.

The other two French ships eventually arrived at the Juan Fernández Islands. Captain Jean-Baptiste Vecard, of the *Baron de Bertel,* later wrote to Monclova that they had sent a launch ashore and captured a small English boat, some arms and marine supplies, and three of the six men whom the English had left behind when they fled from Captain Vermont's *St. Joseph.* As Viceroy Monclova noted, Vecard finished his letter by "offering me his ship and asking for my orders so that he could obey them." The viceroy called a meeting representing the committee of the merchant consulate's tribunal, which unanimously agreed that Monclova should write to thank the Frenchmen for their zeal and direct them to the port of Callao, where they would be well received.

Despite their gratitude, the merchants of Lima were already ambivalent about the French presence. With few or no new goods to sell for years, and no Tierra Firme Fleet expected in the near future, their only hope of covering their losses lay in preventing any incursions on their monopoly. That way, when the Spanish fleet finally arrived for a Portobelo fair, they would be able to demand high prices for their merchandise. The merchants sent a lengthy memorandum to Monclova, arguing against allowing the two recent French arrivals to sell any cloth in Callao. Because of the conflicting advice Monclova received from the audiencia, the king's counsel *(fiscal)* in Lima, and the representatives of the merchants' tribunal, he delayed making a decision about French sales pending news about market conditions in Callao.

By the time he received that news it was April—autumn in the Southern Hemisphere—and he had heard about ship movements elsewhere in the Southern Sea. The *corregidor* of Piura, the official in charge of that district, reported that he had captured the two English vessels that had fled the Juan Fernández Islands. After confiscating their cargoes and any supplies he needed, he set the vessels and their crews free "without doing any harm to the persons on board."

Monclova was not disposed to leave the English roaming free in his jurisdiction, however. He and his war committee decided to send two armed ships in search of the enemy. One was the principal dispatch ship *(patache)* of the

Armada of the Southern Sea, called the *Santa Cruz*, and the other was a good-sized, privately owned ship called the *San Francisco de Asís*. Each of the vessels carried twenty bronze cannons of twenty-pound caliber when they left Callao on May 24, plus crews of 160 men, ammunition, food, and supplies. That pair of ships, hardly worthy of being called a fleet, nonetheless represented a very large outlay of cash in difficult times. With instructions from Almirante Pedro de Alzamora, the principal military officer of the Armada of the Southern Sea, they were ordered to search for the English enemy vessels and engage them.

A few days after the *Santa Cruz* and the *San Francisco de Asís* left port, Captain Vermont asked permission to take the *St. Joseph* in search of the English as well. Monclova and the committee representing the merchants' tribunal accepted his offer and sent him out with a patent as a "captain of sea and war of the royal armada of Spain" so that he would be treated and aided as such by Spanish vessels and ports in the viceroyalty. The *St. Joseph* left Callao on June 25 and cruised the coastline as far south as Manta but returned without seeing the English. The two armed Spanish ships glimpsed the smaller of the English ships near the port of Paita but could not overtake it. Then, receiving news that an English ship had been sighted near Guayaquil, the *San Francisco de Asís* set out alone under Captain Don Francisco de Mendieta, who reasoned that his ship was large enough to capture or sink the English vessel unaided.

The *Santa Cruz* remained in Paita to protect the port. Mendieta sighted an English ship between Punta de Mero and Tumbes and followed it for seven days before getting within cannon range. Finally, on August 2 he came close enough to bombard the English vessel, shooting down the fore-topmast and sail and doing other damage, but he was unable to come within musket range. Darkness ended the engagement, and Captain Mendieta soon gave up the chase, returning to Paita to rejoin the *Santa Cruz*. Though the two vessels cruised as far as the Isla de la Plata, they did not sight the English vessel again and returned to Paita. From their reports, it was clear to Monclova that the English were not eager to fight, especially after the losses they had sustained.

The three men captured by the French ship *Baron de Bertel* were held in the royal jail in Callao. Monclova's lieutenant in the port of Manta captured nine more Englishmen when they put in for supplies and forced them to burn their launches and small boats so that their compatriots could not use them. He sent the captured men to the jail in Callao, where they gave testimony to Monclova's general auditor for warfare *(auditor general de la guerra)*, Don Juan

Fernando Calderón de la Barca, the senior official for criminal cases *(alcalde del crimen)* in the royal audiencia of Lima. Another nine Englishmen surrendered in Panama, reportedly with Dampier's permission.

According to the official testimony, the English prisoners said they had left the Irish port of Kinsale in September 1703 with corsairing patents from the queen of England. In exchange for the patents, Queen Anne would share along with the corsairs and their sponsors in any booty captured. After stopping briefly on some islands near the Brazilian coast, they sailed through the Strait of Magellan. The Duke of Ormont, viceroy of Ireland, had warned them not to make the dangerous journey alone but to wait until other ships being readied in England joined them. Captain Dampier ignored the advice, however, "saying that he had much experience in these seas, because he had been here on orders from King William years ago." The men recounted their skirmishes with Spanish and French vessels since arriving in the Southern Sea and noted the prizes and cargoes they had captured; their testimony agreed with information that Monclova had received from other sources. He had no way of knowing how many more English corsairs might be headed toward the coasts of Peru, but he had every reason to worry.

At the same time, the French presence in the area continued to grow. In early June Monclova heard from Don Diego de Zúñiga, an oidor of the Audiencia of Chile, that a French ship had arrived in the port of La Concepción on May 13, followed by another vessel eight days later. One carried forty cannons, the other carried thirty-six, and both held corsairing patents from the Count of Toulouse. The corregidor of Arica, Don Juan de Mur, confirmed the news when the ships arrived there in mid-June. The captain of one of the ships, Pierre Perre de Cutray, of the *St. Charles,* sent a letter to Viceroy Monclova saying that he had left St. Malo in late December 1703, sent by the French Royal Company of China, with the blessing of Louis XIV and a patent from the Count of Toulouse. He noted that he had sailed for Canton via Peru because of the danger he would have faced in taking a [more southerly] route through the Spice Islands, which were reportedly thick with English and Dutch ships. As he had done in other cases, Monclova allowed the Frenchmen to proceed to Callao and instructed Spanish officials to accommodate their resupply, following the guidelines provided by Philip V three years earlier. The *Baron de Bertel* had already arrived in Callao by then, and Captain Vecard offered to go in search of the English if the viceroy wished him to do so. He said he would leave his cargo in Callao while he was away, but he presumably would have had to sell some of it to pay for the supplies and additional men he would need to pursue the English.

Viceroy Monclova was in a very difficult position. If he wanted French assistance against the English corsairs, he would have to breach the monopoly of local merchants once again. He convened the committee of the merchant tribunal on July 5 to discuss the matter, and they agreed that Monclova should permit the French to sell the *Baron de Bertel*'s cargo on the same terms conceded to the *St. Joseph*'s a few months earlier, because Callao still had a great shortage of clothing for sale. The captain of the *St. Charles* was told to sail from Arica to Callao, where the French would be allowed to exchange enough goods to secure needed supplies and provisions, but no more. The same terms would apply to the *Sancti Espiritus,* one of the first three French vessels in the area, as soon as it arrived in Callao. At a further meeting on August 21 the committee discussed the situation at length and decided to tighten the prohibition on trade for any French ships that might arrive later. As far as the merchants of Lima were concerned, their French allies and their English enemies might as well have been acting together to drive them to ruin.

The first three French ships left Callao for France on September 22, 1704. They constituted a tiny minority of the 241 vessels that sailed from Callao between 1701 and 1704, and the only foreign vessels,[23] but their presence marked an unsettling change for commerce in the viceroyalty. In his letter to Philip V in October of 1704 Monclova emphasized that he had treated the French with all the respect that the king had mandated in January 1701 and June 1703 because of the "close links and the union of the crown of Your Majesty with that of France."[24] In particular, he had allowed them to exchange trade goods for the supplies and other items they needed for careening their ships. In the absence of royal orders to the contrary, he wrote that he would apply those same rules to any other French ships that might arrive.

At the same time, Monclova had to consider the rights and privileges of Spanish merchants in Lima and elsewhere in the viceroyalty. He reported that he had repeated and reinforced orders to all the officials in his jurisdiction to "impede free and open commerce with these ships, which I recognize to be greatly prejudicial to the interests of the merchants, to the dispatch of the fleets, and consequently, to the fulfillment of the obligations and contracts that they have with Your Majesty." He justified allowing the *St. Joseph* and the *Baron de Bertel* to sell their cargoes by noting that poor citizens needed clothes and he needed help against the English. Despite these needs, he advised the king, it would be far better to discontinue French voyages into the Southern Sea; once the French arrived in the vicinity, the extended coastlines and open beaches made it very difficult to prevent them from trading. Moreover, enforcing the ban on illicit commerce might easily be seen as a hostile act by Spain's French allies. It would be far better to avoid all these problems by banning French voyages at their source.

At the very end of his letter Monclova mentioned the "little time remaining when I can maintain myself in these responsibilities, since I must suppose that very shortly the Marquis of Castelldosrius, my successor, will arrive on the galleons that we await each day." He signed the letter in a very shaky hand on October 8, 1704, and dispatched the packet from Lima on its long journey toward Madrid. In fact, Monclova would be relieved of duty only by God. He died in Lima on September 15, 1705, still serving as viceroy because his successor had not yet arrived.[25]

Ironically, given the struggles with the French that had marked most of his life, Monclova ended by being considered a good friend of France and a loyal servant of the new Bourbon king of Spain. As late as 1704 he was mentioned in French court circles as an ideal candidate for the presidency of the Council of the Indies in Madrid.[26] King Philip V even honored him with the status of grandee of Spain, second class, on May 5, 1706, unaware that by then Monclova was far beyond the jurisdiction of any earthly power.[27]

Monclova's nearly twenty-year tenure in Peru coincided with one of the most sustained crises in the history of the viceroyalty, which was exacerbated by the collapse of the fairs at Portobelo. The schedule of the Tierra Firme Fleet and its escort of galleons, which traditionally brought goods for the Portobelo fair every year, became increasingly erratic in the late seventeenth century, arriving every other year, then every third or fourth year, then every five years. Historians have not yet sorted out all the reasons for the decline, but Louis XIV's determination to break Spanish control over transatlantic trade surely contributed to it. Although fleets and individually licensed vessels and dispatch boats continued to serve New Spain and the Caribbean, the last major Tierra Firme Fleet with an escort of galleons arrived in 1696.[28]

The fairs' unpredictability had serious repercussions in Peru. Moreover, because enemy raids in the late seventeenth century hit hardest in the Caribbean, the viceroy often had to shift revenue for defense from Lima to Panama in what one historian has called a "veritable river of money."[29] All of these circumstances hurt the economy of Peru, including the wealthy and powerful merchant community in Lima. Living at the far reaches of the American empire, they relied on their commercial monopoly to balance some of the risks inherent in a trading network that spanned the Atlantic and included the pirate-infested waters of the Caribbean. There is no question that they charged high prices in the markets they held captive. They also funded coastal defense and royal administration in Peru and acted as prominent patrons of religion, education, and the arts. Their prosperity was arguably essential to the continued viability of the viceroyalty.

By the end of the seventeenth century the merchant community's monopoly and everything it sustained had come under attack from several quarters. Merchandise brought overland illegally from Buenos Aires found a ready market in Upper Peru (today's Bolivia), where merchants from Lima had previously controlled supplies and prices. According to Guillermo Céspedes, those same merchants "defined Buenos Aires as a nest of smugglers."[30] And the arrival of Dutch, English, and French interlopers in the Southern Sea provided sources of moderately priced goods to residents no longer well served by the erratic fleet system and the Portobelo fairs.[31]

With the advent of the Bourbon monarchy, the merchants of Lima felt the same ambiguities regarding the French presence that Viceroy Monclova expressed in his letters to the king. They welcomed the French as allies against the English but not as rival traders. Publicly, the merchant consulado of Lima would maintain that stance and argue strongly that their exclusive rights to provide goods to the viceroyalty should be sustained and defended. They knew, however, that the coastlines were so extensive, and the royal officials so thinly spread, that an absolute monopoly would be nearly impossible to enforce. Therefore, privately and individually many Lima merchants actively colluded with the French to introduce contraband or "illicit" goods into the viceroyalty. Were they hypocritical? Of course. Were they mistaken to defend their monopoly, when free trade was the wave of the future? Not necessarily. They feared that free trade would ruin them by flooding the market with cheap merchandise, while they had to sustain the costs of defense, government, religion, and culture in the viceroyalty. So as good businessmen they hedged their bets and diversified their investments, working in public to protect what remained of their monopoly and in private to breach it.

Into this highly complex and multivalent atmosphere sailed the armada of 1706 under the Count of Casa Alegre, bound for Cartagena and then for Portobelo and the first fair in a decade. To say that the armada's arrival was anxiously awaited on both sides of the Atlantic, as well as in the Southern Sea, would be a considerable understatement, but the nature of the anxiety varied greatly from one interest group to another. The crown wanted the Portobelo fairs revived and a regular flow of trade and revenue reestablished. Ordinary consumers wanted a regular and reliable source of merchandise. Royal officials wanted their salaries paid and enough money in the public coffers to properly fulfill their duties. And the merchants of Lima wanted to make a profit. The revival of the Portobelo fairs might further all of those aims, but their success was by no means assured.

Given the situation in 1705, with English pirates in the vicinity and the worrisome "Pacific invasion of the French," the merchants had less reason than others to trust in the fairs. If they accepted the risk of attending in person or sending representatives and funds to Portobelo, they wanted to make sure the goods brought back to Peru would make a profit. Given the high overhead costs that the fairs entailed, the goods would have to be priced accordingly and the merchants' exclusive trading rights would have to be protected. If the Peruvian market was flooded with cheap contraband goods, they would face heavy losses, perhaps even financial ruin. Viceroy Monclova's trading concessions to French vessels in 1703 and 1704 had been understandable, with the threat of pirates and no other help in sight. But if the Tierra Firme Fleet actually arrived, its escort of galleons would be able to handle the English threat and make sure that the fair would take place. Then the viceroy could enforce the ban on illicit commerce and assure their profits. In short, the merchants' willingness to participate in the Portobelo fairs depended on the attitude and actions of the new viceroy, who would arrive with the galleons.

That individual, usually known by his title as the Marquis of Castelldosrius, came from the most prestigious branch of one of the most distinguished families in Catalonia. He descended from the noble lineages of Oms, which claimed to have been in royal service since the time of Charlemagne, and Sentmenat, which had ancient roots in the Sabadell district of Barcelona. Over the course of the Middle Ages both families had consolidated their positions by well-chosen marriages among themselves and to members of other distinguished lineages. The future viceroy was born on Christmas Day 1651 and named Manuel de Oms de Santa Pau olim de Sentmenat y de Lanuza, but his name is generally rendered as Manuel de Oms olim y Sentmenat.[32] The ancient lineages of Catalonia and the Balearic Islands had a very strong tradition—some would say an obsession—with preserving and defending the integrity of their descent. One result of this tradition was the practice of stringing together as many family names as possible to demonstrate one's impeccable lineage. When this intricate "dance of the surnames," as one historian has called it, became too complicated, a family might simplify a bit, retaining only the best names and perhaps an echo of the past by using the Latin *olim* (lit., before).[33]

Because Manuel's older brother died in 1646, he was the family's principal heir from the moment of his birth in 1651.[34] When his father died in 1652, the one-year-old inherited the family fortunes, much richer in honor and prestige than worldly wealth. The family's net income from holdings in land, credit paper, and other property barely surpassed 2,000 Catalan libras a year, grossly insufficient to maintain the family's honor and traditions of public service. Despite these modest resources, Manuel received an excellent education and developed a polished literary style replete with classical allusions. He was also groomed for a career that was appropriate to his station in life and that would generate income as well as serving God and the king. The church was not an option for the scion of a noble family, leaving the military as his best point of entry into royal service. In 1673 he married his cousin Doña Juana de Oms y Cabrera, further consolidating the Oms lineage. The following year, during the second major war with Louis XIV's France, he received a promotion to the rank of *maestre de campo*. As part of his duties, Don Manuel raised an infantry regiment and served with distinction in preparing Catalonia against the threat of a French invasion. From there he moved into positions of increasing authority, as military governor of the port of Tarragona in 1677–80 and viceroy and captain general of Mallorca in 1683–88.[35]

In 1689 King Charles II elevated Don Manuel to the titled nobility as the Marquis of Dosrius, named for one of the family's properties in Catalonia, and appointed him to the Council of War in Madrid.[36] The Count of Oropesa, president of the Council of Castile and perhaps the richest nobleman in Catalonia, sent Dosrius to Portugal as a special envoy in 1691. Beyond his family traditions, Dosrius had more than enough personal reasons to work hard in royal service. He and his wife had ten children, all of whom had to be provided for in a manner befitting their distinguished lineage.

The Spanish mission to Portugal in 1691 ostensibly involved nothing more than to congratulate the king and queen on the birth of their son and heir, Prince João. The queen of Portugal was the sister of the new German queen of Spain, María Ana of Neuburg, so the mission had a dynastic dimension as well. With his cultured manners and diplomatic gifts, the Marquis of Dosrius carried out his duties in Lisbon with more than the required grace. He even wrote a theater piece, or *comedia*, in honor of the infant prince.

Dosrius's mission to Lisbon was far more than a courtesy call, however.

Louis XIV of France had begun another land grab in 1688, and Spain had allied with most of the rest of Europe against him.[37] Portugal remained neutral, so the Marquis of Dosrius served as a well-placed spy for Spain in Lisbon, with the ultimate aim of enticing Portugal into the alliance against France. As the war dragged on, the marquis stayed in Lisbon, becoming a great favorite at the court. He even stood in for the king of Spain as godfather to one of the Portuguese princesses. In 1696 Charles II officially appointed him ambassador to Portugal and amended his title to Marquis of Castelldosrius, in honor of Don Manuel's plans to build a castle on his estates.

Castelldosrius's promotion proved to be a financial burden to him, however. Spanish royal finances were in sad shape in the mid-1690s, after decades of economic distress and monetary upheaval and a seemingly endless series of wars. The Spanish economy showed signs of recovery, but the government still found itself financially embarrassed on a regular basis. To carry out his ambassadorial duties, Castelldosrius had to empty his pockets and go deeply into debt besides. The history of his personal finances, arranged through agents in Catalonia, was as complicated as the most intricate courtly dance, with loans arranged to pay off other loans and money shifted to where it was most needed in the short term.[38] In the long term he could trust that the crown would reimburse him, but meanwhile he had to fend for himself.

The war against France finally ended in 1697, after nearly a decade of indecisive attrition on both sides of the Atlantic. Among the more notable actions in the Americas, French forces invaded and occupied Cartagena de Indias in 1697. The English pirate William Dampier described Cartagena as "a city so well known that I shall say nothing of it. . . . [The monastery of Nuestra Señora de la Popa] is a place of incredible wealth, by reason of the offerings continually made here, and for this reason often in danger of being visited by the privateers, did the neighborhood of Cartagena not keep them in awe."[39] The city's wealth and strategic importance made it an obvious target for Louis XIV.

Cartagena de Indias was founded in 1533 and soon became important as the most secure harbor in the Caribbean. French and English pirates and privateers raided the city several times in the course of the sixteenth century, and Francis Drake was able to capture it with a large force and extort a huge ransom from the inhabitants in 1586. The government of Philip II responded by investing in state-of-the-art fortifications for the city and its harbor. Drake's attacks on Cartagena and other Spanish ports also persuaded the Spanish king to send a large fleet against England in 1588. From the late sixteenth century on, Cartagena grew in size and stature as the main port for the Tierra Firme

Fleet, and it was the exclusive entry port for African slaves in Spanish America from 1595 to 1615.[40] With the fortifications in place, and a daunting natural setting, Cartagena remained secure for most of the seventeenth century.[41]

The French attack in 1697 was led by M. Jean-Bernard Desjeans, the Baron de Pointis, aided by an auxiliary assemblage of buccaneers under M. Jean-Baptiste Ducasse, at that time governor of the French colony on Hispaniola (fig. 12).[42] De Pointis distrusted his buccaneer auxiliaries, who went off marauding and arrived late off Cartagena. To get them out of his way, he sent them inland to attack the hill surmounted by the monastery of Nuestra Señora de la Popa and devised a plan for a frontal assault on the city from the sea with his own forces. Although he had received warnings about the perils of such an approach, he chose to ignore them because Cartagena seemed to face a calm sea unprotected. He almost paid with his life for that bit of arrogance. As he approached the shore in a canoe to select an invasion site, the baron encountered firsthand the perils of "the neighborhood of Cartagena" (see map of Cartagena de Indias and its immediate area). As he would later write,

> One would not have thought that in a great bay, shelter'd from the winds that usually reign upon this coast, where ships find a good anchorage, and the sea calm, it should be impossible to get ashoar; but scarce were we come to it, when the waves breaking upon the rocks even with the water, did but little miss of filling my *canoa* quite full of water at once: . . . We were then, notwithstanding all our draughts and memoirs, oblig'd to agree, that Carthagena was inaccessible on this side: For if in so calm a day, the sea was so boisterous as we found it, what were we to expect in other weather? In short, the stay we made in this country, hath shewn us by experience, as well as inform'd us by the relations of the inhabitants, that the sea upon all this coast and in all seasons, is a natural and invincible rampart; and that Carthagena is approachable only by the lake, which makes the harbour.[43]

Having learned his lesson, de Pointis entered the great "lake," or harbor, through the shallow, narrow passage at Boca Chica. With the escape routes from the city blocked, he forced local officials to sign a treaty of surrender and pay an enormous ransom in exchange for a promise not to sack the city. Unfortunately for the citizenry, the baron refused to pay Ducasse and his men what they thought was their fair share of the loot. The outraged buccaneers extorted more ransom from the hapless residents of Cartagena and then sacked and burned the city anyway. De Pointis feared that he would be blamed for this gross violation of a solemn treaty, but Louis XIV was evidently pleased enough with his share of the loot to overlook the lapse. As for Ducasse, Louis XIV rewarded him with a knighthood and a promotion to admiral. None of this brought the French crown much benefit or lasting advantage, however, and only added to the anger and loathing that citizens in Spain and its colonies felt toward the French.

Louis XIV had strained the French economy almost to the breaking point in his frontal attack on Spain and its empire, without much success. A better way presented itself at the end of the century. Barring divine intervention, Charles II of Spain was sure to die childless—and soon, by all accounts. Because of dynastic marriages over the past two centuries, the Spanish Habsburgs were closely related to many of the other ruling houses of Europe, as we have seen. One of the leading candidates to succeed Charles II was an Austrian Habsburg; another was a Bavarian; and the third was a French Bourbon, one of Louis's grandsons, Philippe d'Anjou. The French king realized that one way or another he would gain more by simply biding his time than by continued warfare.

When William III of England and the Netherlands drew up a treaty in 1698 for the dismemberment of Spain's empire in Europe and abroad, Louis signed on. The Habsburg emperor balked, however, expecting that his family would get the whole Spanish inheritance someday soon. News of the partition treaty inevitably reached the Spanish court. King Charles, justifiably angry and offended, showed his favor for the Habsburg contender to succeed him, and his strident German queen and her faction aimed to see that he held firm in that resolve. A small but influential group of Spaniards nonetheless continued to favor the French candidate, convinced that only France could defend the empire against partition. As they quietly worked behind the scenes to neutralize the influence of the unpopular queen and her faction, Charles appointed the Marquis of Castelldosrius as his ambassador to France.

For a variety of reasons, France was perhaps the most difficult and important posting for a Spanish ambassador at the end of the seventeenth century, as well as one of the most expensive. Diplomats generally had to supplement official funds when they served in such posts so that they could entertain and make an impressive showing at the foreign court. Given Castelldosrius's meager estate, he was not the most likely choice for France, but his personal qualities and distinguished record nonetheless commended him to the king and his advisers. Though Charles II appointed him to the post in 1698, it took some doing for Castelldosrius to extricate himself from his creditors in Lisbon. He submitted accounts of his expenses to the Council of Finance in Madrid, which approved them for (eventual) reimbursement. With their assurances, and Castelldosrius's guarantees to his principal creditor that the money would be repaid, he finally left Portugal in 1699. On the way overland to France he stopped briefly in Barcelona to attend to family business and was feted by the Catalan elite.[44] The French court would receive him far less graciously.

Castelldosrius arrived in Versailles in the autumn of 1699, at the age of forty-eight, just as the court was leaving for Fontainebleau. Louis refused to let him come along, presumably in retaliation for the king of Spain's delay in receiving Louis's minister d'Harcourt. In any case, Castelldosrius had his first audience with Louis only after the court returned to Versailles. The gossipy but generally trustworthy memoirs of the duc de Saint-Simon describe Castelldosrius as "a very poor Catalan gentleman" whose appointment to France was a kind of exile for him after the prestige and success he had enjoyed in Portugal. He reported that Castelldosrius raised only two matters with Louis at their first meeting, both of them stronger on piety than on international import. One can almost see the twenty-four-year-old Saint-Simon smirking condescendingly when he wrote that Castelldosrius "made the prettiest speeches in the world." First, the new Spanish ambassador presented Charles II's request that the Sorbonne revoke its condemnation of the books of the Spanish nun María de Ágreda. In the mid-seventeenth century Sister María had maintained a long correspondence with Philip IV of Spain in which she often pointedly reminded him of his duties and his responsibilities to God and his people. The French king presumably had little interest in refurbishing the reputation of a nun who meddled in politics. Second, Castelldosrius presented Charles's request that Louis establish as dogma throughout his realm the Immaculate Conception of the Holy Virgin. Given that the Catholic Church did not proclaim the Immaculate Conception as dogma until 1854, the notion was, shall we say, a nonstarter in the France of 1699. Writing some time later, Saint-Simon concluded his first mention of Castelldosrius with some surprise: "Who would have believed that this ambassador would have turned out as he did just fourteen months later, and that this very exile would have made the ambassador's fortunes complete?"[45]

Saint-Simon was alluding to the dramatic sequence of events preceding and surrounding the death of Charles II in November 1700. As all of Europe jockeyed for position in the Spanish imperial sweepstakes, Castelldosrius proved to be an ideal intermediary between Spain and France. Louis granted frequent audiences to the Spanish ambassador in 1700, including one very long chat in which the two men met privately, without the French foreign minister, the

Marquis de Torcy. Saint-Simon noted the extraordinary nature of such a private meeting, "which Castelldosrius would not discuss then or later, but from which he emerged looking very pleased."[46]

In Madrid the Habsburg and French factions continued lobbying for the Spanish inheritance right up to the king's final agony; the Bavarian candidate had died in 1699. In the end, King Charles, the pathetic remnant of the Spanish Habsburg line, made the necessary choice, though not necessarily with a full heart. In a new will signed just a few days before his death he named Philippe d'Anjou, the second grandson of Louis XIV, as his successor, acknowledging that only the Bourbons had the resources to hold the empire together against the pack of predators circling in the near distance. Louis himself could be viewed as the top dog in that pack, of course, and Charles knew it. Nonetheless, by stipulating in his will that Bourbon Spain and Bourbon France must remain separate, and that the empire would be Spain's alone, he and his advisers hoped to make the best of a bad set of choices.[47]

When Charles II finally died on November 1, 1700, the Spanish court was immediately informed of the will, which came as a great shock to the Habsburg ambassador, and the news passed quickly to the French court at Fontainebleau, where it had an equally stunning effect. Louis and his advisers spent days discussing whether to accept its terms or to carry out the terms of the partition treaty instead. Castelldosrius received the latest dispatches from Spain and assured Louis that the Spanish people were anxious to welcome his grandson as their new king. Secure in that knowledge, Louis agreed to accept the Spanish will. The seventeen-year-old duke was not overjoyed with his new responsibilities, but he could hardly go against his grandfather's wishes.[48]

The formal audience confirming these events took place at Versailles on the morning of November 16. Louis invited Castelldosrius to his chamber as soon as he arose; his grandson had already entered through a private doorway. Presented to the duc d'Anjou, his new sovereign, Castelldosrius fell to his knees and kissed the duke's hand in the Spanish fashion, thus becoming the first Spaniard to pay homage to the new king. He then made a graceful speech to the young man in Spanish. Louis responded to the speech himself, noting that his grandson did not yet understand Spanish. As he concluded, he pointed to his grandson and said to Castelldosrius, "If he follows my counsel, he will tell you, you will be a great lord, and soon; he could do no better right now than to follow your advice." At that point, Castelldosrius responded in French with a remark that is often misquoted and misattributed: "What joy! There are no more Pyrenees and we are but one."[49] That was truer than he knew. Much of the rest of Europe soon declared war against the Bourbons in the War of the Spanish Succession, which forced France and Spain close together to defend the Bourbon accession in Spain and the integrity of the Spanish empire.

Castelldosrius remained at the French court for several more years, enjoying the favor of both Louis XIV in France and Philip V in Spain. In a curious way, Louis XIV had shaped Castelldosrius's career from the beginning. By provoking wars in the 1670s and 1680s, the French king had provided opportunities for the young Manuel d'Oms to rise swiftly in Spanish military and diplomatic circles. Once Castelldosrius became a key player at the French court, Louis's favor, however self-interested, propelled the impecunious marquis into a position of influence and status that he could never have achieved on his own. Judging from his own remarks in the years that followed, Castelldosrius felt a genuine and deep admiration for the French king. He also gloried in the sophisticated culture and refinement of the French court. Long before French fashions, entertainments, and literary affectations became the rage in Bourbon Spain, Castelldosrius adopted them wholeheartedly at their source. And the intensely status-conscious French courtiers who had scorned him when he arrived seemed to grow genuinely fond of him. Saint-Simon himself wrote a surprisingly warm description of Castelldosrius that deserves to be quoted at length because a few phrases are usually excerpted out of context and used to his detriment:

> The king, who always treated the marquis of Castelldosrius with great distinction and much familiarity after the acceptance of the will, sent him large sums of money at different times, as he was very needy without ever speaking about it; he accepted [the gifts] with grace because they came from the grandfather of his master. He was a very good, honest, and gallant man whose head was never turned, nor was he ever lacking [in wit and grace] in these extraordinary and brilliant times. [Above all, he was] a polite and considerate man who made everyone love and esteem him.[50]

For Castelldosrius's loyalty to the House of Bourbon, Philip V named him viceroy of Peru in 1702 and a first-class grandee in 1703. Given the reputation of Peru as a land of immense riches, Saint-Simon assumed that the viceregal appointment made Castelldosrius's fortune, and many scholars have repeated that notion without question.[51] In any case, it certainly marked the pinnacle of his career. Because of the war, there was no proper fleet to the Indies in the years 1701–6. Preparations began every year, only to be postponed for more opportune times. In the meantime, Castelldosrius continued to serve Philip V as

Spain's ambassador to France, though he was also technically a member of the Council of War in Madrid, which recommended that the crown pay for moving Castelldosrius and twelve members of his entourage to Peru.[52] That same arrangement had been made for the Count of La Monclova, but the journey was nonetheless bound to cost Castelldosrius considerably more than the subsidy allotted. When he finally received the order to report to Cádiz to prepare for embarcation in 1704, he borrowed 6,300 pistoles from French merchants in the Compagnie de la Mer Pacifique (Pacific Ocean Company) before leaving Paris.

Castelldosrius must have left Versailles with distinctly mixed feelings. Despite all prognostications for his good fortune in Peru, taking up responsibility for the viceroyalty during a world war for the empire's survival can only have been a daunting prospect. Once he reached southern Spain, he found that the fleet had been postponed yet again, and he eventually had to bear the cost of supporting his entourage in Jeréz de la Frontera for another two years. That was no small matter. Castelldosrius was taking with him twelve French gentlemen, two pages *(pages)*, two personal attendants *(ayudas de cámara)*, five lackeys *(lacayos)*, one surgeon, three musicians, two cooks, two cooks' helpers, and two pastry chefs. Judging from their surnames, twenty-seven of the thirty-one persons were non-Spaniards, and all but one of them was French, the lone exception being the Milanese music director for the palace orchestra.[53] The Council of the Indies complained about the numbers, and especially the presence of so many foreigners, but other viceroys had also traveled with large entourages, and the council ultimately gave its approval.[54] By the time Castelldosrius finally left Cádiz in 1706, he owed creditors in Spain another 200,000 pesos (equivalent to 1.6 million reals or 145,454 ducados).[55] Still, the fabled wealth of Peru had been making Spaniards' fortunes since the days of the Pizarro brothers, and Castelldosrius had every reason to hope that it would serve him equally well.

The complicated and often astounding story of Castelldosrius's tenure in office in Peru and his machinations regarding the Portobelo fair of 1708 have engaged the interest of generations of historians.[56] The records include thousands of official documents, including seventy-one fair-sized packets covering the investigation of his tenure as viceroy.[57] No one can remain neutral about Castelldosrius; the fewer documents one reads, the easier it is to take sides. Some historians praise him as a cultured and honest man and an effective viceroy during his brief tenure. Others denigrate him as one of the most corrupt officials in the whole of Spanish imperial history, based on charges made against him at the time.[58] Everything depends on the documents one reads and accepts as plausible. In what follows, I try to follow the path of interpretation supported by the bulk of the evidence. Castelldosrius's actions as viceroy and his interactions with the Count of Casa Alegre, commander of the *San José,* tell us a great deal about how that ship came to meet its end and what that meant to the Spanish crown.

The *armada de galeones* of Tierra Firme, with the Count of Casa Alegre as its captain general, finally left Cádiz on March 10, 1706, and arrived in Cartagena de Indias on April 27 after an uneventful crossing—a lucky break in wartime.[59] Like other captains general before him, Casa Alegre immediately began informing himself about enemy movements in the vicinity. This time Spain's principal enemies in the Caribbean were English and Dutch rather than French. He also checked on the state of preparations for the Portobelo fair. In more settled times, with a predictable fleet schedule and regular dispatch boats plying the Atlantic, the merchants in Lima would have known months in advance when the galleons were due to arrive in the Caribbean. The Armada of the Southern Sea would then have been readied to transport a contingent of merchants, with money and merchandise from the whole community, as well as revenue for the crown, on the voyage from Callao to Panama. They would have finished the journey by crossing the isthmus and making their way to Portobelo. But the times were anything but settled in 1706. The authorities in Lima received no word about the galleons until after they arrived in Cartagena. Even had they received advance warning, there had been so many false notices and disappointed hopes over the past ten years that they might not have believed it.

Castelldosrius had promised to repay his creditors in Spain immediately upon his arrival in the Indies, and he expected to continue on from Cartagena to Portobelo without delay, using his authority as viceroy to commandeer transport. Viceroys held extraordinary powers in the Spanish empire, literally acting as the king's proxy. Among his other attributes, a viceroy held the title of captain general of the military forces in his jurisdiction. For a lieutenant or second in command *(teniente general)* in that military capacity, viceroys tended to choose a family member or close friend, assuring a unity of purpose in coordinating military actions. When the teniente embarked on a fleet, he assumed the title of captain general. In other words, a viceroy held broad and impressive military powers, but they were suspended when a naval fleet was in port. That fleet's captain general assumed the ultimate military authority for the duration of his visit, whether or not the viceroy or his lieutenant was also in the vicinity.

In 1706 the Count of Casa Alegre, captain general of the Tierra Firme Fleet that ferried Castelldosrius to his viceroyalty, took on the ultimate military authority as soon as the fleet arrived in Cartagena. He shared the new viceroy's determination to see that the Portobelo fair take place as soon as possible so that his armada could collect the king's revenues at the fair and carry them back to Spain. But he also had broader responsibilities for the defense of the region. His concern for wartime security was bound to clash with Castelldosrius's anxiety to reach Lima, and their differing priorities collided almost as soon as the fleet arrived in Cartagena. Although Casa Alegre was new at commanding the Tierra Firme Fleet, he was wise enough to rely on more experienced military officers, such as his almirante, Don Miguel Agustín de Villanueva. Bolstered by Villanueva's counsel regarding military matters, Casa Alegre held firm in various tests of will with Castelldosrius; and because he outranked the viceroy, he was destined to win.

The immediate focus of their clash was Castelldosrius's need for transport to take him and his entourage from Cartagena to Portobelo.[60] General Casa Alegre initially designated three ships for Castelldosrius's use and ordered them refitted and supplied. Castelldosrius complained a month later, however, that "the days passed, and with them the favorable breezes that blow in these seasons," and he began to suspect that the general had changed his mind. He was right. News had arrived that five enemy ships and a fire ship were in the vicinity of Cartagena, making it highly inadvisable to weaken the fleet or to leave the city unprotected. News had also arrived confirming rumors that the Count of La Monclova had died in September 1705. As a result, the whole viceroyalty had been under the interim governance of the Audiencia of Lima for the better part of a year. That made Castelldosrius even more determined to reach Peru as soon as possible so that he could collect the king's taxes personally and persuade the merchants to attend the Portobelo fair.

Casa Alegre treated Castelldosrius with the utmost courtesy and followed the guidelines for proper behavior and deference to the letter, but he refused to compromise the security of Cartagena and the fleet under his care. He called a meeting of all the civil and military officials in the area, including the viceroy, to discuss the general situation. Based on news Castelldosrius received "from various quarters," he inferred that the meeting was really designed to ratify the general's delay in releasing the three ships to him, and he refused to attend. At the meeting, Casa Alegre used what Castelldosrius called the "specious pretext" of the threat of enemy attack to postpone providing the ships and asked for a written vote on the matter.

The next day, the captain general, accompanied by the almirante and the *auditor de guerra* of the fleet, called on the viceroy at his residence to report that a plurality of those in attendance had supported his stance. Nonetheless, he assured the viceroy that he had ordered the ships' outfitting to continue. Castelldosrius thought that was merely a ruse, however, because he had seen only a few men bringing ballast stones to the largest ship at Half-Moon Beach. He asked the general to reconsider his position and to call another full meeting of all the officials in the area. Casa Alegre complied and once again paid a courtesy call on Castelldosrius to report the vote to him. At the moment no ships could be spared to take Castelldosrius to Portobelo, Casa Alegre regretted to say. With that, there was little Castelldosrius could do but complain, and complain he did, in a blizzard of letters to Casa Alegre, the civil and mercantile authorities in Lima, and the king himself.[61]

Castelldosrius's anxiety was personal as well as professional. His own finances, precarious at the best of times, became more ruinous by the day, as he supported his entourage in the pestilential summer heat of Cartagena. In his letter to the king on May 25 he noted that he had served thirteen years in embassies and in waiting to take up the viceregal appointment in Lima. Now, the unconscionable delay meant that he did not know "how, or with what I can maintain myself in this city, where there is little or no silver, and the climate is so contrary to health." Castelldosrius was not the first viceroy to suffer through such circumstances. In Cartagena he heard stories about "many governors and ministers, good and useful men, who, lacking the means to sustain themselves, and after suffering a thousand indignities and assailed by hunger and their sense of honor, lost their lives while fleeing from here in canoes or traveling overland, as the last recourse in their impossible situation."

In his anger and frustration, Castelldosrius blamed everyone who stood in his path to Portobelo. In addition to the general, he faulted the almirante, Villanueva, "to whom the general defers in everything," for stressing the potential danger from enemy ships, a threat that Castelldosrius considered exaggerated at best. He also cast doubt on the honesty and competence of the armada's leaders in general, who had allowed most of their men to come ashore. He complained that the three merchants' representatives in Cartagena, who had voted in both meetings to support Casa Alegre and Villanueva, "seem to have conspired to oppose me since I was named to this post, for reasons that are not clear." He conjectured, however, that they wanted to prevent any trade goods reaching Portobelo in advance of the fleet. After so many years without an official fair, the first goods to arrive in Portobelo would fetch inflated prices and depress the market for the subsequent fair. Instead of giving him the ships he needed, Castelldosrius concluded, Casa Alegre had merely sent a small canoe to Portobelo with news of the armada's arrival, a summary of the situation, and a request that the Lima contingent "come down" for the fair. Castelldosrius pointedly ended his letter by observing that nothing would make the merchants less likely to leave Lima than news of enemy ships near Cartagena.

Castelldosrius's packet of letters sailed back across the Atlantic with the first available ships, and the king and his Council of the Indies duly considered his complaints. Their response could not have been more circumspect. In a very brief letter to General Casa Alegre dated January 11, 1707, the king and his council noted that Castelldosrius had written commenting on the matter of finding transport to Portobelo, but they left out all of his accusations of wrongdoing. They merely said, in the politest possible terms, that they would like to know what Casa Alegre had to say about the events.

Despite Castelldosrius's best efforts and incessant complaints, he had to remain in Cartagena for three months before he could arrange to travel to Portobelo, where he arrived on July 21, 1706. He wrote to the king ten days later, reporting on his arrival and relating as much information about the state of affairs in Lima as he could gather without actually being there. The bad news came first. Despite his exhortations, Castelldosrius had reluctantly concluded that the merchants would not travel to Callao for the trip to Panama and Portobelo without his presence and direct intervention in Lima. Because the fair could not begin without them, and as it was already quite late in the season, the whole timetable had to be pushed back, making it virtually impossible for the galleons to return to Spain in 1706. Two hundred years of experience had taught Spaniards to avoid the late-summer hurricane season at all costs, except under the most dire circumstances. As desperately as the crown needed the revenue expected from Peru, it would have been madness to attempt a return crossing of the silver galleons in wartime during hurricane season.

Castelldosrius devoted much of his long letter to explaining how he had finally managed to reach Portobelo and justifying the additional expenses he had incurred. He complained that the long stay in Cartagena had done visible harm to him and all but two or three members of his family, in addition to the frustration, expense, and pointlessness of remaining there when he was needed in Peru. He had even been tempted to do as many officials had done in the past, "going to Portobelo in canoes and other vessels of little or no safety, which contrary winds would have rendered especially risky and doubtful at the present time." He assured the king that the danger alone would not have stopped him for a single instant. He had decided against making the trip in small boats only because he would have had to leave behind in Cartagena many officials who were necessary for his administration in Peru. Hearing that a twenty-four-gun hulk had been captured and taken to Santa Marta, he had begun negotiations to buy or lease it for the voyage from Cartagena to Portobelo. Instead, fate came to his rescue in the form of a French frigate and a packet boat in Portobelo. A letter from Castelldosrius persuaded their captains to come to Cartagena, where they anchored at Boca Chica within days. Another French corsairing frigate in Portobelo, the *San Juan Baptista*, agreed to help as well.

On July 15 Castelldosrius and part of his family embarked on the *San Juan Bautista*, and the rest of his family sailed on the other frigate, together with as many governors and ministers as would fit. The rest of his entourage had to make do with the packet boat and two sloops that happened to be going the same way. They all arrived in Portobelo without incident on July 21 but had no desire to stay. If Cartagena was unhealthful in the summer, Portobelo was even worse. It had long been known as the "Spaniards' graveyard" because of the pestilential fevers that flourished there in the hot season. Castelldosrius took ten days to make all the arrangements for the overland journey to Panama City. When he wrote to the king on July 31, he said they were departing immediately. But more delays and a harrowing journey to Panama followed. Castelldosrius had hoped to greet the Peruvian merchant fleet in Panama and send them on their way to Portobelo, and he wrote to the audiencia and the merchant consulado in Lima with orders and timetables for preparing the fleet in September and October 1706. Nothing happened except inconclusive meetings in Lima and one missed deadline after another. At the end of December, Castelldosrius was still in Panama, feeling the strain of the long delays. The only bright spot from his point of view was that in Panama he could exercise his full civil and military authority as viceroy of Peru without being subject to General Casa Alegre's overarching authority on the other side of the isthmus.

On December 31 Castelldosrius wrote two extraordinary letters to Lima, one to the audiencia and the other to the merchant consulado. In the first, he again urged the audiencia to put the full weight of its authority behind efforts to ready the fleet at Callao. The tone of his letter was desperate and emotional; he said that no less than the survival of the monarchy depended upon the audiencia's efforts. He included fulsome praise for the young king, arguing that he merited an offer, "not only of our fortunes, but also of our lives, as he has exposed his own life to danger [in battle] for the conservation and universal glory of the kingdom." Castelldosrius emphasized that his first task was to prevent illicit commerce, and he urged the members of the audiencia to do everything they could to stop it. He reminded the president of the audiencia that he had served "five years in the embassy of France, at the feet of the Most Christian king [Louis XIV], and he instructed me well to know how much against the royal mind it is to permit the excesses that some private individuals attempt, abandoning his grace and favor."[62]

Castelldosrius wrote to the merchant community in Lima the same day, with a related message. He urged the merchants to set aside any doubts that he knew the intentions of both kings [of Spain and of France] and assured them that he would deal truly and honestly with them. They would have a viceroy who, after his service to God, would devote his time "to nothing more than the service of [the king] his Master, the public good, and his own conscience [*propio punto*], which he has known how to conserve in thirty-nine years of public service from one place to another; and who is not so imprudent as to offer to do things that he cannot accomplish, and therefore to expose your Graces to disappointment with him later."[63] In Lima that message could be read in several ways, but certainly as a threat as well as a promise.

At about the same time, Castelldosrius asked the Lima merchants for a personal loan of 200,000 pesos so that he could repay his Spanish creditors by the first available fleet. He recognized that the Lima merchants would need the money returned for the Portobelo fair, and he promised they would have it. It may seem surprising that they would advance such a sum to a man they had never met, but Castelldosrius had a trusted ally in Lima arguing his case. Don Antonio Marí, a lifelong friend from Catalonia, had gone on to Peru when Castelldosrius and the rest of his entourage were still stuck in Cartagena. Marí managed to persuade the merchants in Lima to advance the money and send it immediately to Panama. However wary they may have been, it made good sense to ingratiate themselves with the new viceroy. They were less than anxious to follow their money down to the fair, however, despite the exhortations of Castelldosrius and Marí.

In addition to laying bare Castelldosrius's increasing frustration, his letters and related documents reveal much about his character. In his years as a diplomat, he had managed to win the respect and trust of at least three kings and their courts, and it would be logical to assume that he accomplished this with loyalty, charm, and amiability alone. Saint-Simon described Castelldosrius as honest, modest, and highly intelligent, but there is no hint that he thought Castelldosrius had a powerful personality. Castelldosrius's letters from Cartagena, Portobelo, and Panama reveal a different side of the new viceroy, or rather several different sides. His strong sense of duty to the king is predictable, given his background. But his impatience and self-righteousness come as a surprise; those traits would later lead him into questionable actions and open confrontations that belied his training as a diplomat versed in the subtleties of court politics.

On the other hand, court politics had obviously taught him that knowledge was power. In his war of words with the captain general, Castelldosrius made sure that he knew what was going on, even at meetings he chose not to attend. Sometimes he gathered information himself, as when he visited the beach where ships were being outfitted, but at other times he relied on information from "various quarters." In other words, scarcely off the boat in an alien land, he demonstrated an impressive ability to establish an intelligence-gathering network of reliable informants. Castelldosrius's letters also suggest how he was able to accomplish this feat: he had brought most of the network with him. Castelldosrius traveled with a large entourage, many of whom he had appointed to offices in Peru. Some were French, but he had also recruited several Spaniards in Cartagena. Arriving with a portable administration was not unusual for a new viceroy; in fact it was traditional. A viceroy's broad power of appointment was considered one of the major benefits of the post. He could reward loyal retainers, consolidate family influence, pay back social debts, collect fees from new appointees, and enhance his own power and prestige by appointing his own men. In a vast area such as the Viceroyalty of Peru he could arrive with a ready-made network of loyal subordinates and avoid the need to start from scratch in building an effective administrative structure.

Like the viceroy, the new appointees could expect to profit from their posts by collecting fees for a variety of services to augment their basic salaries. A French visitor to Peru a few years later passed a harsh judgment on these practices that many later writers have adopted. Noting that most subordinate officers held their jobs for only three to five years and thereafter faced a mandatory review, he claimed that they all viewed their term "as a Jubilee, which is to come but once in their lives; at the end whereof they will be laugh'd at, if they have not made their fortune." Even honest men became corrupt, the visitor claimed, assuming that they would be charged with maladministration regardless and that the only way to clear one's name would be to bribe the judges with "part of what they have wrong'd the king and the subjects of."[64]

The realities of colonial administration were rather more subtle than that.

The crown expected officials to charge fees for their services. That way, part of the cost of colonial administration was shifted from the crown to the citizenry. The mandatory review, or *residencia*, of an official's term in office took those expectations into account, while working to keep outright corruption and abuse of authority to a minimum. Throughout the Habsburg centuries the system worked fairly well, and it is difficult to see how an empire so large, diffuse, and expensive to administer could have functioned otherwise. The crown simply had to rely on the basic competence and loyalty of officials in the field and to trust that their self-interest did not undercut their ultimate duty to the crown. Viceroys benefited from their ability to appoint subordinate officials, to be sure, but they had every incentive to appoint men who were competent, and that enhanced the effectiveness of the overall administration.

In the late seventeenth century, in an attempt to draw more patronage power back into the hands of the monarch, the crown tried to recapture some of the appointment powers hitherto exercised by its viceroys. Early in the tenure of Melchor Portocarrero in Peru, before he became the Count of La Monclova, the government in Madrid decided to select various officials rather than leave their appointment to the viceroy. Portocarrero complained to the king openly and pointedly in 1690 about the implications of that break with tradition:

> The time is coming when I will not be able to accommodate a single relative or dependent of mine . . . who are persons with obligations and who have come to these remote realms trusting that they would be able to achieve what all those who have followed other viceroys have achieved; . . . and I . . . I will be left with no more authority than that exercised by the king's representative in some city or other . . . because all sorts of people—whether they are members of the secular or regular clergy, or gentlemen, or men of business, or other persons with obligations—through a relative or through a friend, are all dependent on the favor of the person who is in charge of the government.[65]

Portocarrero was not just arguing from his own self-interest. He understood that the patronage system held the empire together with ties of personal loyalty and that the viceroy played a key role in that system. Far distant from the oversight of bureaucrats in Madrid, appointees who did not have a local patron to please might easily drift away from loyalty to the crown.

With the change of dynasty in 1700 a new element entered the picture. The Bourbons were not immediately accepted as the legitimate rulers of Spain, despite the last will and testament of Charles II. With a war being fought over who would control Spain and its empire, Philip V and his ministers were anxious to establish their own networks of loyal supporters. One way to do that was through granting offices in the Indies. Castelldosrius owed his appointment as viceroy to his demonstrated loyalty to the new dynasty, and Philip V had every reason to suppose that he would continue to uphold the crown's interests in Peru. Castelldosrius sailed to the Indies with explicit orders to revive the Portobelo fairs, to resuscitate the Armada of the Southern Sea, to defend the viceroyalty against foreign incursions, and to renew the flow of tax revenue to the crown. The king expected Castelldosrius to use his office to restore his personal finances as well, but that would not necessarily have an adverse effect on his service to the crown. Events would prove how difficult it was to try to achieve all those aims at once, however.

Castelldosrius's letters from Portobelo and the circumstances of his arrival there remind us how indebted he was to the French, both financially and politically. Without French help he would not have been appointed viceroy, and he had needed both French money and French ships to get from Cartagena to Portobelo. His entourage also contained a sizeable contingent of Frenchmen, though evidently he had not obtained the necessary permission for them to enter the Indies. In the two centuries of Habsburg rule it had been a straightforward matter to define foreigners, who were generally barred from office-holding and even immigration to the Indies without special license. With the advent of the Bourbons in Spain the situation became more complicated, but there is no question that Spanish officials in the Indies thought the Frenchmen in Castelldosrius's entourage needed more than the usual licenses to immigrate.

They expressed their disapproval by barring entry to all the Frenchmen who accompanied Castelldosrius. It took several months to sort things out, but he eventually prevailed. The English governor of Jamaica, who tended to view the whole drama in broad geopolitical terms, reported to London in March 1707 that governors supporting the Bourbons had supplanted those "who were supposed to be in the interest of King Charles" (i.e., the Habsburg pretender to the Spanish throne).[66] More accurately, governors loyal to Castelldosrius had supplanted those who were not.

Castelldosrius's letters also remind us how much he had riding on his ability to carry out the king's mandate. Philip V was counting on Castelldosrius to provide revenue from Peru to fund the war effort. Assuming that the war ended well for him, Philip seemed likely to stay in power for decades to come; he was only twenty-three years old in 1706. Without the king's continued favor Castelldosrius would have no chance to advance his career. He was fifty-six years old in 1706, no longer young but presumably still able to plan for another decade or more of service, and he had ten children to place in society. By successfully carrying out the king's mandate in difficult times, he would have an additional claim on the king's favor. Castelldosrius was also counting on the Portobelo fair to generate funds to pay his personal debts and begin restoring his finances, eroded after so many years in expensive diplomatic postings. The note of anxiety, bordering on hysteria, that often creeps into his letters from Cartagena, Portobelo, and Panama suggests the precariousness of his position. Only when he reached Lima would he be able to assume the full power of his viceregal authority and get to work, both for the king and for himself.

Castelldosrius was able to arrange the final leg of his journey early in 1707. He and his entourage finally arrived in Lima in March, and he lost no time in dispatching his new appointees to their offices in the main population centers of the viceroyalty.[67] By May 22, when he officially took possession of his post, his administration had fully settled in. Castelldosrius soon realized with alarm that "illicit commerce" with French interlopers in the Southern Sea was rampant and largely outside the control of the authorities. If the merchants engaged in that commerce expected Castelldosrius to turn a blind eye to their activities, they were badly mistaken. As he noted in a letter to the king at the end of August, "The merchant body in general laments and complains quite rightly that the illegal traffic has greatly weakened it, and yet the individual members of that body are themselves the ones who cause the general decline, for they have no concern whatsoever for the common good when it conflicts with their own private interests."[68] It is doubtful that all the merchants in Lima were involved in illicit commerce with the French, but enough of them fit Castelldosrius's description to justify the generalization. The collapse of the Portobelo fairs had presumably led many of them to violate the law, just as it had starved the viceroyalty of needed revenue.

The *avería* tax, collected from merchants at the fair, supported the fleets that protected trade, including the Armada of the Southern Sea, whose primary purposes were to carry the merchants between Callao and Panama for the fair and to defend the coast. The last avería contract with the merchants of Lima, in 1662, had specified that they pay the tax only in years when an armada de galeones arrived in Tierra Firme and that the contract would continue in effect until ten fleets had made the trip. Because the regular fleet system collapsed in the late seventeenth century, the terms of the 1662 contract were not fulfilled until the 1706 galleons arrived. Castelldosrius was supposed to negotiate a new contract as soon as he could. His ability to do so hinged on the merchants' attitude toward the fairs, and after decades of unpredictable fleets, and no fleet at all since the beginning of the war, they had understandably lost confidence in the system. It would take all of Castelldosrius's skills, along with major concessions, to reach a new agreement.[69]

Once his subordinate officials took up their posts, the viceroy ordered them to produce an accurate accounting of the financial situation. He learned to his dismay that far from being the cash cow that Madrid and Paris imagined, the viceroyalty had been running a deficit for years, with about 1.5 million pesos in annual income and 1.7 million pesos in annual expenses. The expenses included everything from a cavalry regiment to the chaplains in the cathedral choir in Lima. With ongoing efforts to recover from the 1687 earthquake, plus added wartime expenses and disruptions and no subsidies from the crown, by 1707 the viceroyalty had debts of over 5.5 million pesos and only 600,000 pesos on hand, all of which Castelldosrius immediately spent on defense.[70] In short, royal finances in Peru were a shambles when Castelldosrius arrived.

Without public revenue and private profits generated by the fair, Castelldosrius had little hope of restoring the viceroyalty's solvency or of financing its continued operation. How could the viceroy prod the merchants into participating in the fair at Portobelo? Without their cooperation, there would be no fair, no defense for the Pacific coast, no revenue for the crown, and no hope of stifling smuggling in the long term. It seems that Castelldosrius devised a plan to reverse all those negative factors and in the bargain to restore his own fortunes and reward his entourage. The plan involved taking control of the illicit commerce and saddling it with a punitive level of taxation. With breathtaking speed, considering the distances and surface area involved and the fact that he was a complete newcomer to Peru, Castelldosrius took control of the illicit trade away from smugglers and local merchants alike. Referring to the illicit commerce, Geoffrey Walker notes that Castelldosrius

> had no hope of stamping it out immediately, but he evidently succeeded in organizing and taxing it for the king, and channeling some of the profits into his own hands and those of his subordinates.

> A *de facto* trading company run by the viceroy's associates absorbed control of existing groups involved in illicit commerce. In exchange for paying a tax to the viceroy's company—reputedly worth 25 percent of the total volume in some places—the merchants could continue doing business as they had in the past few years. The volume of illicit trade at the port of Pisco south of Callao grew large enough to be dubbed the "Pisco fair"! The viceroy's company issued re-

ceipts for the tax, which allowed the merchants and their goods free passage. If they refused to pay, they saw their goods confiscated as contraband, with the denouncer claiming a share as legal compensation. Either way, Castelldosrius and his network benefited. The whole system was set in place and functioning toward the end of 1707. At the very least, it speaks well of Castelldosrius's organizational skills.[71]

Walker uses evidence of the viceroy's brilliant and unorthodox plan to revile him as corrupt, but I draw a different conclusion. Castelldosrius and his subordinates undoubtedly reaped short-term gains from the illicit commerce, as his enemies would later charge, but he had promised the king that he would revive the Portobelo fair, and he knew that the two activities were incompatible, as did the crown.[72] He seems to have gathered all the strands of illicit commerce into his hands not only for short-term profit but also as the quickest way to amass the resources necessary to stifle smuggling and turn the merchants' ambitions back toward the Portobelo fair. There is little doubt that he had the organizational skills to do so. Moreover, we should not forget that he had been on intimate terms for five years with Louis XIV of France, one of the greatest political manipulators of his day or any other. That Castelldosrius crafted his overall plan ad hoc, once he understood the desperate nature of his situation, is even greater proof of his organizational skills.

Jolted out of their lethargy by this turn of events, the merchants of Lima soon added real conviction to their habitual pleas to stamp out illicit trade. Their two-faced strategy of condemning illicit commerce as a group and practicing it as individuals had become considerably less profitable. As a result, they began to clamor wholeheartedly for its abolition. Their change of attitude is usually presented as a rejection of the regime imposed by Castelldosrius and his administration, but there was more to it than that. A few years earlier the diffuse nature of the illicit trade had made it virtually impossible to control, as Monclova had acknowledged in 1704. That is one reason why many merchants had hedged their bets by taking part in it. Castelldosrius dramatically altered the situation by showing that he could organize, control, and tax the illicit trade. That meant he could also suppress it, thus restoring the central place of the Portobelo fairs and the exclusive trading privileges of the merchants in Lima. Presumably that would have been more profitable to them in the long term than the uncertain and diminished profits from smuggling. Nonetheless, they needed positive as well as negative inducements to participate in the fair.

Meanwhile, the Spanish crown had a pressing need for cash. Philip V expected a great boost for his war effort when the armada returned, and that effort could not wait for long-term solutions. In the fall of 1707 Castelldosrius used every expedient he could think of to gather a respectable sum of money to send to Madrid. These included unpaid salaries from vacant offices, unclaimed legacies, income from ancient *encomiendas,* donations made under pressure from anyone with money and pretensions to royal favor, and even half the annual salaries of the corrigidores in the viceroyalty. In a few months' time Castelldosrius gathered a total of 1,379,310 pesos for the crown, an astonishing accomplishment at a time when there was a deficit of 5.5 million pesos and virtually no cash on hand.[73] In sixteen years the Count of La Monclova had sent a total of only 1.2 million pesos to Madrid.

While supervising the collection of these extraordinary taxes for the king, Castelldosrius continued to negotiate with the merchants in Lima, trying to persuade them to go to the Portobelo fair. The only term they would accept was a promise to stifle the illicit trade so that the goods they brought back from Portobelo could be sold at a profit. Castelldosrius obviously had to demonstrate his good faith, so he issued orders barring illicit goods from the viceroyalty and expelling French interlopers. Eventually news of his abrupt about-face would reach the Spanish court, with predictable results: the anti-French forces were delighted, and the pro-French forces were dismayed and angry.[74] But that was in the future. In the short term Castelldosrius had accomplished three of his immediate objectives: he had collected a respectable amount of money for the king, he had found the resources to outfit the Armada of the Southern Sea for the trip from Callao to Panama, and he had persuaded the merchants to participate in the fair.

The viceroy's actions also had a negative side. He had temporarily frozen a major source of his own income, namely, the fees for permitting, organizing, and taxing illicit trade through his trading company and his network of subordinate officials. He had also alienated the French in Peru, who had come to expect much friendlier treatment; some of them could easily turn to piracy if the illicit commerce dried up. That was a risk Castelldosrius evidently thought he had to take. A contingent of the Lima merchant community finally left Callao on December 19, 1707, with more than 7 million pesos to finance their trading mission to Portobelo. The little fleet also carried the money and treasure that Castelldosrius had collected for the king. Despite the potential danger from pirates, they reached the Panama port of Perico safely on January 20, 1708. A ship coming from Guayaquil with money for the fair joined them on

February 8, and the caravan of merchants and money began the trek across the Isthmus of Darién. On the other side, galleons from the Tierra Firme Fleet were awaiting their arrival. At long last the Portobelo fair was about to begin.

The Tierra Firme galleons had stayed in Cartagena since their arrival in April 1706, while Captain General Casa Alegre monitored reports of enemy movements in the Caribbean and awaited news from Lima and Madrid. In terms of communication times, Madrid was much closer to Cartagena than Lima was. During the two years that the Tierra Firme Fleet remained in Cartagena, the king sent periodic orders to Captain General Casa Alegre, as well as to Viceroy Castelldosrius in Lima. In late October 1706, anxious for the funds he expected from Peru, the king sent a series of missives announcing that Louis XIV was dispatching a French squadron to the Caribbean to escort the treasure galleons back to Europe.[75] Another spate of royal orders in early November announced the departure of that squadron and ordered Captain General Casa Alegre to place his fleet under the protection of the French for the return voyage and to obey orders from the commander of that squadron.[76] And who was that worthy gentleman? None other than Ducasse, who had visited Cartagena eleven years earlier in command of the buccaneers in the Baron de Pointis's expedition. Together they had extorted a vast ransom from the citizenry and nonetheless had sacked and burned the town. It is not hard to imagine what the Count of Casa Alegre, captain general of the Tierra Firme Fleet, anchored in Cartagena, thought about the king's order, but he was duty-bound to obey it if he took his fleet to Havana to meet the French squadron. Because the Portobelo fair still had not taken place, Casa Alegre had a perfect reason not to sail to Havana. Ducasse returned to Europe without the Tierra Firme Fleet.

The months dragged on, and still there was no movement in Lima, Cartagena, or Portobelo. In July 1707 the king notified Casa Alegre that Ducasse would be sent to the Caribbean on escort duty again. He ordered Casa Alegre to return to Spain with Ducasse whether or not the Portobelo fair had been held, indeed even if it were being held when he received the order.[77] The king sent Castelldosrius copies of his dispatches and orders to Casa Alegre. He also sent Ducasse a copy of the order placing him in command of the combined fleets from New Spain and Tierra Firme for the return voyage. Ducasse sailed for the Indies in early October 1707, under a nine-month contract with the Spanish crown to escort the treasure fleets home.

Casa Alegre did not join Ducasse in Havana this time either (fig. 13). Periodic news about English ship movements from their base on Jamaica persuaded Casa Alegre to keep the Tierra Firme galleons in Cartagena, ostensibly to protect the port and the district from the English. In the aftermath of the 1697 French attack on the city, local and viceregal authorities had done what they could to strengthen Cartagena's defenses, with the works supervised by the military engineer Juan de Herrera y Sotomayor,[78] but a war fleet in port provided the best defense of all. The viceroy sent word to Cartagena in December 1707 that the merchants from Lima had finally gone down to the fair, carrying his remittances for the king with them. That was all the more reason for Casa Alegre to delay his departure for Havana.

Casa Alegre may also have had other reasons. It is hard to believe that he welcomed the prospect of relinquishing command of his fleet and subordinating himself to Ducasse. Having resisted ceding command to Don Francisco Navarro in Veracruz in 1687,[79] he was not likely to hand his fleet over to an erstwhile French pirate. Nonetheless, he had to put the best face on his unwillingness to leave Cartagena, to avoid being accused of disobeying the king's command. He accomplished this feat in the time-honored Spanish manner: he obeyed but did not comply with the king's order to join Ducasse.[80] Ironically, the captain general of the New Spain Fleet of 1706 complied with the king's orders and sailed his fleet from Veracruz to Havana, arriving in late May 1708. The irony involves the identity of that fleet's captain general: Don Diego Fernández de Santillán, Casa Alegre's own nephew. Don Diego and his fleet reached Spain safely under Ducasse's protection in late August 1708. In addition to public and private revenues, they carried a huge amount of tobacco, much of it purchased on the king's account. On the outbound voyage in 1706 Don Diego had carried an order to buy 3 million pounds of tobacco for the king, paying for it with 200,000 pesos in royal revenues.[81]

While the Tierra Firme Fleet remained in Cartagena in 1706 and 1707, Casa Alegre allowed most of his men to go ashore, subject to immediate recall but also subject to the attractions and perils of life on land. Scarcely a month after the fleet arrived in Cartagena two of the soldiers disappeared.[82] By the time of the muster, on July 19, 1706, seven more soldiers, five apprentices, and five sailors were gone as well. Three more men had fallen sick in the pestilential climate of the Caribbean in summer. They were being nursed in private homes in the city, as was customary in the absence of a proper hospital. Another man, the chief pilot, Captain Benito Alonso Barroso, died in early August. His death represented a serious loss to the capitana of a fleet in wartime. To replace him,

Casa Alegre chose Captain Roque de Fuentes, chief pilot on the *San Joaquín*, whose earlier disagreement with Almirante Villanueva presumably made him eager to accept the new assignment.[83]

Before the end of 1706 another fifty-four men failed to report for muster on the *San José:* thirteen died, and the other forty-one, including the head squadron leader, Pedro de la Palma, deserted. By the time the *San José* had been in Cartagena less than a year the captain general had lost close to 15 percent of his complement of men. The attrition continued through 1707 and the early months of 1708—a fairly common occurrence among Spain's Indies fleets. As long as the ships remained idle in port, this was not a matter of great concern. Casa Alegre promoted or shifted men to posts that needed filling and signed on others when the need arose. For example, to replace his missing head squadron leader, he installed Don Pedro Baloes on Christmas Day, 1706.

At the end of 1707, nearly two years after leaving Spain, Casa Alegre received word that the merchant contingent from Lima had finally left Callao for Panama. They sailed in four ships of the Armada of the Southern Sea, commanded by Captain General Don Antonio de Zamudio, Marquis of Villar de Tajo. The viceroy saw the fleet off in Callao, where he had been residing since the end of September to oversee preparations for the departure.[84] Those preparations included registering and loading the money that the merchants were taking or sending to the fair. As the viceroy noted in his letter to the king,

> Although according to the registers of the masters of silver, [the fleet] is carrying around 5 million [pesos] in gold and silver, I must believe that the portion of gold will bring the total to 6 or 7 millions. And although my vigilance, and that of the Prior and Consuls of the Tribunal of the consulado, has worked to see that everything be registered, it is not easy to persuade myself that this has been achieved; even so, I console myself that this sum will in any case pass to the dominions of Your Majesty and will circulate among his vassals, in utility and benefit of the royal service of Your Majesty.[85]

Upon receiving the news that the small fleet had left Callao, Casa Alegre readied the Tierra Firme galleons to sail and left Cartagena on January 5, 1708. As captain general of the galleons, Casa Alegre held responsibility for overseeing the fair and everyone connected with it. During his sojourn in Cartagena he had already overseen a small fair in the nearby town of Santa Marta. His responsibility for the Portobelo fair would once again bring him into conflict with Viceroy Castelldosrius, if only by proxy.

Castelldosrius had borrowed 200,000 pesos from the merchants in Lima before he even arrived in Peru, as we have seen, in order to repay his debts in Spain. He had promised to repay the debt before the Portobelo fair and devised an ingenious way to make good on that promise. Traditionally, the Lima merchants paid a tax of 7 percent on the silver and 0.5 percent on the gold they brought to the fair. The revenue collected was earmarked to cover the 350,000 ducados owed to the crown for the avería tax. Two merchants from the Lima contingent were designated to collect the tax at El Boquerón, on the route between Panama and Portobelo. If the sum collected was more than 350,000 ducados, the surplus was refunded to those who had paid the tax.

For the 1708 fair, Castelldosrius persuaded the two tax collectors to hand over the first 200,000 pesos they collected to his Lima creditors. In other words, he planned to used a goodly portion of the sum earmarked for the averías to repay the money he had spent traveling to his viceroyalty. The crown was ultimately responsible for those expenses, but Castelldosrius may have doubted that he would ever be repaid. He had surmounted that obstacle by shifting royal tax revenues directly to his Lima creditors. Although defensible, Castelldosrius's plan was highly irregular.

The tax collectors carried out the plan faithfully, but too many people were involved for it to remain secret, and Captain General Casa Alegre got wind of the scheme. He learned that what remained of the revenue collected would scarcely begin to cover the 350,000 ducados for the avería. Exercising his authority as captain general, he threw the two tax collectors into jail, sent soldiers to confiscate most of the revenue, and postponed the opening of the fair until he could get things sorted out. At that point the licenciado Francisco Medina, an oidor of the Audiencia of Santa Fe, investigated the case and found insufficient cause to continue holding the merchants and the money. Judge Medina therefore released the merchants' representatives and returned most of the money confiscated by Casa Alegre—a total of 431,250 pesos, or just over 313,600 ducados—to representatives of the merchant community. To the master of silver for the galleons he turned over only 50,000 ducados from the tax collected at El Boquerón.[86] Viceroy Castelldosrius had finally won a battle with the captain general, but at the expense of funds needed for the fleets. The Portobelo fair took place thereafter in an atmosphere of ill will and mutual recrimination between the Lima merchants and the royal and naval officials associated with Captain General Casa Alegre and the Tierra Firme Fleet. In retrospect, their discord was an omen of things to come.

The merchants finished their business at the fair at the end of May 1708. The contingent from Lima had brought 7 million pesos—just over 5 million ducados—to trade in Portobelo. Even if we assume, for the sake of argument, that all of the money was going back to Spain to pay for goods bought at the fair, that was still a far cry from the 20–35 million pesos that often changed hands at the sporadic fairs held during the late seventeenth century.[87] Nonetheless, all things considered, the merchants in Portobelo could be pleased with the immediate outcome of the fair.

They did not know, however, that as the fair was taking place in Portobelo, new developments in Peru were putting fresh strains on the viceroy's promise to stamp out illicit commerce. The war in Europe had soaked up extraordinary sums, and Louis XIV insisted upon being repaid quickly for the help he was providing his grandson in Spain. He therefore dispatched a ship called *L'Aimable* to bring home some of Peru's legendary silver to repay his loans. When *L'Aimable* and its squadron reached Callao in May, Castelldosrius told Captain Michel Chabert that his treasury was empty, but he eventually put together a package of local loans to send more than 300,000 pesos back to France.[88] While Castelldosrius was negotiating with bankers and merchants in Lima to secure the money for *L'Aimable,* however, other French ships were smuggling merchandise into ports up and down the coast. Did Castelldosrius permit the smuggling to occur in order to profit from it, as his enemies later claimed, or did he tax the trade as usual once he realized he could not stop it? Either way, when the merchants of Lima found out about it, they accused Castelldosrius of double-dealing and worse for his failure to end the illicit commerce. In their fury, they began a campaign to have him removed from office, a campaign that would hound the viceroy to his grave and beyond.

Unaware of these developments, the merchants' representatives in Portobelo headed home in May 1708. Before they even left Panama, however, English privateers under Thomas Colb captured seven of the fourteen sloops *(balandras)* in their fleet and more than half of their merchandise.[89] Storms along the coast later forced the remnant of the fleet to land in Paita instead of Callao and to travel overland the rest of the way to Lima.[90] Some of the men would not reach home until more than a year after the fair. Because the illicit trade had continued in their absence, local markets were all but saturated with goods by the time they returned to the capital of the viceroyalty.

Fig. 1. Portrait of Philip V of Spain in 1701, by Hyacinthe Rigaud. This portrait of Spain's first Bourbon king was reportedly commissioned from the official painter at the French court as a memento for Philip's grandfather Louis XIV. The Prado Museum, Madrid

Fig. 2. Portrait of Louis XIV, king of France, in 1701, after Hyacinthe Rigaud, oil on canvas, 289.6 × 159.1 cm. The French king reportedly ordered the original of this portrait as a gift for his grandson Philip V of Spain. Louis liked the painting so much, however, that he kept it for himself, and Rigaud's workshop later made several copies as well. The J. Paul Getty Museum, Los Angeles

Fig. 3. Spanish Galleons, Great Vessels, with high aftcastles, for Voyages to the West Indies. From
P. Jacques Guéroult du Pas, *Recuëil de veües de tous les differens bastimens de la mer
mediterranée, et de l'ocean, avec leurs noms et usages* (Paris: Pierre Giffart, 1710). Courtesy of
the James Ford Bell Library, University of Minnesota, Minneapolis

Fig. 4. Stern of a Spanish galleon of sixty-four guns, with a depiction of St. Joseph and the Child. The drawing was included with a memorandum from Francisco Garrote, at La Carraca in the Bay of Cádiz, to Martin de Sierralta, 9 November 1699. Originally filed in AGI, Panamá, leg. 161, fol. 708, it was later extracted and moved to a special section for illustrations. According to Garrote, "The attached sketch was made for me by an important designer of decorations for ships' sterns, in order to execute it on the two galleons." Given the date, the location, and the indications of gunnery and decoration, this could well be the stern of the *San José* built by Pedro de Aróztegui at Usúrbil. I am grateful to Javier de Solís, the Count of Casa Alegre, for calling my attention to this drawing. AGI, Mapas y Planos, Ingenios y Muestras, 189

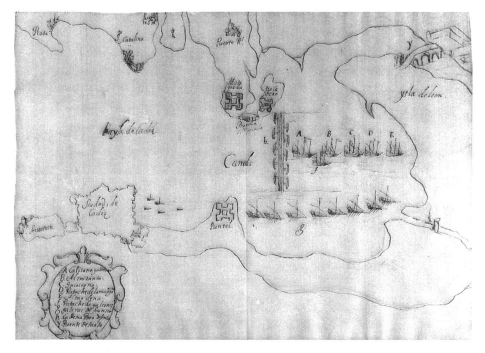

Fig. 5. When word arrived that anti-Bourbon forces were planning an attack on Cádiz in 1702, Don José Fernández de Santillán was in charge of defending the bay. This previously unknown sketch shows the deployment of five galleons and a dispatch ship behind a chain, supported by a contingent of French galleys. The galleon *San José* served as capitana of the Spanish squadron, with the *San Joaquín* as almiranta. Aided by the natural defenses of the site, this small contingent was able to prevent the entry of an Anglo-Dutch fleet estimated at 180–200 vessels. Photo courtesy of Javier de Solís, the Count of Casa Alegre, from AGI, IG, leg. 2560

Fig. 6. The Anglo-Dutch attack on Vigo in 1702. Paul Decker II was the artist, and Johann August Corvinus the engraver. From a collection commemorating anti-Bourbon victories in the War of the Spanish Succession, published in Augsburg by Jeremias Wolff in 1715. Photo courtesy of Javier de Solís, the Count of Casa Alegre

Fig. 7. The capture of Gibraltar by Admiral George Rooke in 1704. Paul Decker II was the artist, and Johann August Corvinus the engraver. From a collection commemorating anti-Bourbon victories in the War of the Spanish Succession, published in Augsburg by Jeremias Wolff in 1715. Photo courtesy of Javier de Solís, the Count of Casa Alegre

N. Guérard le fils fecit

A Llamas ou moutons du Perou   E Plan de la desazogadera
B Trapiche ou moulin a minerai   F Profil de la desazogadera
C Buiteron ou cour ou l'on petri le minerai G La pigne
D Bassins a laver   H Fourneau a tirer le vifargent

Fig. 8. Silver mining operations at Potosí, in the Andes Mountains of today's Bolivia. The famous outline of the immensely rich mountain of silver appears in the background, with installations used for crushing, washing, and smelting ore in the middle ground. The foreground depicts llamas, or "sheep of Peru." Illustration from Amédée François Frézier, *Relation du voyage de la Mer du Sud aux cotes du Chili, du Perou, et du Bresil: fait pendant les années 1712, 1713 & 1714* (Paris, 1716). Reproduced by permission; The John Carter Brown Library at Brown University

Fig. 9. The church and monastery of San Francisco in Lima, 1673. This engraving, by Pedro Nolasco, shows its ornate facade, principal cloister, and gardens. From Miguel Suárez de Figueroa, *Templo de N. Grande Patriarca San Francisco de la provincia de los Doze Apóstoles de el Perú en la ciudad de los Reyes arruinado, restaurado y engrandecido de la Providencia Divina* (Lima, 1675). Reproduced by permission; The John Carter Brown Library at Brown University

Fig. 10. The city of Lima as it appeared in 1685, with fortifications completed while the Duke of La Palata served as viceroy. Versions of the same city plan appeared in several later depictions of Lima, although serious earthquakes in 1687 and 1746 damaged or destroyed many of the buildings shown in the 1685 plan. This version appeared in Jeremiah N. Reynolds, *Voyage of the United States Frigate Potomac: Under the Command of Commodore John Downes, During the Circumnavigation of the Globe, in the years 1831, 1832, 1833, and 1834* (New York: Harper & Bros., 1835). Reproduced by permission of The Huntington Library, San Marino, California

VIEW of LIMA.
"The City of Kings" before its destruction by
the great Earthquake of 1746.

32 S Francisco	4 Hospital de Sacerdotes	48 Recol dela concep.ʰ
33 S Ildefonso	35 S Pedro	49 N Carmen
	36 Trinidad	50 S Clara Mon
	37 S Phelipe e ley Real	51 Descalzas Mon
	38 Vniversidad	52 el Prado Mon
	39 Caridad	53 cole del Cercado
	40 collegio de Donzellas	54 Ped de Alcantara
	41 S Thomas colleg	55 Refugio de Incurabl
	42 R noviciat	56 Convalescencia de S.a
	43 S Pedro Nolasco	57 Beaterio de la Merced
	44 S Catalina	58 S Rosa de Viterbo
	45 S Andres Hospl	59 cara de Moneda
	46 S Anna Hosp	60 S.tʰ del Beat Toribio
	47 S Bartholome Hs	61 N.S de cachaenos

J Sculpsit
STREET, 1808.

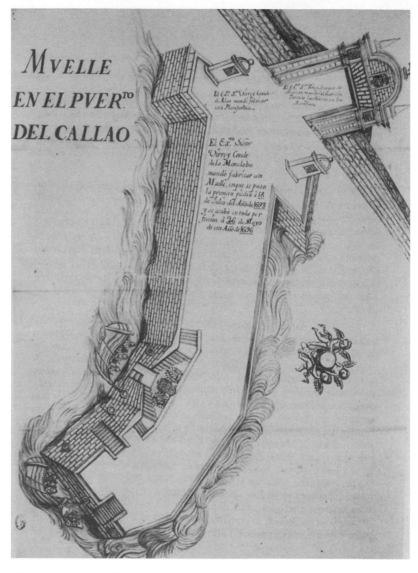

Fig. 11. Dock built at Callao, 1693–96, on orders from the Count of La Monclova, viceroy of Peru. AGI, Lima, leg. 90

Fig. 12. Map accompanying the Baron de Pointis's account of the French attack on Cartagena in 1697. Note the sandbar blocking what had been the main entrance to the harbor, which left only the narrower entry at Boca Chica and the Pasaje de Caballos. The latter is shown on the map as a channel near the lower right corner, which is inaccurate; it should be located nearer the top right of the map. Reprinted from *Monsieur de Pointi's expedition to Cartagena* (1699); reproduced by permission of The Huntington Library, San Marino, California

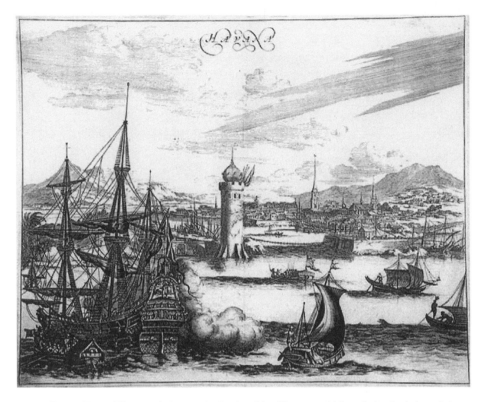

Fig. 13. View of Havana, Cuba, ca. 1671, by Arnoldus Montanus. Although the depiction of the fortifications and the tower is somewhat fanciful, the engraving illustrates the importance of the city and its port. Included in John Ogilby, *America: being the latest, and most accurate description of the New World...* (London, 1671). Reproduced by permission; The John Carter Brown Library at Brown University

CHAPTER FIVE

The Last Voyage of the San José

Back in Portobelo, Captain General Casa Alegre could be pleased with his success in amassing tax revenues for the king. A careful accounting drawn up in Portobelo on May 20, 1708, listed every maravedi. The account was written on seven and a half sheets of folio paper, which were then sewn together.[1] Each sheet bears a round hand stamp that reads "1709," presumably added later by officials in Madrid. The packet is archived in a large bundle titled (in Spanish) "Letter-accounts of the treasures remitted by royal officials in various jurisdictions on the fleets from Tierra Firme in the years 1559 to 1723 . . . in five sections." The account seems to be complete to the date when it was written. All together, with a few additions to the sum that Castelldosrius had collected for the viceroyalty, the sum remitted to the king totaled 1,551,609 pesos, 7 reals.

As Casa Alegre prepared his galleons to return to Cartagena, he oversaw the lading of the king's revenue in money and other treasure, as well as private remittances.[2] The *San José* and the *San Joaquín,* as the two largest, strongest, and most heavily armed ships in the fleet, would carry nearly all of the officially registered treasure, public and private, divided evenly between them and carefully registered by each ship's master of silver *(maestre de plata).* Spanish law stipulated that the capitana and the almiranta of a fleet should divide the treasure between them, though fleets sometimes deviated from this standard practice. The third vessel in the chain of command, the gobierno *Santa Cruz,* would carry a much smaller amount. Don Nicolás de la Rosa, the irascible Count of Vega Florida, commanded the gobierno and did not get along well with the captain general. Spanish prisoners later told their English captors that "upon some difference between the admiral and [Vega Florida] at Porto Bello, orders were given that no more money should be shipped on board her."[3]

Meanwhile, in Havana Ducasse and his squadron waited for the fleets from New Spain and Tierra Firme to join them for the return voyage to Europe. A correspondent in Jamaica for the *London Gazette* reported, "We have advice by an Englishman, who hath lately made his escape from Havana, that Monsieur du Casse is there, that his sailors are very sickly, and that Monsieur du Casse himself had been nine days indispos'd, when [the Englishman] came away."[4] Ducasse had orders to provide an escort for both fleets, but only from Havana, the final leg of their journey to Spain. The captains general of the two Spanish fleets held responsibility for taking them to Havana.

In addition to the registered treasure for the king and private parties, a sizeable amount of unregistered treasure may also have been loaded as contraband. Captured Spanish crewmen later told the English that the small amount of treasure on the gobierno *Santa Cruz* had been "privately brought on board her in the night, and belonged to some of the passengers, except what others might have about them, or were in trunks."[5] But what about unregistered treasure on the *San José* and the *San Joaquín* and on Indies fleets in general? Careful scholarly investigations of fraud in the late sixteenth century indicate that about 10 percent of the treasure that arrived in Europe never appeared in the registers.[6] Other estimates, especially those based on the total production of silver and gold in the Indies, have often ranged far higher. The highest estimates do not take into account that much of the treasure mined in America stayed in America for both public and private needs, fueling the economic growth of the Spanish colonies. We cannot assume, in other words, that all discrepancies between mining production and registered treasure are explained by contraband shipments to Spain.

Moreover, any attempt to give a single global figure for smuggled treasure is bound to distort reality, because the level of smuggling varied over time as circumstances varied. The late seventeenth and early eighteenth centuries probably marked the heyday of smuggled receipts from the New World, in large part because of well-founded fears that the crown would seize private treasure in its desperation for cash. When that happened, the owners of the treasure would be compensated with interest-paying government bonds, but they would lose the use of their capital in the short term. This drastic action occurred with some regularity, especially in wartime, inducing some merchants and other private parties to risk dire penalties by avoiding registration.

The crown could do no more than stay alert to the likelihood of smuggling and work to combat it. Royal officials suspected that contraband on the New Spain Fleet of 1704 amounted to ten times the value of registered treasure; to compensate, the crown levied a hefty fine on all merchants involved with the fleet that year.[7] In legend at least, the Tierra Firme Fleet planning to return to Spain in 1708 is thought to have carried an unprecedented cargo of bullion and other treasure, most of it unregistered. To what extent do the available documents support that legend? We will examine the evidence further in a later chapter, but here we will focus on the fateful voyage that gave rise to the legend of the *San José*.

On the return trip to Cartagena from the Portobelo fair the Tierra Firme Fleet included sixteen ships;[8] another merchant ship joined them en route. Seven of the vessels mounted artillery. Casa Alegre's capitana, the *San José*, carried sixty-four guns and just over 600 men. Don Miguel Agustín de Villanueva's almiranta, the *San Joaquín*, also carried sixty-four guns, as well as about 500 men. Vega Florida's gobierno, the *Santa Cruz*, officially carried fifty guns and about 300 men, though on that occasion she reportedly mounted forty-four guns, with another eleven in the hold.[9] Because of his assignment in the fleet, Vega Florida is often called simply the *gobernador*, literally, the commander of the gobierno. Four other ships also mounted guns on the trip from Portobelo. The first was a large hulk *(urca)* owned by Don Francisco Nieto and added to the fleet in Portobelo, with thirty-four guns and about 140 men. The official name of the hulk was *Nuestra Señora de la Concepción*, although most documents refer to her simply as "Nieto's ship" (la Nieta).[10] Another armed vessel was the French frigate and former privateer *Sancti Espiritus*, presumably the same ship that had arrived in the Southern Sea in 1704. The English knew the *Sancti Espiritus* in her former life as the *Gosport* and often refer to her as such. On the voyage from Portobelo she carried thirty-two guns and about 300 men. A French merchant ship carried twenty-four guns and about 200 men, and a Vizcayan patache called *Nuestra Señora del Carmen* carried twenty-four guns and about 150 men. Unarmed merchant ships and small craft rounded out the total of seventeen vessels. Although English documents often refer to the Spanish vessels as a fleet of seventeen warships, in fact only five vessels, the two galleons among them, were large and well armed.

Almost within sight of Boca Chica, the entrance to Cartagena's harbor, the fleet encountered an English squadron under Commodore Charles Wager made up of four ships: Wager's *Expedition*, with seventy guns; the *Kingston*, with sixty guns; the *Portland*, with fifty guns; and the fire ship *Vulture*, which probably was not armed.[11] The English ships had been patrolling the entire coast since early March in anticipation of the galleons' return from Portobelo, and the Spaniards knew it. In the ensuing battle between the warships from the evening of June 8 to the early morning of June 9, the *San José* sank with nearly everyone aboard, and the gobierno surrendered after a prolonged battle. All the Spanish merchant ships escaped at the start of the battle and made it safely to

Cartagena, as did the almiranta, the *San Joaquín*. Nieto and his crew deliberately grounded and burned the damaged urca after the battle rather than let it fall to the enemy. The English lost no ships, but both sides sustained damage to their vessels and crews. This bare account of the action can only hint at the human dimensions of the battle, including months of deliberations about strategy and tactics on both sides, as well as logistical difficulties. The complexity of the human story reveals itself in the written record, as we shall see.

Given the magnitude of the disaster on the Spanish side, it comes as no surprise that local officials took statements from dozens of witnesses shortly after the battle. Don Joséph Zúñiga y de la Cerda, as governor and captain general of Cartagena,[12] immediately sent word to surviving officers that it would serve the king for them to make declarations regarding the battle and the events leading up to it. Some of the resulting testimony taken by notaries in the weeks following the disaster has a matter-of-fact tone, dry and analytical. Several witnesses, however, related their experiences in anguished, personal, and sometimes bitter tones, denouncing those they considered responsible and characterizing their own behavior as blameless and disinterested, dedicated only to the king's service. Everyone knew that any departures from standard procedures, and of course any dereliction of duty, would likely result in severe punishment.

Several key issues permeated the testimony, which responded to the same set of questions: Had anyone seen Wager's squadron in the area, and if so, had that information reached Captain General Casa Alegre in Portobelo? Had the captain general convened meetings *(juntas)* of senior officials to discuss the departure of the galleons, and if so, what had happened in those meetings? Why had Casa Alegre decided to leave Portobelo for Cartagena when he did? How had the battle unfolded? Under what circumstances had the gobierno *Santa Cruz* surrendered? And above all, what had happened to the *San José?*

The first several questions centered on knowledge about the English presence in the area and how military and civilian officials had responded to that knowledge. Virtually every Spanish declarant agreed that the English presence had been common knowledge in the weeks before the armada left Portobelo. The key issue was how officials had handled that knowledge. According to Don Pedro García de Asarta, the captain of sea and war on the almiranta, Governor Zúñiga had learned of the extent of the English threat from the "declaration of a Frenchman whom the English had made prisoner, and who jumped into the water to flee near the Rio Grande de la Magdalena, and he arrived at . . . [Cartagena,] where the said governor received his declaration."[13] The Frenchman reported that the English had four ships patrolling off the coast, two warships of seventy cannons, one ship of fifty cannons that some witnesses called a frigate, and a vessel of thirty-four cannons that they called a fire ship *(brulote)*. Governor Zúñiga assumed the obvious, namely, that the English were planning to attack the convoy as it returned from Portobelo.

In the meantime, a small French sloop under Captain Luis (presumably Louis) Baron arrived in Cartagena to help with Spanish defenses in the Indies.[14] Governor Zúñiga immediately sent the sloop to Portobelo with his adjutant, Don Pedro de Fuentes, who carried letters and official reports to General Casa Alegre regarding the English presence. The French sloop also carried letters from private citizens in the area who confirmed the intelligence reports gathered by Zúñiga. One of them noted that more English forces were on Isla Fuerte, southwest of Cartagena, near the mouth of the Cenut River.[15] On the way to Portobelo,

> the captain of the aforesaid sloop said that off the coast of Darién the sailor on watch at the top of the mast said he sighted land, to which [the captain], who is also a pilot and experienced with that coast, responded, "Take a good look," because, given the current position charted for the ship and its course, it could not be land. And he sent another man to the top, who said he saw small islands or ships taking soundings, and that there were men, some on deck, and others in the rigging. As the men on the sloop were verifying whether they were seeing small islands, land, or ships, a strong storm came up and obliged them to head out to sea, and, distancing themselves, they lost sight of the aforesaid, remaining in doubt of their identification, the captain and pilot being twenty leagues from land at that point.[16]

Whether or not they saw ships, and if so, whose ships, there was no question that English patrols were in the well-trafficked area between Portobelo and Cartagena. Don Laureano Ximénez Moreno, a merchant, testified that the insecurity of the seas in the region was very well known in Portobelo, nor had the news of four English sails off Cartagena escaped him, "even though he had come with the armada as a merchant and was in seclusion at home attending to business."[17]

Knowledge of the English presence in the area, though hardly unexpected, added a new layer of complications to Casa Alegre's decision making about his return voyage to Cartagena. Following standard procedure, he convened a meeting of the senior military and civilian officials in Portobelo at the time. They met in the houses leased by the president of the Audiencia of Panama, the Marquis of Villa-Rocha, Don José Antonio de la Rocha y Carranza. The following men attended the meeting:

—Don José Fernández de Santillán, Count of Casa Alegre: captain general of the armada

—Don José Antonio de la Rocha y Carranza, Marquis of Villa-Rocha: president of the Audiencia of Panama

—Don Miguel Agustín de Villanueva: almirante of the armada

—Don Nicolás de la Rosa, Count of Vega Florida: *gobernador del tercio* (commander of the fleet's infantry contingent)

—Don Sebastian de Xijón: *almirante ad honorem* and captain of sea and war on the *San José*

—Don Pedro García de Asarta: captain of sea and war on the *San Joaquín*

—Don Joan Andrés de Hordas/Ordaz: royal overseer *(veedor)* of the fleet

—Don Joseph Fermín de Larragoyti: royal accountant *(contador)* of the fleet

—Don Antonio Ron/Erron: former fiscal for the Audiencia of Quito, traveling to Spain

—Don Francisco de Medina: Former judge of the Audiencia of Panamá; newly appointed to the Audiencia of Santa Fé, the judicial district that included both Cartagena and Portobelo

—Don Antonio Rodríguez Cortés: representative of the merchant community

—Don Francisco de Quijano Ceballos: representative of the merchant community

—Don Juan Martín de Isasi: master of silver on the *San José*

All of them would play a role in the later battle, and several would live to testify about it. One of the most interesting accounts of the junta's discussions came from Judge Medina, the same judge who had clashed with General Casa Alegre before the Portobelo fair. Governor Zúñiga thought highly of Medina and commended his report to the Council of the Indies. Unlike the thirty other men testifying, Medina preferred not to give simple testimony before a notary. Instead, when the notary Andrés de Solís came to call at his residence in Cartagena on July 4, Medina simply declared that he would give a full account in a separate communication to the council.[18] He did so on July 22 in a long and very personal letter to his patron, Don Bernardo Tinajero, the fiscal on the Council of the Indies.[19] Leaving no room for doubt, Medina blamed Captain General Casa Alegre, and more particularly his almirante, Don Miguel

Augustín de Villanueva, for all the dire events that had befallen the fleet after the Portobelo fair.

Zúñiga's endorsement and Medina's position as a judge make it easy to accept the latter's account as a fair and honest assessment, but his personal history complicates matters. As Medina noted in his letter, he had been appointed to the prestigious post of oidor of the Audiencia of Panama after a rapid rise in royal service. In 1695, however, his career had come crashing down around him when King Charles II requested his resignation based on charges of wrongdoing. Medina blamed his disgrace on "the reverend Bishop and the royal officials [in Panama] at that time, [who were] violators of the royal mandate." His "calvary," as he called it, ended only in 1708, when the Spanish judicial system exposed widespread corruption in the Panamanian audiencia and exonerated him from the false accusations. As a result, Philip V called Medina back into service and promoted him to the Audiencia of Santa Fe, on the recommendation of Bernardo Tinajero and the Council of the Indies. Relieved and very grateful, Medina prepared to take up his new post, "leaving my retirement in the wilderness, where I had maintained myself for almost thirteen years in order to deny fuel to the fires of malice burning against me." His letter reveals a passionate resolve to justify the faith placed in him by the new king and Tinajero.

Medina's ordeal did not end with his exoneration, however. When he arrived in Panama, his enemies in the government tried to prevent him from going to Portobelo, but he found a way to get there anyway. Alerted by those same enemies, Captain General Casa Alegre detained Medina on board the *San José* in Portobelo for a few days but eventually released him as he learned the full story.

Shortly thereafter, perhaps in retaliation, Judge Medina decided to free the two representatives of the consulado of Lima whom Casa Alegre had arrested in the dispute over averías for the fleet. That cannot have endeared him to the captain general, and it is possible that lingering resentment about his humiliation in Portobelo colored Medina's testimony regarding subsequent events. In any case, Medina tells us, after the fair ended,

> the general called a junta to determine the departure of the armada for Cartagena, motivated by news from the governor [of Cartagena] that some English ships of the line were patrolling in sight of the city, evidently planning to surprise the galleons when they returned from Portobelo. And I, having received various reports that [supported that notion] about the enemy's intentions, questioned various prisoners who had just arrived from Jamaica, and they affirmed

that there were strong preparations there for such an action, and that as many as eight ships had departed Jamaica, each one carrying fifty to sixty-four cannons of 36-pound caliber. Most of the ships were well manned with English crews experienced in war at sea. And with this and other evidence I argued against the return of the galleons [to Cartagena] at that time, and the majority of those attending the junta agreed and resolved to reconnoiter the route first. [Nonetheless,] a few days later, the general decided that the galleons should leave, without having carried out the precautionary measures prescribed in the first junta. I continued to insist upon my opposition, fearing the ruin later borne out by events . . . and pondering the inconsolable pain that such an occurrence would inflict upon the loyal hearts of your Spanish vassals. My arguments resulted in such a breach between me and the general that he ordered me to leave the capitana [the *San José*] and move to the merchant hulk of Don Francisco Nieto.

In short, Medina argued that taking the ships and their treasure along a known return route from Portobelo to Cartagena, when the enemy had superior forces in the area waiting for them, virtually assured the disaster that followed. Ironically, Medina's repeated disagreements with Casa Alegre explain how he came to escape the tragedy of the *San José:* the captain general ordered him off the ill-fated capitana.

Medina may have held a grudge against Casa Alegre, but nearly every other witness to the tragic events of June 8 also faulted the captain general's decision to leave Portobelo. On July 11 Don Joséph Canis de Alzamora responded to the call to give testimony, the first fleet officer to do so. Canis had served as captain of sea and war on the gobierno *Santa Cruz* since 1706, and he had served the crown for many years before that as well. Like Medina, Canis attended the two junta meetings called in late May to discuss the situation. At the meeting, the captain of the sloop that brought news about the English ships reported that some of his men thought they had seen sails off the coast of Darién as well, but he had not been able to confirm the sighting.

Although Canis did not identify the sloop further, it was one of the French vessels that had arrived in Cartagena to assist the Spaniards and that Governor Zúñiga had sent to Portobelo to warn the fleet about the English threat. According to Canis, everyone present at the junta except Villanueva agreed to send the sloop out again on a ten-day reconnaissance mission to discover whether there really were other English ships off the Panamanian coast; its captain agreed to the plan. Villanueva rejected that plan and argued that the galleons should leave Portobelo without any further delay.[20]

Although most of the witnesses agreed about the tenor of the discussion in the junta meetings, their testimony varied in many details. Governor Zúñiga's adjutant, Fuentes, testified that when he gave the letters to Casa Alegre in Portobelo, the captain general said he already knew about the English, and when Villanueva saw the letters, he did not give the news much value, saying "that it was nothing to worry about, and he stayed with this opinion, supporting and pushing for the departure of the galleons."[21] Fuentes hinted that Casa Alegre had been the recipient of Villanueva's pushing, testifying that the captain general initially favored sending the French sloop to explore the route from Portobelo to Cartagena before departing with the fleet. Once the sloop had taken on supplies for the voyage, however, Casa Alegre changed his mind.[22] He cancelled the reconnaissance mission, attached the French sloop to his command, and took the fleet out of Portobelo a few days later. The timing suggests that Villanueva had somehow persuaded the captain general to depart.

That was certainly the rumor that spread on the streets of Portobelo, aided by hearsay testimony from witnesses to the subsequent disaster. One witness who knew more than most about the sea was Don Pedro de Medranda, who was on his way to Spain to complain that the Audiencia of Panama would not honor his royal appointment to command the Armada of the Southern Sea. Medranda traveled on the gobierno in the ill-fated fleet. He testified on July 9 that he "had heard tell from very creditable persons" that all the attendees at the juntas save Villanueva and Casa Alegre "had resolved against the galleons' departure until the route had been reconnoitered; despite this resolution, the said general of galleons and his almirante, Don Miguel Agustín de Villanueva, had decided to dispatch them, saying that 'the sea is broad and many are its paths.'"[23] In other words, Medranda's declaration portrayed Casa Alegre and Villanueva as both cavalier and wrongheaded.

Did Casa Alegre truly disregard an overwhelming vote against his departure, which would have been a serious breach of standing procedures? Not everyone testified that there had been a formal vote, and several witnesses described the juntas' deliberations in more ambiguous terms. Don Martín de Zamudio de las Infantas was a *regidor perpetuo* (permanent alderman) on the Lima city council and a member of the cultural elite in the viceregal capital. He had traveled to Portobelo to catch a ride to Spain with the Tierra Firme Fleet. We may presume that he was related to Don Antonio de Zamudio de las

Infantas, the captain general of the Armada of the Southern Sea. In reporting on the juntas that met in late May, Martín Zamudio noted Villanueva's argument that "the four [English] ships lacked sufficient force to prevent the departure of the galleons." Zamudio said that the president of Panama had responded that "if they had enough strength and manpower to oppose the English, then they ought to sail, and if not, not." Zamudio also mentioned that although everyone but Villanueva favored sending the French sloop out to explore the route before reaching a decision, Casa Alegre had said that the matter was too important to be decided that way or by a vote in the junta. And thus, "without anyone's accord but his own, he resolved on the departure of the said galleons."[24] In Zamudio's testimony we see Casa Alegre in command, not as a pawn of Villanueva's, and we see the juntas as less than staunch and unified in their opposition to the departure. When Governor Zúñiga summarized the packet of letters regarding the armada's voyage, he noted that "the president of the junta, the Marquis of Villarocha, ordered the departure, considering the strength of the fleet, and that most witnesses agreed with the general and the almirante that "la mar era ancha, diversos sus rumbos," echoing the phrase attributed to Villanueva by Medranda, but without Medranda's imputation of arrogance on the part of the almirante.[25]

Another passenger on the *gobierno*, Josép Alzamora Ursino, described the events in similar terms, noting that "the various juntas that were called [to consider the English threat] were reduced to consultations, because they did not take votes restricting the power of the general to resolve the matter, with the effect that he decided [by himself] on the departure of the said galleons."[26] Josép Múñoz de la Trinidad, a lawyer from Lima and a passenger on the gobierno, testified that "he knew that [Governor Zúñiga] had sent repeated warnings to the general of galleons that these coasts were infested with English enemies, about which there were different consultations, and in which he knew that the president of Panama was always of the opinion that their departure was not opportune; regardless, the general resolved to do it."[27]

In contrast with most of the other witnesses, Don Francisco Serrano de Reina y Céspedes, a former governor and captain general of Puerto Rico, suggested that Casa Alegre had based his decision to depart on a clear-eyed analysis of the respective strength of the English and Spanish fleets. Serrano said that he had known about the English presence in the area, "having heard the general of galleons say in his house that the English had scant force with respect to the armada of galleons, which had three ships of the line—the capitana, the almiranta, and the gobierno—plus two French navíos [here meaning small warships], the patache *Nuestra Señora del Carmen*, and Nieto's navío [or hulk], which had been reinforced with forty men."[28]

According to Esteban Trave, the condestable (gunnery sergeant) on Nieto's ship, the French captain of the sloop had told him about the English ships off Cartagena. Trave also had heard the captain say to the governor's adjutant that one of his men had seen up to thirteen or fourteen sails off Portobelo but had not been able to confirm the sighting. Trave's hearsay testimony marked an important inflation of the number of potential enemy sails sighted by the sloop near Portobelo—from three or four to thirteen or fourteen.[29] It makes sense to think either that Trave had simply misunderstood what the French captain said, which is easy to do when one is dealing with a foreign language, or that the latter had misspoken. Nonetheless, if Trave spread the inflated rumor around Portobelo, it would have added to the cloud of apprehension hanging over the fleet's departure.

It comes as no surprise that Almirante Villanueva presented the decision to depart, as well as the discussion in the juntas, in a way that justified his actions. In his letter of July 22, 1708, Villanueva reported that

> the general convoked a junta de guerra in the residence of the president of Panama, and after a long discussion it was resolved that the departure should be carried out, adding to the three flags [i.e., ships of the line] the reinforcement of Nieto's urca with the infantry company of Don Joséph Canis, plus the French frigate *Sancti Espiritus*. Forming a line with these five ships together, providing protection to the merchants, was considered a very superior force of galleons, according to those who made declarations [in the junta]; and were the governor of Cartagena to send news that the enemy force had increased, [the galleons] should then change course, going to Havana without making a stop in Cartagena.[30]

Villanueva's characterization of the reasoning behind the departure sounds plausible enough, but his conflation of the juntas into one meeting and his bland characterization of the resolution to depart hardly capture the tenor of the discussions or his role in them, according to many other witnesses.

The bulk of the testimony centered on the ensuing voyage from Portobelo to Cartagena and the battle that sank the *San José*, drowning all its officers and nearly all of its crew. The fleet that left Portobelo was quite small compared with most war fleets of the period, and it was miniscule compared with the merchant fleets that had dominated the Indies trade in the sixteenth century. It was even smaller than typical escort squadrons for those fleets in the seventeenth century, with only three ships of the line. As various witnesses noted,

Casa Alegre had transferred a small force of infantry to Nieto's merchant urca and added it to the line of battle, along with the French frigate *Sancti Espiritus*. The five ships were not equally well prepared for battle, however. The three principal ships carried the only heavy guns and most of the experienced sailors, gunners, and soldiers.

Nieto's ship was as long in the keel as the *San José* and the *San Joaquín*, but it had been built as a cargo carrier—a hulk, or urca—without the heavy internal bracing and other reinforcements that distinguished Spanish warships. Some of the witnesses referred to the ship as a navío rather than an urca, and the word *navío* would later become the preferred term for Spanish warships. In this context, however, the term *navío* simply served to distinguish it from an unarmed or lightly armed merchant vessel. Don Joséph Canis de Alzamora, captain of the infantry company that Casa Alegre transferred from the almiranta to Nieto's urca, complained that the vessel lacked sufficient men and arms to be a credible combatant. Besides the 48 men in his company, there were 30 sailors, 34 apprentices, some pages, and the urca's officers—about 140 in all—but Canis thought that scarcely 20 of them were fit for combat. As for gunnery, the urca carried twenty-two eight-pound iron cannons on the lower deck and five iron cannons on each side of the upper deck, toward the rear, but no experienced gunners except the sergeant, Esteban Trave. Canis testified that the captain general had promised to provide gunners for the urca and that Canis had reminded him of this at various times on land and aboard ship—the last time when they were setting sail—to no effect.[31]

The contramaestre of the urca, Antonio Hernández Romero, later amplified Canis's testimony with vivid detail. In Portobelo Hernández "heard the said captain [Canis] make various representations to the general to provide him with men and gunners, but he could not; and when we were on board and setting sail, the general passed by in his ship's boat, hurrying the departure along, and [Canis] again represented to the general that he did not have gunners to handle the artillery pieces, nor men to fight, and he called on all those on board to be witnesses to what he said."[32] Gunnery Sergeant Esteban Trave corroborated the story as well, reporting that "Canis, in response to Casa Alegre's order to set sail, repeated that he had neither men nor gunners to fight, and that the said navío lacked everything [necessary]; but the general said to make ready to depart, and pulled away from us in his boat and left; at that, Captain Canis complained aloud about the harm and prejudice [this would cause] and made witnesses of everyone on board the navío."[33]

Because of the lack of gunners, Nieto's urca would be of limited use in the artillery battle that lay ahead. General Casa Alegre surely knew this and presumably did all he could to find men to handle the artillery. Did he hope that the mere presence of guns on the urca would fool the English into thinking that his fleet had superior strength? Did he hope that if a battle ensued nonetheless, the urca would serve as a decoy, attracting the English away from the better-armed and better-manned treasure ships? There is no way to reconstruct his thinking. Canis was well aware that he had been placed in an impossible situation, and he did what he could to document it. By calling upon all on board the urca to witness his representations to the captain general, he provided an excuse for the urca's failing to distinguish itself in battle.

Casa Alegre took his armada out from Portobelo on May 28, having quashed all opposition to the departure. The three ships of the line, plus Nieto's armed merchant hulk and the French sloop *Sancti Espiritus,* provided most of the armed support for the merchant and support vessels.[34] The smaller French ship and the Vizcayan dispatch vessel also carried arms, as noted above, but could offer little protection for any other ship. Most of the witnesses say nothing about the voyage from the time they left Portobelo until the battle eleven days later. The few who mention the intervening days reveal details that are ominous in retrospect. Don Pedro de Medranda, who had hoped to command the Armada of the Southern Sea, noted that they made little progress the first day out. On the second day they got only as far as San Blas Point before the wind stopped. There, in sight of land, they stayed becalmed for two days more before continuing along the Tiburon coast.[35]

Meanwhile, Commodore Charles Wager's squadron was hoping to intercept them. Wager had left Port Royal, Jamaica, in his flagship *Expedition* on May 1—May 12 by the Spanish calendar (see appendix 1). The warships *Kingston* and *Portland* accompanied him. They joined the fire ship *Vulture,* which was already patrolling off Cartagena. Wager had waited as long as he could in Port Royal for expected reinforcements to arrive from England, but in the event he departed without them. He knew that the galleons would soon leave Portobelo for Cartagena, and further delays in his departure from Jamaica might cause him to miss them altogether.[36]

As Wager and his squadron patrolled the area, they kept a sharp eye on the horizon, watching not only for more English ships but also for the Spaniards. The commodore's objective was to intercept and if possible capture the Spanish galleons and merchant ships returning from the Portobelo fair, and timing was everything. First he had to be informed as soon as the fleet left Portobelo. On May 20 by the Spanish calendar the *Portland* and the *Kingston* anchored in the Bastimentos keys off the Panamanian coast southeast of Portobelo to replenish their supplies of water and information. The *Expedition* and the *Vulture* stayed out to sea. The Bastimentos keys served as a major nexus for international shipping traffic in that part of the Caribbean. As one of the Spanish officers noted, "There were always from thirteen to twenty English and Dutch ships doing business there, with one or two armed ships to protect them."[37]

The logs of various officers in the English squadron provide a sense of the volume of shipping traffic in the area, from the European military vessels carrying the war over the Spanish succession into the Americas to a range of privateers, traders, pirates, and fishermen. The officers of the *Portland* mentioned various ships anchored nearby when they stopped in the Bastimentos: three Dutch vessels; an English merchant ship; a privateering sloop with six prizes, which soon sailed for Jamaica; and the queen's ship *Severn Dolphin*.[38] Many of those ships carried news about the Portobelo fair and the whereabouts and doings of the Spanish plate fleet, as the English called it. The *Kingston* and the *Portland* learned from them that the galleons were still in Portobelo.

Likewise, Casa Alegre soon learned that the two English warships had been in the Bastimentos. The juntas that met in the house of the president of the Audiencia of Panama in the week before the armada departed discussed their presence at length. One of the arguments Casa Alegre used to justify his sudden departure was to "avoid giving the English squadron time to hear about our movements from the Bastimentos, or giving the two ships of fifty cannons that were in the Bastimentos time to join the squadron."[39] Casa Alegre and his officers knew that the safety of the galleons and merchant vessels in their care depended on avoiding, evading, or defeating the predators. He took a calculated risk in departing when he did, given that avoidance no longer figured on his limited list of options.

Evasion required keeping the English from learning about the movements of the armada, a difficult task at best. The officers were well aware that once the armada passed the Bastimentos, English sympathizers would try to alert Wager's squadron of their whereabouts, so they kept a sharp lookout for fast ships in the vicinity. García de Asarta reported seeing two small ships enter the Bastimentos the morning after the fleet set sail from Portobelo. Two days later the lightly armed but fast Vizcayan *patache* was sent to chase another two ships. Both turned out to be known merchant ships based in Cartagena, one heading toward Portobelo and the other heading for home. The latter joined the Spanish fleet.[40]

The English on patrol also kept a sharp lookout for sails in the distance that might bring reinforcements from Jamaica, more news about the galleons, or the galleons themselves. One sail they sighted on May 23 (June 3) turned out to be "a sloop from the Bastenmentues giving us an account the Galloons sailed from PtaBell last Monday, designing for Carthageen. He [the sloop] left sight of them Wednesday."[41] Captain Windsor identified the sloop as "from the Severne"; it may have been the same *Severn Dolphin* that had been anchored near Windsor's *Portland* in the Bastimentos. The sloop stayed with the English squadron for several days and then continued on toward Jamaica.[42] Now the English knew that the galleons were on the way and that they had made little progress their first few days at sea.

Commodore Wager could then gauge their likely trajectory, sail directly toward Cartagena, and decide upon an opportune moment to attack. In the months that his squadron had been patrolling the coast, whenever they came near Cartagena they had used the monastery of Nuestra Señora de la Popa as a landmark because it was situated on a hill above and behind the city. Although the hill was less than 400 feet above sea level, it was the highest point in the vicinity. The English logs render Spanish placenames in an impressive variety of spellings, some no doubt designed to mock Catholic sensibilities, but whether "Mother La Pope" or "Nostra Sinior de la Pappa," their references to the prominent landmark are unmistakable. Wager was biding his time, waiting for Casa Alegre to come to him and presumably hoping that the reinforcements he expected from England would arrive in time to join him. Given what the English must have known by then about the Spanish fleet—three heavy warships and another two with considerable artillery—it was wise to better the odds before attacking. That tactic could be sustained only for a few days, however. If Casa Alegre and the fleet got inside Boca Chica, the main entrance to Cartagena harbor, Wager would lose them altogether.

The Spanish fleet made much better progress from June 1 on, once the wind picked up, but Casa Alegre took care to see that his collection of disparate ships stayed together for security. That meant that the slowest vessels set the pace. On June 7 the armada finally reached the Islas de San Bernardo, fairly close to Cartagena. Instead of sailing after sundown, however, at about six in the evening Casa Alegre maneuvered the *San José* around to point her prow toward the northeast and wait for the gobierno and the merchant vessel *Rey David*, which were bringing up the rear. There the armada remained until dawn on June 8, when the captain general and the rest of the vessels resumed their course toward Cartagena.[43] It turned out to have been a fatal delay.

Sailing northeast, almost in sight of the entrance to the harbor at Boca Chica, the Spaniards saw the English squadron to the north. Witnesses on various ships reported sighting the English squadron hours apart, which suggests that the Spanish fleet was strung out all along the route, a result of their differing sailing speeds. On board Nieto's urca, Trave (the gunnery sergeant) and Ximénez Moreno (the merchant from Portobelo) both reported seeing four alien sails to windward at 8:00 or 9:00 AM, when the urca was between the islands called Ciruelo or Ziruelo and Tesoro.[44] According to Ximénez, "Very quickly we knew that they were coming toward us with a fresh wind behind them, and later we recognized that they were English."[45] Judge Medina recalled only that men on the urca had sighted the English "before midday."[46] One witness on the gobierno, General Medranda, did not mention having spotted the English until about 2:00 or 3:00 PM , though the wording of his testimony is ambiguous;[47] in any case, he seemed surprised that General Casa Alegre continued the voyage after sighting the enemy sails. Perhaps he hoped to lead the armada to safety before the English closed in, but he sent an order to all the merchant ships to get downwind of his warships, a clear sign that he knew a battle was likely.

To enter Boca Chica and Cartagena harbor, the armada first had to round Tesoro Island. Everyone knew that, including the English. The winds were variable all day, starting out from west-southwest, which helped to propel the armada toward the harbor. By afternoon, however, the wind had shifted to the northeast quadrant—headwinds, in other words—making it more difficult for the ships to make headway around the island. At about 4:30 or 5:00 PM Casa Alegre apparently gave up the attempt, turned the capitana toward the northwest, and prepared for battle.

Medranda's detailed testimony left no doubt that he blamed Casa Alegre alone for the armada's situation on the afternoon of June 8. The captain general had decided on the departure, the course, and the pace of the voyage from Portobelo; the rest of the armada had simply followed his lead, a point Medranda repeated several times.[48] If any of the other senior officers—the Count of Vega Florida in particular—had alternate plans in mind, he had kept them to himself.

After opposing their departure from Portobelo, Vega Florida's best defense in any future inquiry was simply to obey the captain general's orders, do his duty, and let the captain general take the blame if anything went wrong. He saw his worst fears confirmed when they sighted the English squadron lying in ambush off Cartagena. It must have been small comfort to know that he had been right about the folly of leaving Portobelo before scouting the route. When he was debriefed a few weeks after the battle, Vega Florida recalled that the captain general,

> having arrived in sight of the Yslas de San Bernardo on the 7th of June, leaving them on the starboard side, . . . continued his course from the east-southeast, and they saw from the gobierno the Yslas de Barú; and before the sun set the capitana turned, heading toward the sea with the prow to the northwest. Remaining sheltered [*quedándose a la capa*] until the 8th day, he set sail for the port of Boca Chica, and almost at midday four sails were seen headed toward the armada with the wind behind them [*con viento bonansible por la brisa*], and the armada continued toward the port with all its sails hoisted, until arriving very close to land, which was the Ysla del Sirhuelo [Ciruelo], and not being able to get around it, the capitana reached a convenient place and turned about, with the prow to the northwest, and in her wake the almiranta, the other ships remaining downwind.[49]

Medina, the judge of the Audiencia of Santa Fe, had less knowledge about the sea than many of the other witnesses, but he was more forthright in blaming Casa Alegre for failing to sail through the night of June 7:

> The armada left Portobelo on the 28th of May, and the second day out two vessels were seen off the port of Nombre de Dios; and on the 7th of June we sighted the Islas de San Bernardo, where the general anchored, losing the favorable wind that would have been sufficient to take us out of danger and carry us to the port [of Cartagena] by dawn. And on the 8th he made sail toward Boca Chica, and from the top of the mast before midday four sails were sighted, which approached the armada from the windward side, having the advantage of a favorable breeze, flying English flags and blocking the armada from rounding the Isla del Tesoro.[50]

Medina's testimony added one interesting detail to Medranda's story: the armada had sighted two ships off Nombre de Dios, perhaps the same suspicious ships seen in late May and mentioned in the juntas in Portobelo. Medina's certainty that the armada could have sailed safely into Boca Chica at night shows the confidence of hindsight and betrays a lack of knowledge about the difficulties of that trajectory. Nonetheless, men more experienced at sea than Judge Medina also faulted Casa Alegre for stopping on the night of the seventh.

Captain Canis, on board Nieto's urca, added more precision to the events of the day of the battle and made oblique references to lapses in the captain general's command:

On the 8th of June the men in the topmast sighted four sails to the north around nine in the morning, and the wind having shifted to the east-northeast, the galleons followed the coast of the islands on the lookout for this port [Cartagena]. And the north-north west wind having died, the said ships fell in behind the galleons. And the capitana continued the same course east that it had taken before, without having made any sign to put the ships into battle formation according to the orders that had been issued in Portobelo. And the gobierno at that point was more than two leagues behind. And about four thirty in the afternoon the capitana tacked back out to sea, and in its wake the almiranta, and downwind of the said capitana and almiranta was the urca with all its sails deployed, trying to take its assigned position. After the capitana raised the sign to assume battle order, the declarant [Canis] was waiting for the gobierno and the French frigate *Sancti Espiritus* to take their place in the vanguard, so that the declarant with the urca could enter the battle line.[51]

Once Casa Alegre decided to turn and fight, the armada formed the battle order that had been decided upon. The gobierno was supposed to be in the vanguard, followed by the French frigate *Sancti Espiritus* and then by Nieto's urca. The capitana was supposed to come next—in the center of the Spanish line—followed by the Vizcayan patache, and the almiranta in the rear guard.[52] That was the plan, at least. In the event, the gobierno had trouble getting into position, even with all its sails aloft, though Vega Florida eventually maneuvered it into place. Nieto's urca had even more trouble, as it measured 60 codos (about 110 ft.) in the keel and was considered large even for a merchant ship. Heavily laden, it was very difficult to maneuver, and when the battle commenced it was close behind the capitana in the battle order rather than ahead of it.

Josiah Burchett later wrote the best-known summary of the battle from the English point of view, based on official English documents. According to Burchett, the Spaniards,

finding they could not weather the Baru, a small island, so as to stand in for Cartagena, . . . stretched to the Northward with an easy Sail, and drew into an irregular Line of Battel, [with] the admiral [i.e., the capitana], who wore a white Pendant at the Main-top mast Head, in the Centre, the vice-admiral [i.e., the almiranta], with the same Pendant at the Fore-top-mast Head, in the Rear, and the rear-admiral [i.e., the gobierno], who bore the Pendant at the Mizen-top mast Head, in the Van, about half a Mile from each other, there being other Ships between them.[53]

Don Pedro García de Asarta described the position of the Spanish line of battle in confusing terms that differ from the descriptions of other witnesses:

> Friday the 8th at dawn we were to the northwest of the Isla de Barú, sailing east-northeast; and to the north we saw four sails. With wind coming from the northwest, the ships were cleared of all encumbrances for the battle, making way from the southeast and turning away from the land. And at about half past four in the afternoon, not being able to get around the Isla del Tesoro, our capi-tana changed course in order to form a battle line, and the other ships in the convoy did the same; but the gobierno, finding itself somewhat downwind, could not take its place; and in the poor form that could be managed (for the cap-itana not having been able to maneuver [into proper position]) the battle began, the almiranta in the rear guard. And the enemy having [the weather gauge], the almiranta found itself, with the course change (because one could not steer any closer to land), in the vanguard.[54]

It is not clear whether García de Asarta meant to obscure the position from which the almiranta began the battle; virtually every other witness said that the ship was in the rear guard, not the vanguard. He may have been trying to reconcile conflicting information from his commander, Almirante Villanueva, and the other witnesses, a problem that will concern us later.

Caesar Brookes, captain of the English fire ship *Vulture,* provided an eye-witness account of the start of the engagement from the other side:

> About 3 we made in all 14 saill of shipps, one birgantine, and 2 sloops, who all stood to [the eastward] till about 5, then tack'd to [the westward] & drew into a line of battle to receive: the first [captain] or he with a pendant at [the main-topmasthead] in the center in a ship of 66 gunns, the 2d [captain] with a pen-dant at his [fore-topmasthead] in the Reer in a ship of 66 gunns, & the 3d w/th a Pend.t at his [mizzen fore-masthead] in one of 44 gunns in the Vann, the other 3 being a Biscayer of 54 gunns, another shipp of . . . gunns, & the Gosport of 32 gunns, the other ships & vessells bearing away at our begin.g to engage. [The commodore] ordred me to put my men on board the Portland and prime, which I did, and [the commodore] ordred the Kingston to engage [with] the 2d. [cap-tain], the Portland the 3d; and he himselfe took up the first. At about 3/4 past five they began to engage, the Barue bearing SE 4 [leagues] distant.[55]

Brookes's testimony introduces one of the most vexing issues for modern scholars trying to reconstruct the battle: what did English witnesses mean when they referred to the "Barue" (often spelled "Brew") or to the "Grand" or "Great Brew" and the "Little Brew"? Spanish testimony refers to "Barú" or "Isla de Barú" but makes no reference to a grand or little Barú. The Spaniards do, however, distinguish between Barú or the Isla de Barú and a small group of islands southwest of Barú, which they called the "Islas de Barú." The English referred to these islands as the "Friends Islands," so at least their testimony does not confuse the various "Brews" with the Islas de Barú.[56]

The best clue to sorting out this issue comes from the geography of the area. Extending south from the entrance to Cartagena harbor at Boca Chica is the stretch of land the Spaniards called Barú or Isla de Barú. Its most prominent feature was a hill about 240 feet high, which would have been a likely reference point for ships at sea. At the southern end of Barú a small peninsula with a hill about 244 feet high would have served as another likely reference point. In fact, it is the only reference point for Barú in modern navigational usage. It makes sense to assume that the " Grand" or "Great Brew" mentioned in English documents was the larger northern part of Barú and that the Little Brew was the smaller southern part. This is confirmed by later testimony from the *Kingston.*[57] Because Captain Brookes testified that the "Barue" lay southeast of his ship, he presumably was referring to the 74-meter hill of the "Great Brew," as it is likely that he could not have seen the "Little Brew" from his position. Brookes's fire ship, *Vulture,* was close to Wager's flagship at the start of the battle and therefore close to the engagement between the *Expedition* and the *San José.* A notice in the *London Gazette* would report that the battle occurred "between the Brew and Friends Islands,"[58] that is, between the Isla de Barú and the Islas de Barú, using the Spanish terms for those places, and that agrees well with Captain Brookes's log.

The most extended and vivid description of the battle from the Spanish side occurred in the testimony of Don Laureano Ximénez Moreno, the merchant from Portobelo who was traveling on Nieto's urca. As a civilian in the middle of a naval battle, he had no specific duties except to stay out of the way. He therefore turned his mind to following the action, and his detailed testimony displays both the immediacy of an eyewitness and the analytical skills of someone accustomed to mastering detail:

> At four thirty or five in the afternoon, the English Commander came even with
> our almiranta and fired a broadside, and the declarant noted that our almiranta

was so quick and ready that when the enemy fired the first shot, the response came with such alacrity that the cannon shots practically met in midair. The commander of the patache fired a round and received a blast in return. Then the [English] commander moved along to fight with our capitana; and because the urca of Don Francisco Nieto was near the stern [of the capitana], Captain Don Joséph Canis said we could not pass up the occasion and fired a broadside, to which the enemy responded, doing damage to the said urca. The shot tore holes in various sails and shredded the foresail, splintered the mainmast, broke various timbers inside the hull, and punched holes in the prow of the launch. The blast also wounded [four men], and one man very soon thereafter had to have his arm amputated by the surgeon. The [English commander] then went on to engage the capitana, and because the enemy ships had the wind behind them, the large cloud of smoke from the gunpowder prevented us from seeing the action, but the French ship that was off the bow of the capitana should have been able to see it in detail, as she was also exchanging fire with the enemy.

Night fell, and for the above reason [the men] could not distinguish one ship from another. And because the capitana was very close, at about seven thirty or eight at night the men aboard the urca saw various flashes of light rise upward from the deck of the capitana, which they presumed were grenades and other munitions, and at the same time they saw through the gunports [on the capitana] that there was fire inside the ship as well, and afterwards they saw more fire; and with the confusion they disagreed about whether or not the capitana had burned.[59]

The ship on which Ximénez traveled—Nieto's urca—was sailing closer to the *San José* at that point than any other ship in the small armada, but even so, according to Ximénez, the men could not be sure what was happening on the capitana because of smoke, confusion, and the distance between the urca and the *San José*. Captain Canis, who led the infantry contingent on the urca, had command of the ship during battle. His report is much less equivocal than Ximénez's, though he places the timing of the *San José*'s loss later than other witnesses do:

At that time, which was already the end of the afternoon, the English ships began to fire at the almiranta, which returned the fire, and the battle continued without ceasing. The English flagship maneuvered to come even with the capitana, because of the space between the capitana and the almiranta. As it passed by, the declarant fired some cannons from the urca and continued firing until the English commander began to fight the capitana.

At that time, which was already close to nightfall, the said urca continued firing all the shots that it could, depending upon the room the flagship left for it. And the said urca took a hit from a twenty-four-pounder, which dismounted a cannon on the lower deck, damaged the launch and the opening and ladder to the castle, and took off a man's arm before lodging inside the ship. And the ship received various other shots from cannons and other munitions [*palanquetazos*] that damaged the rigging and brought down the mainmast. And with the capitana and the almiranta still fighting, as were the urca and the patache behind them, at about nine at night the declarant saw a great fire break out, with enormous flames but little noise. [Some sailors climbed] to the top of the mainmast with fire flasks and grenades, launching them into the air to provide light, so that everyone on the urca affirmed that [the fire] was from the capitana, because it was in the windward quadrant from the urca at a distance of about six ship-lengths. At that, I ordered the gunnery sergeant, Esteban Trave, and some sailors to climb on the poop deck [*toldilla*], and they said they could not see the capitana.[60]

In other words, in the time it took Trave and his men to move to the highest point at the rear of the ship, the capitana vanished from sight. They must have had little doubt that they had witnessed a major disaster. The only question was whether the capitana had sunk because fire had burned through the hull at the water line or because an explosion, presumably of the powder magazine, had opened up the side. On that point witnesses on the nearest Spanish vessels remained unsure; there had simply been too much smoke and confusion for them to see properly. They all mentioned the fire, but several also said that they had not heard the kind of noise they would have expected from an explosion.[61]

One eyewitness did mention hearing something that might have been an explosion. Don Luis de Arauz served as captain of the principal patache in Casa Alegre's fleet, a lightly armed small vessel called *Nuestra Señora del Carmen*. His assignment in battle formation was to stay close to the capitana. Arauz does not seem to have given his testimony until long after the battle—October 18, 1709—and his statement suggests that he broke his silence only to counter charges that he had deserted his post in the heat of the action and had failed to notify the almiranta of the loss of the *San José*.[62] In describing the beginning of the battle, Arauz asserted that all on board "awaited the glorious triumph of the arms of His Majesty and of the Spanish nation, even the most timid not doubting a complete victory, God willing."[63] After the sun set the capitana was engaged with the three large enemy vessels, according to Arauz.

He did what he could to help the capitana, but the patache mounted only twenty-four guns ranging from six- to four-pound caliber, whereas they were up against "warships of seventy guns firing thirty-two-pound caliber balls."[64]

The battle continued vigorously, with incessant gunfire from one direction or another and a horrific clamor from the artillery, which had heated up with the repetition of volleys, especially the artillery of our capitana, the whole of which looked like a volcano; the combat continued in this manner until after eight at night, when [we noticed] a great flame, which, seeming to have its origin in the interior of the capitana's hull, flared out through the gunports and hatches, climbing up to the bunting, and [we heard] at the same time an indistinct noise, with the dense smoke that covered that whole vicinity augmenting the confusion, [and] in an instant the patache [remained] inside that same darkness, without [our] being able to verify with evidence the misfortune that was already being lamented on board; and trying to relieve the men's [anxiety] with invented consolations, [when] the smoke cleared I tried to sight the capitana in the precise location where it would have been, and not seeing more than the three enemy ships with their lanterns to leeward, [this provided evidence] of the misfortune, and I immediately fell into doubt about what I should do; and in order to proceed with more certainty, I called together the officers of the ship and passengers of intelligence, and the sealed orders were opened, and after a brief consultation it was determined with uniformity to go in search of the almiranta, which we expected to find quickly, given the order of battle, first of all to report the great fatality and also to benefit from the security provided by her protection; to this end the foresail was set and the ship was turned around, with men stationed at the prow to be on the lookout for her.[65]

They did not see the almiranta that night, though Arauz had expected her to be directly behind the patache. The location of the almiranta turned out to be a very sore point for Almirante Villanueva, as we shall see, and it colored the testimony of several of the witnesses, including García de Asarta, the almiranta's captain of sea and war. His description of the sinking includes detailed information that does not appear in other testimony. Yet because the almiranta was nowhere near the capitana when it sank, García de Asarta cannot have witnessed the sinking firsthand. Instead, he presumably gathered information from a variety of sources, including from men who survived the tragedy, but phrased his testimony as if he had been an eyewitness.

The English commander came a bit closer and fired a charge at the said [almiranta], as did the third and fourth [ships in the English line], the latter being more to windward. And these ships being more nimble, sailing around and reloading, were giving and receiving shots until, coming upon the capitana when night had already fallen, they fired their charges (the enemy ships having come together), at which time fire was seen twice on our [ships], which was thought to be from the small French ship, though according to what was known later from those who escaped from the capitana [the fire] was on her. But [there was neither] the noise nor the clamour that the explosion of a powder magazine occasions, and a short time thereafter she opened up and sank.[66]

García de Asarta conveys an appropriate sense of the confusion of battle, but his description of the sinking and the lack of an explosion is clear and unequivocal. Did that clarity come from the survivors' tales? From other witnesses who saw the fire but heard no explosion before the *San José* disappeared? In any case, only Arauz's testimony from the patache mentions hearing a noise that may have been an explosion.

By contrast, all of the testimony from English sources says that the Spanish flagship "blew up." Commodore Wager, on the *Expedition*, had exchanged gunfire with the *San José* for several hours, hoping to capture it and the rich cargo he knew it carried. The logs of both the captain and the master of the *Expedition* describe the battle briefly and leave no doubt that the *San José* blew up, but they provide little detail.[67] In reports of the engagement, Wager and others on board the *Expedition* mentioned the enormous heat of the explosion and the burning planks and splinters that fell on nearby ships thereafter. Nonetheless, the explosion does not seem to have broken the *San José* apart, because very little debris remained after the ship went down. The captain of the *Portland*, Edward Windsor, supplied what may be the crucial bit of evidence about the *San José*'s fate. In his log for the day after the battle he noted: "& in the 2d broadside the Admirall of the Galloons gave the commodore she blew up."[68] If, as Windsor noted, the *San José* blew up immediately after firing a broadside at the *Expedition*, one or more of her guns may have set off a fatal chain of events that sank the ship.

Several scenarios come to mind. One or more guns on the *San José* may have misfired or blown up, causing a fire and opening up the side. The fire may have set off the powder magazine, which could have blown in several directions. If it blew sideways, the hull would have opened up, sinking the ship, but without leaving much debris, which would agree with the testimony of several witnesses. Because the *Expedition* was closest to the *San José*, however, any amount of flying debris would have threatened the men on the English flagship.

The officers of the *Kingston*, sailing as vice-admiral in the English fleet, corroborated the testimony of the captain and master of the *Expedition*. The *Kingston* had been close enough to the *Expedition* before the battle to both see and hear Commodore Wager and had followed the *Expedition* along the Spanish battle line. Four officers on the *Kingston* gave depositions on board the *Expedition* two months after the battle: 1st Lt. James Thornton, 2nd Lt. Thomas Whitaker, Master Patrick Balnevis, and Pilot Ralph Kelly. All four confirmed the report that the Spanish admiral (i.e., the *San José*) had vanished following an explosion. They described the action in virtually identical terms, phrased in the first person plural and presumably following an agreed-upon script. In the words of 1st Lt. Thornton, "When we got abreast of the Vice Admirale [the *San Joaquín*] the Comodore called to us to engage him, so we bore down within about half Gunshott and gave him a broadside in which his Maintopsail yard came down, and afterwards fired severale shot at him, but he fale astern. Then this deponent, being on the Gundeck, received orders from his captain to point the guns to another ship upon the bow, to which we gave one broadside as we went by him. About half past seven the Spanish Admirale blew up alongside the Comodore."[69]

The captain of the English fire ship *Vulture* had been ordered to transfer his men to other ships for the battle. He primed his vessel and stood by during the fighting in case Commodore Wager found a use for the fire ship. He too reported that the Spanish admiral, after battling Wager's flagship for several hours, "blew up and sunk immediately."[70] Judging from the available testimony from both sides of the action, a huge fire, probably accompanied by an explosion, sank the *San José*. Yet it remains curious that only the English were sure about the explosion. Can the wind have been such that most of the Spanish ships did not hear it? Arauz's testimony from the nearby patache mentioned hearing only an "indistinct noise," which seems to support that notion.

In any case, the *San José* disappeared and took with her Captain General Casa Alegre, all of his officers and passengers, and nearly all of his crew. Various sources estimate the human toll at anywhere from 575 to 650 men.[71] Several English sources reported that eleven men survived, though other reports mentioned as few as seven and as many as seventeen survivors.[72] The *Portland* picked up one man at ten o'clock on the morning after the battle; the *Expedi-*

tion picked up another three. About five o'clock that afternoon, the *Kingston* "came up w/th the wreck of the Admiralls ship, from off which we took seven of his men . . . it being dark when we had done."[73] Spanish records suggest that four more men survived the disaster. It is not clear who rescued them, but we know their names and something about their lives.[74] They will reenter the story later.

The men on board the other ships in the Spanish fleet did not know the full extent of the disaster, but they were undoubtedly stunned and disoriented when they lost sight of the *San José*. According to García de Asarta, after seeing the fire, "everyone remaining confused for the lack of a signal, and no one thinking that such a misfortune could have occurred, the most immediate [ships] . . . believed that the capitana had changed course."[75] Nieto's urca had battle orders to stay with the gobierno, and Ximénez related that

> Captain Don Joséph Canis called to the men who were on lookout at the prow [asking] whether they could see the gobierno and the French navío [i.e., the *Sancti Espiritus*], and they responded that they were still visible off the prow, at which point the captain said that it was his duty to continue calling out to the men at the prow, and these questions and the answers that they gave continued all night, in the style that is customary on warships. And a little while after the fire occurred on the capitana, new shots were heard faraway that continued all night, at which they wondered if it might be the capitana. But they were not able to approach where they heard the guns, both because [the urca] was leeward of the position and because it had been ordered not to leave the gobierno. All night long the men called out from the prow to Captain Don Joséph Canis that they could still see the gobierno and the French navío *Sancti Espiritus* and that they continued onward in front of the urca.
>
> And at dawn on Saturday the 9th they saw only three ships: one was the patache, the other that of Captain Juan López de Dios, and the other the small French ship. And seeing that the gobierno was not there, the said captain, Don Joséph Canis, began to shout with great fury at the men who had been on guard at the prow; and the declarant, having come out on deck at hearing these voices, saw and heard a sailor respond to the said captain, saying, "My lord, they told me to keep quiet." Which sailor it was, the declarant does not know.[76]

Some of the crew had apparently decided that they had seen enough battle for one night. By reporting that they still had the gobierno and the French warship in sight, they avoided any chance that Captain Canis might take them elsewhere in search of more action. In his testimony Canis mentioned nothing about the sailors' duplicity nor about his fury when he discovered their deception. He testified only that

> the urca continued following the gobierno and the said French ship downwind because the men in the prow and the waist of the [urca] and the contramaestre reported that they were proceeding with all sails aloft after the south-southwest wind rose again, which course the declarant also followed because he saw neither a lantern nor a signal from our[ships]. On the following morning, the 9th of June, neither the gobierno nor the French frigate *Sancti Espiritus* was anywhere to be seen, but only the patache and the other, smaller French vessel and the ship of Juan López de Dios, which appeared off the prow of the urca at some distance.[77]

While the crew of the urca misled their captain into thinking that they were still following the gobierno, that ship was actually far away, its crew fighting for their lives. The gobierno had begun the battle in the vanguard of the Spanish line, after struggling to get into position. When the men on the gobierno lost sight of the *San José*, they had no way of knowing what had happened to her because they had not heard the sort of noise that would have signaled an explosion. The gobernador, Vega Florida, knew only that three of the four English ships—Wager's *Expedition*, the *Portland*, and the fire ship *Vulture*—converged on his vessel; the *Kingston* was still some distance away, having engaged the almiranta *San Joaquín* in the rear. When the English ships came within shouting distance of the gobierno, "on the starboard side the first commander said in the Spanish language, 'lower your sails for Queen Anne,' and the gobierno responded with all its artillery; and from the same side the order was repeated, and they received in response two more shots."[78]

Captain Caesar Brookes, on the English fire ship, surmised that the gobierno had been too disabled by the early fighting to join the exodus of Spanish ships after the *San José* blew up,[79] but nothing in Vega Florida's career suggests that he would have turned tail in the middle of a fight even if his ship had remained sound. In the event, he had no choice. With the *San José* and the *San Joaquín* nowhere in sight and his own ship damaged, he and his men had to fight against crushing odds. The gobierno mounted only forty-four light guns—sixteen-pounders on the lower deck and ten-pounders on the upper deck. Wager's flagship alone carried seventy-four guns during the battle, ranging from thirty-two- to twelve-pound caliber, and the *Portland* carried fifty-eight guns ranging from twenty-four- to ten-pound caliber. When the *Kingston* joined them at about 10:00, she added another sixty-four guns to the English line. Based on relative firepower, the outcome of the battle was determined before anyone fired a shot.

The English ships sailed in an orderly battle line past the gobierno, each one firing a broadside from starboard, which the gobierno did its best to return. The English repeated the maneuver several times as the night wore on, their guns aimed at the rigging. As Vega Florida reported in his debriefing a few weeks later, "With the first blasts, the fore-topsail [*velacho*] came down, cutting various working lines, and at the second round of fire the topsail [*vela de gavia*] came down with much working rigging, and at the third round the halyards [*drizas*] of the mainmast and foremast, and all the principal cables, tackle, and rigging [*brandales, brazas, y amantillos mayores*] on the mainmast, and the mizzen and mizzen-top."[80] Commodore Wager knew that he had lost a major prize with the sinking of the *San José*, and the *San Joaquín* was nowhere in sight. The gobierno was a distinctly inferior prize, but a prize nonetheless, and he had much more to gain by capturing her than by sinking her. Under English law and custom, naval commanders could claim the lion's share of any ships or goods they captured, even during wartime.[81] In other words, the distribution of value followed the same law that governed prizes taken by corsairs. In stark contrast, Spanish law and custom specifically prohibited private gain by naval commanders and crews during wartime.

Vega Florida had everything to lose and nothing to gain from the battle. Against impossible odds, he stood at the prow directing his men, trying to return the blast from one ship and then reload his guns before the next ship came into range. After about two hours he tried to maneuver the gobierno into position to sail back to find the rest of the Spanish line, but his ship was too damaged by then to respond. His unsuccessful maneuver also gave the English time to come about, so that they were able to pound away at the gobierno from their portside cannons and give their starboard cannons a rest.[82]

According to both Spanish and English witnesses, the gobierno fought on until about two or three the next morning, "without any of the [other Spanish] vessels in the convoy coming to its aid."[83] Captain Brookes, on the *Vulture*, noted that the gobierno had put up "a cunning defence,"[84] but after long hours of battle against three well-armed enemies, her masts and rigging were shot to pieces, and the ship was impossible to maneuver. As Vega Florida noted a few weeks later, "The battle had converted me into nothing more than a buoy on the sea. Mainmast, topmast, mizzen, spars, sails, and rigging were all destroyed."[85] Not even the reserve masts and rigging survived the bombardment.

Many of the gobierno's three hundred men had been killed as well, along with at least one distinguished passenger, Don Antonio de Ron, fiscal of the Audiencia of Quito. Another sixty men or so were wounded and out of action, and those still standing had reached the end of their endurance.

Making matters worse, the gobierno was taking on water because of numerous hits below the water line—twenty-three in all—even though most of the shots had hit the masts and rigging. By the time the crew discovered the leaks, the water was already five to six palms deep. The only choice left to Vega Florida was to fight to the death or surrender, and the latter was an option that he clearly found repugnant. According to Don Martín de Zamudio, the city councilor from Lima who was aboard, the crew and passengers urged Vega Florida to surrender, but even when he saw the damage below the water line, he continued trying to persuade them to look upon the coat of arms of "our king and lord" and fight on. They were not convinced. In Vega Florida's words, "With the enemy continuing to fire their cannons, and the fire ship coming up behind them, they were led to believe that the English were coming to set the ship on fire." And there was no one to come to their aid. In the clear moonlight, there was not the slightest sign of another Spanish ship in any direction. They were on their own, as they had been since the start of the battle.

Vega Florida would later praise all on board for their bravery and zeal in defending the Catholic faith and the king, and he would single out several officers and passengers for special commendation: General Don Pedro de Medranda, Captain Don Diego Joséph Sánchez, and his lieutenant and the regiment's standard-bearer, Don Joan Antonio de la Chica. Nonetheless, the vast majority of the remaining men and civilian passengers were unwilling to die in the fight. Before giving up, Vega Florida asked everyone on board to testify to the ship's notary, Juan de Castro, that he had done everything possible to avoid defeat, a certification that was necessary in Spanish law. With that, he struck the fore-topsail to signal his surrender and asked the English commander for "quarter," that is, honorable terms.[86]

Don Francisco Serrano said that the men continued to act with "indescribable valor" right up to the moment of surrender, reloading all the guns in order to continue the fight,[87] but he was undoubtedly putting the best face on a dismal situation. He presumably did not mean to cast doubt on Vega Florida's decision, though surrender was always a questionable option to the Spanish government. A commander had to prove that he had acted honorably under adverse circumstances. In this case, there is no reason to doubt that. All the testimony from witnesses on board the gobierno spoke of the commander's steadfastness and bravery in the face of hopeless odds. There is one more reason to think that Vega Florida surrendered only under extreme duress: he owned the gobierno outright and had outfitted it at his own expense for royal service. Although he had preserved his honor, when Vega Florida finally accepted the necessity of surrender, he also accepted the certainty of a great financial loss.[88]

Vega Florida's loss was Wager's gain. Or was it? Three English ships had engaged the crippled gobierno from about 9:00 PM on June 8 until about 3:00 AM on June 9. When Vega Florida finally surrendered, which English ship had the right to the prize? Captain Brookes, of the *Vulture*, would have found it difficult to argue that his was the dominant ship in the English assault. But the captain and master of the *Portland* may have thought about challenging Commodore Wager for the prize. Although Captain Windsor mentions nothing about this in his log, Master Christopher Pearson suggests that the *Portland* jockeyed for position with the commodore's flagship in firing upon the gobierno through the night. Then, Pearson testified, when the *Portland* learned that the crippled gobierno "had struck we made all the hast we could to send our boat on board, but the Expeditions boat gote aboard before ours; this was about 3 of the clock in the morning."[89]

Staking the claim for Commodore Wager was a Swede who headed the *Expedition*'s infantry regiment and commanded the ship's boat. Martín de Zamudio referred to him as Enrique Lanz. Lanz conveyed Vega Florida, along with General Medranda and Serrano, to the English flagship, leaving a lieutenant and a few soldiers on board the gobierno to represent Commodore Wager. Medranda did not mention that he had accompanied Vega Florida, perhaps because he resisted identifying himself as a prisoner, but his testimony included specific information that he would likely have acquired only on the English flagship. By removing from the gobierno everyone who had served in a high-ranking military capacity, the English guarded against any Spanish attempt at resistance.

Wager's flagship had also sustained serious damages and loss of life. John Taylor, the master of the ship, noted in his log that "we had five men killed outright, 2 men who had their arms shott off and dyed of their woundes, and severall wounded. Our sailes and rigging shott to peeces, we bent other sailes, [and] knotted and spliced our rigging. . . . We lay by all night by the prize."[90] A later English report said that Commodore Wager had lost fourteen men, while the gobierno had lost ninety.[91]

At about 6:00 AM on June 9, men on the *Expedition* sighted four sails to the east, and Commodore Wager signaled the *Kingston* and the *Portland* to give chase.[92] Once the day had dawned fully, the English assessed the damage to their crippled prize and spent the morning overseeing minimal repairs, finally disarming her guns and lashing them down. They also allowed Vega Florida to visit the gobierno to remove his personal effects. He had various trunks of clothing loaded into his personal skiff and also brought with him several black slaves when he returned to his own captivity aboard Wager's ship. Whatever he claimed as his personal property could not be confiscated by the English as part of the prize.[93] Despite the emergency repairs, the gobierno could barely stay afloat, let alone sail, so Commodore Wager took her in tow behind his flagship.

Later that same day, June 9—witnesses differ about the time, but somewhere around midday—Commodore Wager sent the *Kingston*, the *Portland*, and the fire ship *Vulture* off with orders to capture the almiranta *San Joaquín*. Zamudio noted that some of the English sailors on the gobierno boasted that they were going to burn the almiranta instead of capturing her, presumably because the fire ship went along, but that would have been quite contrary to English interests, as she was thought to carry as much treasure as the *San José*. The three ships returned to report to Wager on the afternoon of June 11, bringing the unwelcome news that the almiranta had eluded them. Though they had been lying in wait for her near the approach to Cartagena, Almirante Villanueva had been able to fight his way clear and enter Boca Chica and safe harbor, where the merchant contingent of the fleet had already arrived.[94] The news must have been some comfort to the captured Spaniards on the *Expedition*, but it was no comfort at all to the English.

A Swedish ship that came back with the English patrol reported that another Spanish warship was grounded on the Isla de Barú. Wager immediately added the Swedish ship to his squadron and sent all four of the ships to either capture or burn the grounded vessel. That night a little after prayers, Medranda, who was with the other Spanish prisoners on the *Expedition*, overheard the English pilot tell Commodore Wager that he had sighted a great fire on land, and then the two men discussed it as being the ship earlier targeted for destruction.[95] Presumably, Medranda understood English, but his captors may not have been aware of that fact. The men held as prisoners on the gobierno saw the same blaze. Zamudio reported that "one night one of the Englishmen in a great hurry roused the declarant and the other Spaniards to come see a ship burning in the distance,"[96] but apparently Zamudio did not know what ship it was, and he seems to have feared that it was the almiranta. The news that Medranda had acquired on the English flagship—that the almiranta was safe—did not filter back to the men on the gobierno, riding behind the *Expedition.*

The gobierno remained in tow behind the English flagship for several weeks, though the English transferred to the *Expedition* everything they could find of value. According to a story that emerged in Vega Florida's later debriefing, "it seems . . . that the English sergeants entered the surrendered galleon and told [the passengers] to show them all the gold that they had and that half of it would be returned [to them]. And after doing so, the English took the gold on board the flagship, [but] they did not comply with the agreement, although different interested passengers went on board their ship [the flagship] to ask that it be returned. And the English only gave to some of them 2, 4, or 6 doubloons, and to other prisoners [they returned] their clothes to wear," as a sort of parting gift.[97] Only when Commodore Wager finally released the Spanish prisoners on the Isla de Barú ten days later did many of them learn that the ship they had seen burning on June 12 was not the almiranta after all, but Nieto's urca.

The three ships the urca had mistakenly followed the night of the battle led her into the Bahía de Barbacoas, east of the Isla de Barú. At the northern end of the bay, a channel known as the Pasaje de Caballos (lit., Horse Passage) served as a traditional alternative entrance into Cartagena's harbor, but only for ships with shallow draught. The passage was very difficult for larger vessels to manage.

Don Joséph Canis de Alzamora, the captain of sea and war in command of the urca, watched from a distance as the Vizcayan patache and the small French frigate he had mistakenly followed went through the channel the next morning.[98] The navío of Juan López de Dios followed them into the channel and anchored there. She made it through the following day (June 10), taking careful soundings to find the deepest part of the channel. While Canis pondered whether to attempt the passageway with the oversized urca, Judge Medina went overland to request help from Cartagena. The urca could not attempt the Pasaje de Caballos that day for lack of wind. Moreover, she was too large to attempt the channel at all without planning the route in advance.

On June 11 Canis sent Esteban Trave, his gunnery sergeant, together with the gunner Sebastián Méndez, to take soundings in the channel, and they reported back that there seemed to be enough depth to make it. Meanwhile, a local resident, Captain Jorge Coret, had arrived by canoe, sent by Governor Zúñiga. The Portobelo merchant Laureano Ximénez described Coret as "very experienced in these parts" and noted that when Coret heard the discussion about whether to take the urca through the channel, he advised against it, saying that "the ship was very large and long, and the channel was very narrow," so that there was a very real risk of losing her in the attempt. Instead he advised taking the urca back around the Barú to Boca Chica, the regular entry point for large ships, assuring Canis that there would be sufficient wind coming off the land to get them back out to sea.

Canis heeded the counsel of "Captain Jorge," but there was not enough breeze to get around the islands of Ziruelo/Ciruelo and Tesoro on the eleventh, so he anchored again. Finally, just after midnight on the morning of June 12, the breeze rose enough to encourage him to raise anchor. Supplementing the wind with a tow line to the ship's boat, powered by oarsmen, Canis maneuvered the urca out to sea. Governor Zúñiga had sent three French launches from Cartagena to help pull the urca through the Pasaje de Caballos, but they did not arrive until about 8:00 AM, long after Canis headed out to sea. He managed to get past Ciruelo but not Tesoro. With the urca still struggling at about 9:00 AM, lookouts in the top spotted three English ships at a distance they estimated to be four or five leagues. These were the *Kingston,* the *Portland,* and the fire ship *Vulture,* sent by Commodore Wager. Realizing that it was impossible to round Tesoro and that the English would soon cut off any hope of escape, Canis and the other officers decided by common accord to turn the ship around and ground it someplace where the men could safely disembark.

Canis carried out the plan, running the ship aground near Captain Jorge's property on the Isla de Barú after firing a cannon toward the English and taking down his infantry company's flag. The *London Gazette* would later report that the English had run the ship aground on the "Little Brew."[99] The story in the *Gazette* leaves no doubt that the English called the southern end of the Isla de Barú the "Little Brew." After grounding his ship, Canis sent most of the men ashore in the urca's two boats and the three French launches sent from Cartagena. Captain Canis, the pilot, Gunnery Sergeant Trave, and Captain Jorge stayed on board and rigged up a mine in the powder magazine, made of six jugs of pitch and bits of iron, with a fuse made of tow. As soon as the boats came back, they set fire to the fuse and rowed ashore. By then it was between 4:00 and 5:00 PM, and the English were almost within cannon range.

The Spaniards spent the night at Captain Jorge's home because English boats remained just offshore and an English warship blocked the narrow channel that led back to sea. Canis and his men could see the urca burning from stem to stern. At about 8:30 PM the powder magazine blew up, and the ship continued to burn all night. Early the next morning the *Kingston* put ashore the seven Spanish survivors picked up from the wreckage of the *San José* and then anchored with the *Portland* and the *Vulture* alongside the urca, which continued to burn despite the efforts of the English crews to extinguish the fire. After Captain Jorge and two prominent passengers from the urca reconnoitered the scene, they reported back to Captain Canis that the fire had reached the hold, which meant that the English would not be able to salvage much of value. Patrick Balnevis, the master of the *Kingston,* confirmed that fact by noting in his log that all they could carry off were odd bits of rigging and one of the anchors.[100] Canis knew that he had done all he could. His surviving men and passengers were safely on shore, and he had deprived the English of a valuable prize. That night he and the others traveled overland toward Cartagena harbor, where, much to their surprise, they found the almiranta, the patache, and the rest of what remained of Casa Alegre's fleet safely anchored.[101] In the absence of superior officers, Almirante Villanueva was in charge in Cartagena.

On June 21, nearly two weeks after the battle, Commodore Wager released the surviving passengers and crew of the gobierno, along with Gobernador Vega Florida, on the Isla de Barú. From there Vega Florida wrote to Villanueva asking for transport to carry his sick and wounded men into Cartagena. Villanueva complied, dispatching five canoes and three large launches, along with three days' provisions, including special food and drink for the sick. Both men followed correct procedures, but their relations were anything but cordial. Vega Florida had strongly opposed the fleet's departure from Portobelo and could well have blamed Villanueva for every misfortune that flowed from that ill-considered decision. Villanueva, whatever private guilt he may have felt for his role in the disaster, could not afford to show it publicly, nor could he permit any aspersions against him to go unanswered. And he held the upper hand. He was the highest-ranking Spanish official in the vicinity, "the command of this armada of galleons that came with the general, the Count of Casa Alegre, having fallen to me." When the captain general of an armada was in port, he outranked all other civilian and military officials, as we have seen. In the absence of a captain general an almirante held the highest rank, and Villanueva assumed command after the death of his captain general. In port, the highest-ranking military officer also assumed the highest civil command, so that Villanueva became the *almirante gobernador* once he reached Cartagena.

The irony of the situation can hardly have escaped Vega Florida. He knew he had to phrase any criticism of Villanueva's conduct before and during the battle in the most circumspect fashion. He managed to do so despite his personal history of temperamental outbursts, his understandable distress at having been left alone to withstand the enemy assault, and the ultimate surrender of his vessel. Even so, after Vega Florida presented his carefully worded report to Villanueva, the latter took great pains to contradict every implied criticism of his own actions and to cast suspicion on Vega Florida's version of events and his actions during and after the battle. Above all, Villanueva had to explain to his superiors in Madrid how and why his almiranta, the *San Joaquín,* had managed to reach Cartagena safely, when the capitana *San José* had been lost and the gobierno had been forced to surrender. Villanueva's distinguished prior history rules out the likelihood of cowardice. Instead the *San Joaquín's* survival seems to have owed to a combination of timing, tactical decisions by both the English and the Spanish, and considerable luck, but Villanueva had no way of knowing whether Madrid would consider that a sufficient explanation.

Villanueva's account differed from the variously worded but consistent accounts that Vega Florida sent to several officials in Madrid. Just as Villanueva presented the decision to leave Portobelo as the result of a perfectly rational assessment of risks, he described the ensuing voyage and battle in a manner designed to present his own actions in the best possible light. For example, in describing the prelude to the battle, Villanueva reported that "the capitana turned toward the sea, putting its prow to the northwest, without having unfurled the royal standard, and shot a cannonball from one of its guns, which was the sign for putting our ships into battle formation, as though he had attached the said standard." At the same time, Villanueva described his almiranta as "remaining in the rear guard in the wake of the capitana, unfurling its banner in the fore-top to make its identity known to the enemies, and putting its boat and bark into the water."[102] The impression conveyed by Villanueva's report was that Casa Alegre had been so nervous and distracted at the prospect of battle that he had failed to follow standard procedures, whereas Villanueva had calmly continued to follow the implicit orders that Casa Alegre should have given. Describing the ensuring battle, Villanueva noted that the ships

fought until after 7:30 at night, the almiranta continuing with the second and third ships [in the English battle line], at which time a fire was sighted in the place where the capitana was; at the time it could not be formally distinguished on which vessel the aforesaid [fire] occurred until the wind cleared the smoke; and the capitana being missing from the group of ships that had been closest to her, the presumption was that she had sunk. And with the darkness of night and the confusion of that sudden shattering event, the nearby ships were separating themselves from the line in various directions, without our being able to see from the almiranta any ships other than those of the enemy, which were distinguished by their lanterns.

In other words, Villanueva reported that his almiranta had engaged both the *Portland* and the *Kingston* until the time that the capitana caught fire. After the capitana disappeared from sight, Villanueva continued,

the two English commandants sailed with the prevailing wind toward the vanguard and resumed firing. And from the almiranta it was judged that they were firing on the capitana and the gobierno, toward which [the almiranta] aimed her prow, maintaining the line and continually exchanging cannon shots with the third and fourth ships [of the English line]. And this was the occasion, as stated in the summary [by Vega Florida], when the English ships fired their first shots at the gobierno.[103]

Villanueva does not explain how the capitana reappeared up ahead and why, in his version of events, the gobierno did not engage the English until after the presumed disappearance and unexplained reappearance of the capitana. Nor is it clear what Villanueva meant when he said that the almiranta continued to engage the third and fourth ships in the English line, whereas he had said earlier that she had engaged the second and third English ships. Was he simply mistaken or confused, or was he consciously falsifying the record in an effort to escape blame? The evidence seems to point to conscious deception, largely because of his claim to have engaged two of the ships in the English squadron. That claim is contradicted not only by Vega Florida's version of events but also by English evidence.

According to Master Patrick Balnevis, at the start of the battle Commodore Wager ordered the *Kingston* to engage the almiranta in the rear guard of the Spanish line. As they engaged, the *Kingston*

gave him [the almiranta *San Joaquín*] two broadsides, in the first of which his main-topsail yard came down upon the capp and he fell astern, but we kept on and hall'd up to the wind; we saw him but a small time longer; he falling astern and to leeward, we still continued on tile the Admirale blew up, who was ahead engaged by the Comandore, after which we did not se any morre of the enemys ships tile about 10 aclock, then came up with the Spanish Rear Admirale, the Comodore and the *Portland* being with him.[104]

Balnevis is ambiguous about how long the *Kingston* continued to engage the almiranta, but he does state that the almiranta drifted out of sight after their engagement, "falling astern and to leeward" before the capitana blew up. Testimony quoted earlier from 1st Lt. James Thornton says much the same thing, noting that after the *Kingston* brought down the almiranta's main-topsail yard, "and afterwards fired severale shot at him, . . . he fale astern."[105]

Could the *Portland* have been engaging the almiranta along with the *Kingston,* as Villanueva claimed? Not according to English testimony. The *Portland*'s master, Christopher Pearson, reported that the *Portland* had not engaged the almiranta at the start of the battle, but had "stretcht ahead and took up the *Gosport* [the French frigate renamed the *Sancti Espiritus*] and a great ship ahead, w[hi]ch I suppose'd to be the Rear Adm.11 [i.e., the gobierno]."[106] In other words, only the *Kingston* engaged the almiranta in the rear guard at the start of the battle, but the *Portland* engaged the gobierno as well as the *Sancti Espiritus.*

The English testimony contradicts every key point of Villanueva's version of events and makes clear that the *Kingston,* the second English ship, engaged the almiranta in the battle on June 8. Wager's flagship, the *Expedition,* first engaged the capitana *San José,* then later sailed ahead to engage the gobierno. The *Portland* was sent to the vanguard at the start of the battle and engaged the *Gosport / Sancti Espiritus* and the gobierno. The fourth ship in the English squadron, the fire ship *Vulture,* was ordered to put most of her men on the *Portland* before the battle began. She stayed close to the *Expedition* throughout the battle. The Spanish fleet originally had seventeen ships, most of them merchants, so a certain amount of confusion in identifying the ships might be expected from English accounts. The English squadron, by contrast, never had more than four ships, and it should have been fairly easy to distinguish among them. It is hard to escape the conclusion that Villanueva embellished his account throughout, doubling the number of adversaries he faced at any given time and extending the length of time that his vessel was actually engaged in battle.

Villanueva's account for the rest of the night seems similarly disingenuous. He related that

about 9:30 [the two English commandants] turned toward land, passing upwind of the almiranta, and the third and fourth ships [of the English battle line] followed their commandants. The almiranta remained alone in the line; and with the doubt of not knowing the motive for this change of course on the part of the enemies, the almiranta nonetheless [would have] exchanged cannon shots with them if it had encountered them again. And recognizing afterwards from the poop that the firing of the artillery continued, I persuaded myself that the capitana and our other ships in the vanguard had also changed course, although I had not seen a signal for this movement, nor did such a change of course seem to be appropriate, given the place where we found ourselves with relation to the islands.[107]

The notion of Villanueva's almiranta's remaining "alone in the line" of battle when there was no longer a line and the battle was far away verges on the comical. He seems to have been intent on assuring the bureaucrats who would read his account that he had remained eager to fight, even as he obliquely criticized the presumed maneuvers of the rest of the Spanish fleet. He continued:

And the almiranta having emerged from this combat with many working cables cut; the tackle, shrouds, and backstays destroyed; the lower part of the mainsail shredded; and the foresail, fore-topsail, and mizzen ill treated; and being unable to carry out any maneuvers, I set the ship perpendicular to the wind and applied myself to repairing the rigging and sails, which works were completed about two o'clock at night [i.e., 2:00 AM on June 9], at which time no form of combat could be distinguished.[108]

That passage, at least, sounds reasonably consistent with the events reported in other accounts. Thereafter, Villanueva returned to his skewed and self-serving version of events, using the merchants on board the almiranta as his foils:

And with the almiranta sailing in the direction of the place where the capitana was considered to be, in order to join with her, the deputy of the merchant community, Don Antonio [Rodríguez] Cortés, made solicitations to me to change course for Portobelo [so as to assure the safety of the] royal treasure and that from private parties, which persuasions did not change my intent, as my first obligation [was to follow the capitana], and [I considered] it a greater danger to undertake a long voyage if the enemies sighted me and pursued me while separated from the rest of the armada than in passing in the midst of the enemy to rejoin [the armada] or reach port, which reasoning [persuaded the merchant representatives] to cease their solicitations.[109]

In the dubious parts of his report, Villanueva projected the image of himself as a dedicated commander focused on his duty to the crown to ensure the safety of the royal treasure. His narration of the rest of his voyage into Cartagena continued to emphasize his attention to duty, but here his version of events was corroborated by numerous witnesses, both Spanish and English.

And Saturday the 9th [of June] having dawned without our seeing the capitana, I continued the return east-northeast. And about seven in the morning five ships were sighted in the southern sector: two to the west and the other three to the east, which sailed toward the port. And so that they would know the almiranta, I ordered the flag flown at the fore-topmasthead. And shortly thereafter [I] executed the Spanish signal of recognition for dispersed ships, but it was not answered with the countersignal by any ship. At that point the almiranta was about two cannon shots' distance downwind from the [floating] foremast of the capitana [the *San José*], to which nine men, soldiers and sailors from her, were clinging, as appears from the declarations of the seven men who were picked up that afternoon by the second English commandant, which, accompanied by the third English ship, was coming up under full sail behind the almiranta at a distance of three to four leagues.

And a little after midday another five sails were sighted from the almiranta to the southeast, which were judged to be the merchant [vessels from our fleet]. And with the almiranta following the same route until five o'clock in the afternoon, the hill of La Popa was clearly sighted, which the pilots said was seven leagues to the east-northeast, and the shallows of Salmedina were about five leagues away, somewhat more to the east. And with that in mind I ordered that the ship sail only until one hour after nightfall; and turning the prow outward, the almiranta remained athwart the wind until the morning of Sunday the tenth [of June]. With the wind from land blowing weakly, I found myself almost in the same place where I had put the ship athwart the wind.

And with the two enemy ships downwind of me at little more than two leagues' distance, I ordered the flag unfurled from the top. And at about nine in the morning they sailed with the breeze as fast as possible to get upwind of the almiranta, which had spied, somewhat distantly off her prow, another two ships that were sailing toward the port. And at one in the afternoon [those ships] were entering [port], and the enemies were approaching the almiranta, which began to coast the edges of the Salmedina shoals, in search of which I had intentionally sailed, so that the enemies could not get upwind of [the almiranta] without danger of wrecking themselves. And knowing that, they turned back out to sea, firing at the almiranta, which answered them with the artillery on her starboard side and her four chasers [*guarda-timones*]. And the two enemy ships repeating a second blast, the second ship struck the square flag and the banner that it flew, and they sailed out to sea, not desiring to come [close enough] to fire their cannons on the downwind side of the almiranta, which reached Boca Chica and anchored at six in the afternoon.

[There] I learned that the capitana and the gobierno had not come into port, although over the two days of Saturday and Sunday all the merchant ships had done so, except the urca of Don Francisco Nieto, which, having been thwarted in getting through the Canal de Barú [i.e., the Pasaje de Caballos], as the patache and another ship had done, stopped [there] until the twelfth day [of June]. And having gone out to sea in order to go around the islands, it was forced by the English enemies to ground itself on those islands, and [after] the people on board disembarked, the ship was set on fire.[110]

Villanueva's successful run into Cartagena proved that he had ample seafaring skills to balance against his instinct to avoid blame. He knew that by positioning himself near the Salmedina shoals he would make it difficult for the enemy to approach close enough to do the almiranta any damage. His account makes clear that the English squadron continued in hot pursuit and that vessels from the scattered Spanish fleet continued to straggle into safe harbor, subtly representing the almiranta as continuing to hold its place in the rear guard, protecting the rest of the fleet. Notably, Villanueva made sure that the almiranta flew her battle flag on the final approach to Cartagena, indicating for all to see that he was prepared to engage the enemy. Witnesses on each of the English ships in pursuit testified that they knew the ship was the Spanish vice-admiral because of that battle flag.

The testimony of the captain of sea and war on the almiranta, García de Asarta, supported Villanueva's account in most particulars. That is hardly surprising, since any aspersions cast at Villanueva's conduct during the battle would no doubt have implicated García de Asarta as well. That may explain the confusion in the latter's description of the battle line and the almiranta's whereabouts and actions in the early part of the battle. García de Asarta also supported Villanueva's assertion that at some point in the battle the almiranta became too damaged to maneuver, and there is no reason to doubt him. The English had aimed to disable her during the initial encounter and then to seize her and her treasure at leisure. In García de Asarta's words,

[We had only] five dead and twenty-three wounded, which is very fortunate, as the enemy was shooting at the [masts and rigging] with such a great quantity of lead and stone shot and [crossed pieces of iron] of about half a *vara* [yard] in size that it seemed like a hailstorm, but not at the hull, as they believed that they could take it with all the treasure, which they supposed they would lose if they sank it. . . ; with all of which the almiranta was left all shivered and without the quick maneuverability of its sails.[111]

Assuming that the *San José* opened up and sank, rather than exploding, García de Asarta had a ready explanation. The ship had become unsound

either because of the bad careening or because of the grounding she had experienced upon leaving Cartagena for Portobelo, the careening having been done at the expense of Your Majesty, though it should have been at [the expense] of [those in charge of the work], as their contracts [specified], about which the [captain] general complained greatly to the royal overseer, who opposed [the work]; one could argue about what would have happened if [the careening] had been carried out at the expense of [those in charge of the work]. [Adding to the causes of the sinking was] the water that the ship took on after the careening, worsened by the [strain caused by the] artillery, which was of equal caliber high and low, of sixteen-pound cannon balls.[112]

García de Asarta filled in the story that Villanueva told about their final approach into Cartagena. When the almiranta lay in sight of Boca Chica on June 10, repaired well enough to maneuver, García de Asarta noted, "The pilots wanted to sail before dawn, because there was some wind, albeit little, but the almirante objected, wondering if he had the men needed for manning the ship, as there were only 256 seamen, including the officers and pages, and a total on board of up to 404, counting passengers and men of all conditions, who planned to remain in Cartagena."[113] Nonetheless, the almiranta set sail and tried to lure the English onto the Salmedina shoals. The brief exchange of gunfire at long range was sufficient to kill one man and rend some rigging on the almiranta and to shatter the mizzenyard on the smaller English ship and damage the cutwater on the larger ship.[114]

García de Asarta also provided additional details about the fate of the survivors from the *San José*. On June 14, with the almiranta anchored in port,

five men from the capitana arrived in Cartagena and related the story of the misfortune, but not of the circumstances of the loss. They said they had escaped on the foremast and were picked up the next day by the second ship in the English line, which put them off on the Isla de Barú, and they brought the news that the gobierno had been taken by the commander [of the English squadron]. And of the seven men who were clinging to the mast, two were picked up by the smaller English ship, and those same two men [later] drowned, confident that,

knowing how to swim and having calm waters, they could catch up to the almiranta, which was coming [their way].[115]

In another of the tragic ironies connected with the loss of the *San José,* the two
men who drowned escaped a major disaster at sea only to succumb to their own
overconfidence by jumping into the water after sighting the almiranta nearby.
Accounts vary as to the number of survivors from the *San José.* Some mention
as few as five, others as many as seventeen. A notice in the *London Gazette* for
August 2 reported that "Captain Tudor of her Majesty's ship *Dolphin,* is just

TABLE 7
Survivors from the wreck of the San José

Name	Category	Job title	Service history
Amuedo y Soto, Domingo	artillery	gunner	Intermittent service; absent for all of 1707
Corzo, Diego	artillery	gunner	Transferred to the patache galleon *Nuestra Señora del Carmen* after the battle
Méndez, Sebastián	artillery	gunner	Transferred to the *San José* from *Nuestra Señora de la Almudena* in February 1708; transferred to *Nuestra Señora del Carmen* after the battle and "his imprisonment"
Villa, Juan Francisco de	artillery	gunner	Transferred to the *San Joaquín* in September 1708
Carrillo, Luis	infantry	soldier	Transferred to the *San Joaquín* 19 June 1708
Estrada, Captain Don Gerónimo	infantry	soldier	Transferred from the gobierno to the *San José* 10 August 1706; collected back wages 25 February 1715
García de Herrera, Pedro	infantry	soldier	Transferred to the *San Joaquín* 19 June 1708
Pérez, Domingo	infantry	musketeer	Transferred to the *San Joaquín* 19 June 1708
Rodríguez, Juan Antonio	infantry	musketeer	Transferred to the *San Joaquín* 19 June 1708
Rodríguez, Julio	infantry	soldier	Transferred to the *San Joaquín* 19 June 1708
Garay, Pedro	infantry	squadron leader	Transferred to the *San Joaquín* after the battle
Gallo, Joseph	crew	sailor	Transferred to the *San Joaquín* 19 June 1708
Ramírez, Domingo	crew	sailor	Transferred to the *San Joaquín* 19 June 1708
Vega, Domingo de la	crew	apprentice	Collected 200 reals 20 May 1717 by royal order

SOURCE: AGI, CD, leg. 578.

now arriv'd from the Spanish coast, who gives an account, that there are no
more men saved of the admiral's galleon that blew up, than 17 out of 7 or
800."[116] My research turned up the names of fourteen men who appear to have
escaped the disaster (table 7). Surprisingly, only three of them were mariners.
The sailors Joséph Gallo and Domingo Ramírez were reassigned to the *San
Joaquín* on June 19, 1708, when they arrived in Cartagena. The apprentice seaman Domingo de la Vega also survived and finally collected the 200 reals in
wages he was owed by the crown in May 1717. The eleven other names included four gunners, two musketeers, four soldiers, and a squadron leader,
Pedro Garay.[117] Did Garay somehow manage to save a few of his men from the
conflagration, or did each survive on his own? We may never know. After the
battle, the men transferred to various other ships in the remnant of the Tierra
Firme Fleet in Cartagena. The fleet would remain there for the better part of
four years before it finally returned home, while naval officials and bureaucrats in Spain and the Indies sorted out the implications of the catastrophic
loss of the *San José*.

CHAPTER SIX

After the Battle

Spain lost much in the battle of Cartagena on June 8, 1708. The Tierra Firme Fleet was deprived of its captain general and nearly six hundred others, several of whom were senior bureaucrats with decades of experience. Their disappearance meant that the remnant of the fleet and its commander could not benefit from their seasoned advice. In Europe, Spain's new Bourbon king, Philip V, lost revenue needed to defend his accession against powerful adversaries. The English were his most formidable enemies on the high seas, but in Europe the Bourbons faced not only the English but the Austrian Habsburgs and virtually every other state except the Italian territories governed or allied with Spain. The loss of royal treasure on the *San José* was bound to have an adverse effect on the war effort.

The English also lost much in the battle. Commodore Wager had planned to capture the *San José*, not destroy her. Although Wager claimed the gobierno *Santa Cruz* as his prize, he knew well that he had lost the two richest ships in the fleet, one sinking and the other escaping. In London, a special postscript to the *Flying Post* reported that "the admiral [*capitana*] was reputed to be worth 30 millions of Pieces of Eight, the vice-admiral [*almiranta*] 20, the rear-admiral [*gobierno*] a rich ship, but much inferior to the rest."[1] John Charnock repeated that estimate nearly ninety years later, noting that the "accumulated riches" on the fleet "were now become almost incredible, amounting, according to some, to little less than fifty million pieces of eight."[2] At the time, the *London Gazette* reported that the captured gobierno was "a ship of 54 brass guns, and very richly laden,"[3] but she carried more cacao than anything else, as did most of the merchant ships in the small fleet. The English had once disdained this raw material for chocolate but were coming to realize its commercial value. Nonetheless, they would have preferred treasure. Josiah Burchett complained that "thirteen Chests of pieces of eight, and fourteen Piggs, or Sows of Silver, was all that could be found" on board.[4] Despite his complaint, the gobierno was still the most valuable Spanish prize that the English captured in the war.[5]

The worst disappointment of the battle, beyond the sinking of the *San José*, was the failure to capture the almiranta *San Joaquín*. Brigadier General Thomas Handasyd, the English governor of Jamaica, wrote an official report on the battle to the Council of Trade and Plantations in London a few weeks later. He left no doubt that the escape of the almiranta caused extreme concern and even shame to the English:

> I herewith send your [lordships] a list of the galleons, and the other vessells that were with them, when they were attack'd by Mr. Wager. I understand Mr. Wager intends to bring the two captains that were then with him to a triall, as soon as the ships expected from great Britain arrive, that they may be able to make up a Court Martiall: By the account that I have had from my own Officers that were on board those ships, and the Lieutenants of them, Mr. Wager has had very foul play, but that will be best known when the Court Martiall meets. The traders that are lately come from Porto Bell, say, that the Spaniards laugh at them and tell them that two of our men of war, one of 60, the other of 50 guns, dare not attack their Vice Admirall of 64 guns [the *San Joaquín*], that they only fired now and then their chase gunns at him, and then sailed ahead of him and gave him their stern guns, at so far distance as not to do him any damage, and never came up to give him a broadside. This talk is enough to concern any true Englishman.[6]

Governor Handasyd's official report and various unofficial dispatches went straight to London, so that the English bureaucracy knew about the disaster much earlier than the Spanish bureaucracy in Madrid. England's Queen Anne and her ministers also learned about the "very foul play" alluded to by the governor, which came out at the courts-martial of Wager's subordinates in Jamaica.

For nearly three weeks after the battle, Wager's *Expedition*, with the captured gobierno in tow, remained off the coast of Cartagena. The *Kingston*, the *Portland*, and the *Vulture* patrolled farther out to sea. As soon as Governor Handasyd learned about the battle, he sent every available privateer to cruise off the coasts of Cartagena and Havana, hoping to prevent the remnant of the Tierra Firme Fleet from attempting to sail to Havana to join M. Ducasse, who had been sent to escort the fleets back to Europe.[7]

Although Wager set his Spanish prisoners ashore and put his men on short rations, the longer he stayed at sea the more his supplies diminished. At noon on June 16 (English calendar) his men sighted three sails in the distance. According to the sign and countersign agreed upon, the *Expedition* lowered both topsails, and the *Kingston* answered by hauling up both courses of sails and firing two guns to windward. By that they knew that all was well and that they were among friends.

After losing sight of one another during the night, the three ships joined the *Expedition* early the next morning. The *Kingston* lent the *Expedition* her stream cable so that the prize could be towed to Jamaica, and by 10:00 AM the squadron had sailed away in company. Although the prize broke loose briefly that afternoon, it was quickly made fast again for the voyage.[8] Commodore Wager was playing a delicate game, undoubtedly planning to bring the captains of both the *Kingston* and the *Portland* up on charges once he reached Jamaica, yet needing their help to get there. According to John Charnock, writing in 1795, Wager moved to the *Portland*, which had not been damaged in the battle, and sent the other ships on ahead. He arrived in Port Royal, Jamaica, on July 13 (English calendar), five days after the rest of the squadron.[9]

Once safely established in Port Royal, Wager had to wait another month before the long-overdue ships arrived from England, bringing enough new captains to make up a court-martial. The court heard sworn statements on July 22 (August 2nd on the Spanish calendar) on board the *Expedition*, anchored in Port Royal, with Commodore Wager and the captains of six English ships serving as the hearing panel. Their sentences were dated the next day, which means that the judges pondered their decision overnight, but no longer.

In addition to testimony from Captain Timothy Bridge, of the *Kingston*, and Captain Edward Windsor, of the *Portland*, the panel heard from other officers on board each ship. The points at issue concerned whether the two captains had been sufficiently zealous in the initial battle and in the various pursuit operations thereafter. Especially suspect was their failure to capture the damaged almiranta *San Joaquín* near the entrance to Cartagena harbor two days after the battle.

Predictably, Captain Bridge, as the senior of the two officers on trial, portrayed his actions as blameless, given the circumstances. In his log, after noting that he had engaged the almiranta at the start of the battle, he wrote:

> At 7 saw a ship blow up a head of me, some of my men at the same time calling out that Comadore Wager was blown up, whereupon my great surprisall. I thought it my duty to make saile to use the utmost of my endeavour in saving himself and what others possible I could. In making saile as the smoke blew

away, I discovered the Comadore to my great satisfaction, and finding the Expeditions fore-tack on board I stood after them, supposing they might receive some damage from some part of the wrack that blew up, they being so very near.[10]

In other words, Captain Bridge argued that his duty to Commodore Wager and to the squadron drew him away from further engaging the almiranta. As for letting the almiranta escape his pursuit two days later, Captain Bridge had written the following in his log for May 30 (June 10):

At 5 this morning see 3 saile bearing from [east-northeast] to [east]; we gave chase to the ship bearing [northeast by east], but at the same time very little wind till towards 10 a clock, we find the chase is the Spanish vice-admiral and pases away for Boga Chega. At 2 this afternoon being near the chase we hauled up the mainsaile in order to engage him, and gave him two broadsides, but my pilot called to me that we must imedially tack, otherwise should be aground, which I do believe was the Enemyes design, to edge us upon the Salmadine shoule, we being but two cables length of the west part of them when we tact. We left of[f] chase, not thinking it safe to follow further; most of our pilotes as we find by experience are often deceived in their knowledge.[11]

Attributing blame for his failure to pursue the almiranta to the advice and faulty knowledge of his pilot, Captain Bridge nonetheless left an ambiguous impression about what the pilot advised after the initial tack.

Another witness, James Thornton, the first lieutenant on the *Kingston*, provided a laconic and neutral recitation of the movement of the ships, presumably to avoid sharing any blame that accrued to his captain. He noted only that after coming close enough to fire a broadside at the almiranta,

the men were ordered from their quarters below to tack the ship, being (as was said) almost ashore on the shoal called the Salmadenas. We fired another broadside at the enemy, but he wearing and we tacking, our guns would not reach him; then the Cap/t ordered we should leave of[f] firing and house the guns, which was done accordingly, and we steer'd away for the Baru and the enemy [steered away] for Cartagena harbour.[12]

Thomas Whitaker, the second lieutenant on the *Kingston*, was far less circumspect, testifying that Captain Bridge had decided not to pursue the almiranta long before they reached the Salmedina shoals. In his words, "This deponent further maketh oath that above an hour before they came near the shoal this deponent, having got ready the starboard guns on the upper deck (the enemy being on that bow), asked his Cap.t if he should get those on the other side ready also, but he answered him no: and that he did intend only to give him that broadside and then tack and would not stand in any further."[13]

Ralph Kelly the pilot, Capt. Bridge's designated scapegoat, also told a far different story from the captain's, damning him with his testimony. Kelly said that on the day in question,

> between two and three in the afternoon we were very near the west end of a shoal called the Salmadenas, which lyes about 3 leagues off Boca Chica, a castle at the entrance of Cartagena harbour, and so near the enemy at the same time as that we might engage him and do execution; but the Cap/n refused to go after him within the showal, although this deponent told him he would undertake to pilott the ship in, so we gave him our broadside & tacked, after which this deponent asked his Cap/n if he would follow the enemy within the Shoal, telling him he was well acquainted there and that there was no hazard, but he told him he thought he had given him his answer already and so left the enemy, ordering this deponent to steer a course for the Baru; and this deponent further maketh oath that he asked his Cap/n if he would follow the enemy within the Shoal an hour before they came to it, and he answered he would not; and in a smale time after took in the small sailes and hall'd up and furled the mainsail; and it is the opinion of this deponent that the Portland might [also] have continued her chace without any danger as to the Shoal.[14]

The implication of dereliction and even cowardice, an implication supported obliquely by Patrick Balnevis, the master of the *Kingston*, could not have been much plainer. In Balnevis's account, after the men on the *Kingston* recognized that the "chase" was the almiranta, "near two in the afternoon, the enemy then bore up to go clear of a shoal called the Salmadenas about three leagues off Cartagena, our Cap/n, not designing to follow him within that shoal, as this deponent heard him say severale times during the chace, resolved to tack; and being then the nearest to him that we were like to be, fired two broadsides & tacked and left him, steering off to sea, and the enemy for Cartagena harbour."[15]

Even putting the most favorable face on the matter, it was clear that Captain Bridge had chosen to break off the chase, a decision that was unacceptable to the hearing board. Although not acknowledging the pilot's implication of cowardice, they found the captain of the *Kingston* guilty of dereliction of duty:

And it did appear by evidence upon oath that the said Capt. Tim[othy] Bridge through misconduct did not use his uttmost endeavour to engage and take the enemy on the 28th of May last at night; and that he did too negligently pursue the chace of the Spanish Vice Admirall the 29th & 30th; and that he left of[f] chace when within shott of the said ship, doubting the pilotts knowledge and being near the shoel called the Salmadenas, though the Pilott offer'd to carry the ship within the said shoal after the said Vice Admirall. But no want of personall courage being alleag'd against him, this court does only find him guilty of the breach of part of the 18th and part of the 14th articles of war, and for the said offence do dismiss him the said Captain Tim[othy] Bridge from being Captan of her Majest.s said ship the Kingston.[16]

The case against Captain Edward Windsor, of the *Portland*, followed similar lines, though mitigated by Captain Windsor's subordinate status. His log reinforced the notion that proximity to the Salmedina shoals had caused him to break off pursuit of the almiranta: "At 4 afternoon [the *Portland*] was within 1 mile & 1/2 of the chace, & at the same time within cables length of the Sallemander [Salmedina shoals], not knowing any thing any thing [*sic*] of it, which oblig'd us to bring to at once, we then giving each other our broad sides; & before we could get clear his weake of the shoale, he was gott a league from us, Bogee Chegee castle bearing [east-southeast] 2 leagues."[17]

Like the officers on the *Kingston*, the officers on the *Portland* had no qualms about contradicting their captain and criticizing his actions. Christopher Pearson, master of the *Portland*, noted that his ship had caught up with the almiranta after an hour's pursuit.

The enemy about that time wore round, brought too the other tack, and stood off. The *Kingston* fird [fired] a broadside at him at a great distance and tack'd, after which we gave him a broadside and wore and follow'd the *Kingston*, who made what sail he could off to Sea. And the Enemy then fired two guns and wore again, going away for Cartagen. This deponent further maketh oath that the two Lieuts. and this deponent did desire their Cap.n to follow the enemy, tho the *Kingston* did not, but he answered he would follow the *Kingston*, and this deponent further doth say that he did not fear the danger of any shoal given as a reason for their not following the enemy.[18]

Lieutenant Ellis Brand corroborated Pearson's testimony, noting that "this deponent doth further say that he proposed to his Capt. to follow the enemy after having wore, but he answered that as the *Kingston* had left of[f] chace he would follow him."[19] The pilot on the *Portland*, Emmanuel Rogers, testified that he had overheard "the Lieutenant and master desire Capt. to continue his chace after the enemy" and that the captain had answered "that since the *Kingston* had left of[f] chace he must follow him." Though Captain Windsor had claimed that they approached the shoal, "not knowing any thing . . . of it," his pilot testified "that they might have continued their chace . . . within the shoal called the Salmadenas without . . . danger, he being well acquainted there."[20]

The heart of Captain Windsor's defense was simply that he had followed the lead of his superior, Captain Bridge, a defense that is difficult to fault. Despite the confident claims from his pilot and others that they could safely have maneuvered around the Salmedina shoals, those claims had not been put to the test. Moreover, had Captain Windsor continued to pursue the almiranta after the *Kingston* departed, he would have borne the full risk of any mishap, and more than his command might have been lost.

The hearing panel at the court-martial acknowledged Windsor's defense, yet still found him derelict in his duty to the crown:

> It did appear, by evidence upon oath, that the said Capt. Edward Windsor was slack in his duty [during the battle and the day after]; and that on the 30th when the *Kingston* & *Portland* chaced the Vice Admirall of the Galleons near the Salmadenas, he shorten'd sail before he came up w.th the said ship & did not pursue the chace of the said ship so farr as he might have done. But it appears that he was lead into these mistakes through want of judgement & having too great a regard to Capt. Bridge of the *Kingston* as a Senior Officer. This court having duly consider'd the whole matter do find him guilty of the breach of some part of the 12th and the 14th articles of war, and for the said offence do dismiss him, the said Captain Edward Windsor, from being Captain of her Majes.ts said ship the *Portland*.[21]

Governor Handasyd, who had nothing but praise for Wager, wrote to the Earl of Sunderland that the two captains had been "brought to a triall, and are broke, which in my opinion is a very favourable sentence."[22] John Charnock's brief biographical note about Windsor, written a generation later, suggests that he was fortunate to have lost only his command for his "improper conduct in the action with the Spanish galleons, off Baru, . . . in consideration of some favourable circumstances in his case. . . . He never was again restored to the service, and is said, by some, to have died of mere chagrin in a few weeks afterwards."[23]

The sentences did not mention any dereliction of duty related to the salvage of Nieto's burnt urca, but the two English ships left the wreck after only a few hours' work. As the *Kingston*'s master, Patrick Balnevis, sourly noted, though they "took out some cower [coir?] and brought one of hir anchors aboard, we might took all out hade we stayed."[24] Balnevis's interest in acquiring supplies and fittings represented the natural concern of a ship's master, who was responsible for keeping his vessel in repair. His comment also raises the larger issue of what could be claimed in wartime and by whom.

As we have seen, Commodore Wager made sure that his ship's boat was the first to reach the Spanish rear admiral (the gobierno *Santa Cruz*) when her commander surrendered after the initial battle. The *Portland* also sent its boat toward the crippled gobierno, but too late to claim the prize. At stake was not only the honor of capturing an enemy vessel for Queen Anne but the full monetary value of the prize. When Commodore Wager claimed the gobierno, he claimed its value for himself. The prize would make the forty-two-year-old Wager a rich man, as well as a naval hero. He would continue serving the English crown for the rest of his life, most notably as First Lord of the Admiralty from 1733 to 1742, the year before he died.[25]

Wager's gain meant a total loss for the Spaniards whose money and belongings traveled on the gobierno. These included the Count of Vega Florida, its commander, who owned the vessel outright; the crown, which owned the arms and munitions aboard; and the merchants, sailors, and other private parties who had gambled that their belongings would be safe on a vessel that carried most of the fleet's contingent of soldiers. As we saw earlier, some of the wealthier passengers, after revealing to the English where they had stowed their money and goods, were set on land with little more than the clothes they were wearing.

At least the almiranta had eluded the English, which must have been a source of satisfaction to the Spaniards, as well as a source of hilarity to the wags in Portobello. With the death of the Count of Casa Alegre on the *San José*, Don Miguel Agustín de Villanueva, commander of the almiranta *San Joaquín*, took charge of all land and sea operations in and around Cartagena and bore the title almirante gobernador. From that position of power he was able to put a positive spin on his own actions before, during, and after the battle, but he faced an array of difficulties far beyond the need to justify his own actions. The primary difficulties involved how to ready the remnant of the fleet for its return to Spain and, most important, where to find the funds to do so.

Villanueva's responsibilities to pay the men in his command and to repair and refurbish his ships put him in conflict with financial officials in the fleet, who were responsible for the funds entrusted to them. Those funds included not only royal revenues but also private remittances. Every peso they released to pay expenses for the fleet meant that less money would reach Europe for public and private needs, and the financial officials suspected (with reason) that they would be blamed for the shortfall. Dissension arose early between Villanueva and Don José López Molero. As the master of silver on Villanueva's *San Joaquín* and the paymaster general of the armada, appointed by Casa Alegre, López Molero would clash with Villanueva on several different levels.[26]

At the end of July 1708, Villanueva wrote a lengthy and frank report to the king from Cartagena about finances, first discussing the royal revenues that were carried on his ship. According to Villanueva, Viceroy Castelldosrius had exempted the merchants of Lima from paying the tax that was traditionally collected at El Boquerón on the way to the Portobelo fair to pay expenses related to the fleet. Instead, the merchants had released considerable funds to Castelldosrius for "other dispositions of the said viceroy, [as well as for] salaries and the cost of guards and emissaries of the said [merchant] consulado."[27] Again according to Villanueva, royal officials in Panama had received only 50,000 pesos for fleet expenses instead of the 350,000 pesos that would ordinarily have been paid at El Boquerón. In his capacity as paymaster general for the armada, López Molero had taken charge of the 50,000 pesos earmarked for fleet expenses. He also had custody of another 582,466 pesos, 3.5 reals, in silver that Castelldosrius had collected for the crown in Peru, proceeding from a tax on the salaries of royal officials; unclaimed estates; a fee for exemption from billeting; the *cruzada*, a religious tax; fees charged for the trade in English goods; and other lesser sources. Villanueva's report accounted for only half of the monies collected by Castelldosrius. As noted previously, the other half would have been loaded onto the *San José* in Portobelo, as custom and regulations required.

Villanueva got the story wrong in various particulars, for example, in giving all the sums in pesos. The tax collected at El Boquerón was accounted for in ducados, a money of account worth 11 reals, whereas pesos were worth 8 reals, which is why they were often called *pesos de a ocho*, or "pieces of eight." Nonetheless, Villanueva was unequivocal about the bottom line: he did not have enough money on hand to repair and provision his fleet. Preparation of the fleet for its voyage to and from Portobelo, authorized by the Count of Casa Alegre, had cost more than the 250,000 pesos allotted for it, according to the accounts prepared by López Molero. Monies collected at Portobelo were supposed to cover the shortfall, but Villanueva found himself unable to pay even the most pressing bills, given the loss of both the *San José* and the *Santa Cruz*.

Villanueva noted that Don Antonio Ron, the former fiscal of the Audiencia of Quito, had received additional funds to convey to Spain for the king. But

Don Antonio had died on the gobierno, and it was not clear what had happened to the king's money. Villanueva was trying to find out. Nor did he know the current whereabouts of a small box of pearls that had been sent from Rio de la Hacha as the royal fifth, the crown's share of treasure, which the Count of Casa Alegre had received in the king's name. Villanueva did not know whether Casa Alegre had left the pearls in Cartagena or taken them with the fleet to Portobelo. If they had been on the voyage to Portobelo, the pearls presumably lay at the bottom of the sea along with the *San José*.

Some of Villanueva's most interesting remarks concern the amount of private wealth that may have been carried on his ship. A precise accounting, he noted, was very difficult to make, "given the character of the fair, and the fact that the largest portion [of the funds] that came down from Peru were in gold, which like a spirit can hide from the most careful examination." Nonetheless, he made a gross estimation based on shrewd observation and experience:

> I consider the silver to reach 3 million, and the gold to exceed 4 [million], though with the caution that in the matter of the gold I am not at all sure that I could find anything of value on the said almiranta today, insofar as the owners and their representatives bring this metal in their boxes of clothing, *grazqueras*, small chests, and desks, and, as I am not permitted to inspect these things because of the privileges conceded to the merchants in the contract regarding the averías tax, I must presume that they will have [taken the gold] ashore. And adding to the said 7 million another million and a half in profits on the merchant ships in this fleet, the overall total (seemingly) would be from 8 to 9 million. And considering that, for the sales celebrated in this city before the galleons went to Portobelo, more than 3 million would have remained secured in [Cartagena] and in the hinterland, the profits of private individuals can be summed up as 12 million.

Right after the battle, Spanish prisoners told their English captors that according to their estimate, counting gold and silver together, some 4–6 million pesos had been carried on the *San Joaquín* and a slightly larger amount, 5–7 million pesos, had gone down with the *San José*.[28] Villanueva's estimate, though nearly twice as high, is certainly plausible. Some of the Spanish prisoners may have had reason to underestimate the amount of treasure carried, perhaps to hide the existence of unregistered shipments. The discrepancy in their estimates of treasure on the two vessels reinforces that possibility. By custom and regulations, the two ships should have carried nearly identical amounts.

Villanueva's certainty that the merchant community had earned profits from the fair and his suspicion that they had smuggled considerable gold in their personal baggage made him unreceptive to their demands after they arrived safely in Cartagena. The phrase he used to describe his attitude toward the merchants was *sumamente duro,* "extremely harsh." When the merchant community in Cartagena voted to demand the immediate release of all registered monies and other valuables carried by or consigned to them, he stalled. Though they argued that they needed the funds to repair their earlier losses and to defend themselves against the zeal of enemy squadrons determined to invade Cartagena, he continued to stall.

Villanueva wrote to Philip V that the merchant community's pretensions to have "free use of the wealth and consignments [on board his ship were] most gravely prejudicial and of no benefit to the public cause and of the greatest disservice to Your Majesty." Instead of releasing the funds to their owners, he said, he had decided to "conserve it all together until I find myself with Your Majesty's precise orders, the observance of which is and always will be the principal objective of my efforts."

Another major point by Villanueva concerned when and how the fleet would return to Spain. He assured the king that he was overseeing the repair and refitting of the king's ships, as well as the merchant vessels, in anticipation of Ducasse's arrival. Villanueva also wrote that he hoped to be able to tell the king in a few months' time of their departure for the Portobelo fair of February 1709, a comment that belied any notion that he was headed for Havana any time soon. As for the return trajectory to Spain, Villanueva wrote that the merchant community would not consider going from Cartagena to Havana without the reinforced protection that Ducasse would provide, "not wanting to risk the remainder of the resources on which they based their hopes for financial recovery," as English commentators noted.[29]

Governor Handasyd assessed the situation in similar terms. He wrote to his superiors in London, "As to the Spanish ships at Carthagene, I do believe none of them will endeavour to join Monsieur du Cass or stir from thence till further orders from Old Spain."[30] The captain general and senior bureaucrats having drowned on the *San José,* there was no one to overrule the merchants' fears or urge Villanueva to join Ducasse in Havana. Meanwhile, the English were also intent on discouraging Villanueva from leaving port. As reported in the *London Gazette,* "It is believ'd, Monsieur du Casse will not continue in these seas, but immediately return to France. All possible measures will be taken to prevent those vessels coming out of Carthagena, which were design'd to join Monsieur du Casse, and all our privateers are order'd to cruize off that port, and the Havana."[31]

Villanueva's final point in his July 27 letter to the king concerned the men in his command—the poor sailors from his own ship, plus the survivors from the *San José* and the crew and infantry company from the gobierno. Villanueva asked the king to authorize his giving them a four-month advance on their wages just before departure for Havana "so that they could satisfy their debts and remedy their lack of clothing." He also asked for authorization to pay the back wages they were owed and to give them another four months' wages in Havana so that they could "collect their provisions" for the return voyage. This last item presumably applied to the soldiers, who had to buy their own food, but not to the sailors, whose food was provided for them.

At the end of his long letter Villanueva inserted a personal plea. Reminding the king that he had often put aside his own best interests in favor of serving the crown, Villanueva asked to be reimbursed for the monies he had advanced to careen and refit his ship before the fateful voyage to Portobelo and for the additional sums he would spend to prepare the *San Joaquín* for the return to Spain. The only way to effect that reimbursement was for the king to order López Molero and the other masters of silver to release the necessary funds. The 50,000 pesos that the almiranta had carried from Portobelo would pay the remaining debts for the earlier careening, including the money owed to him, so that he could satisfy his personal debts—but only if López Molero released the funds. Ending with an expression of hope for the king's kindness and benevolence, Villanueva sent his letter off by way of a Vizcayan dispatch ship heading home, presumably the patache *Nuestra Señora del Carmen*, which had taken part in the battle of Cartagena.

Typically, individual ships carried official business back and forth across the Atlantic in the intervals between fleets. During wartime, however, even official dispatches were rare. Just before the Vizcayan dispatch arrived in Spain in early December, another ship, named the *San Juan* and referred to variously as a *navío* or a *fregata*, left Spain for Cartagena. Although her Cádiz-based captain, Don Juan Phelipe Gámez de Acosta, had obtained the usual permission to carry 40 toneladas of goods for sale, most of his cargo consisted of papers and dispatches from the crown.[32] The *San Juan*'s exit documents were dated November 27, 1708, in Seville, but at that point news of the disastrous battle off Cartagena had not yet arrived in Spain. Any orders or initiatives from the crown were sadly outdated the moment ink touched paper. Likewise, Villanueva wrote his requests to the crown without knowing the desperate situation his king faced in Europe.

Countless government documents echo the sentiments the king expressed in an internal memorandum of August 15, 1708: "the only recourse that, given the present level of public expenses, leaves some room for hope is the relief that the felicitous arrival of the fleet will produce."[33] With revenues from the Indies the war effort could succeed; without them, the king lamented, "the monarchy finding itself in this conjuncture, although my application, my wakefulness, and the zeal of my ministers are dedicated with the greatest care [to the effort], everything is vulnerable to a bad outcome for the lack of means necessary to sustain the armies."[34]

Louis XIV of France, whom the king habitually referred to as "the Most Christian King, my grandfather," provided crucial support for the Bourbon war effort to maintain Philip V on the throne of Spain. That support came at a high price, however. Louis often demanded payment for men, munitions, and logistical support in advance. We have seen how the Marquis of Castelldosrius used all of his organizational and coercive skills to collect more than 1.3 million pesos for the war effort in the first few months of his tenure as viceroy of Peru in 1707. Much of that sum would be paid directly to Louis XIV. Shortly thereafter, Castelldosrius turned over another 300,000 pesos in loans to Captain Chabert, of the French dispatch ship *L'Aimable*.[35]

The squadron of eight ships dispatched under General Jean-Baptiste Ducasse in the fall of 1707 offered the best hope for defending Spain's treasure fleets from the English and bringing them safely home. Officials in Madrid and Paris (and presumably London as well) believed that the combined fleets would carry as much as 20 million pieces of eight when they finally returned. The outcome of the war arguably depended upon whether Ducasse succeeded in his mission. He expected to make the round trip quickly, but when he arrived in Portobelo late in 1707 he found that the merchants in Lima had not yet come to the fair. Until they did so, the Tierra Firme galleons remained in Cartagena, as we have seen. The New Spain Fleet was in Veracruz, just beginning a careening that would take several months to complete. When the Count of Casa Alegre begged off leaving for Havana, Ducasse went without him and soon learned that Havana was even more detrimental to the health of his men than Tierra Firme had been. Moreover, when the New Spain Fleet arrived from Veracruz at the end of May, Ducasse clashed repeatedly with its commander, Don Diego Fernández de Santillán, Casa Alegre's nephew, and with the merchants from Veracruz.[36]

Back in Madrid, memoranda written in May 1707 and thereafter meticulously outlined how to deal with both fleets when they arrived in Spain. The documents discussed various contingencies, depending upon the route chosen and whether the fleets traveled and arrived separately or together. Various memoranda and letters also dealt with how and when to pay off the men on the fleets as well as the men in Ducasse's escort squadron. The last point was especially important, as the king had authorized that agents of the French crown be the first to get funds from the fleets. The Spanish king agreed to pay the full cost of Ducasse's services, which would amount to "413,526 pesos and 168,657 libras, 13 sueldos, and 6 dineros" for nine months' service.[37]

Through the summer of 1708 the king and his ministers made careful plans to require the owners of gold and silver brought in as *pasta* (raw metal) to have it coined at royal mints and pay a minting fee. At the same time, the crown continued negotiations with the merchant community in Seville (called "el comercio de Sevilla"), from whom the king needed to borrow money, though they were suffering from the wartime decline in trade.[38]

Meanwhile, the remnant of the Tierra Firme Fleet, its escort squadron of galleons halved by the battle in June, remained in Cartagena undergoing repairs,[39] but in Havana neither Ducasse nor Diego Fernández de Santillán had any inkling why. Nor did the latter know that he had inherited the title of Count of Casa Alegre following his uncle's death on the *San José*. Despite their disagreements, Ducasse's squadron and the New Spain Fleet left Havana together on July 4–5, 1708, before news of the June 8 battle reached Cuba.[40] All they knew when they sailed for Europe was that the Tierra Firme Fleet had not arrived in time to accompany them, a worrisome development but not without precedent.

English ideas about the New Spain Fleet greatly exaggerated its value and its vulnerability. An Englishman in Jamaica wrote that "the said fleet is very rich, and by the most moderate computation not less worth than eighty million of Peices [*sic*] of eight; and Mons.r Ducass has had a great sickness and mortality in his squadron, and consequently goes home very weak; [and the fleet could be captured] with a great deal of ease."[41] Not quite. Because they suspected that the English would be patrolling the traditional route toward Cádiz and Seville, Ducasse and the New Spain Fleet aimed for the Cantabrian coast. At the end of August 1708 the New Spain Fleet—technically the fleet of 1706—safely anchored in the northern port of Pasajes, near San Sebastián.[42] There they unloaded and filed the necessary reports, no doubt congratulating themselves on a successful voyage.

The 1708 New Spain Fleet, under Captain General Andrés de Pez, also returned home safely that year, without Ducasse's protection. The treasure carried by both New Spain fleets would provide considerable financial and emotional relief for the Bourbon war effort, but at a cost to private individuals. On August 29 a royal proclamation was cried through Pasajes ordering all the newly arrived "factors, shippers, and passengers" to declare within twenty-four hours all the raw silver and gold they carried, whether or not the royal fifth had already been deducted from it, so that it could immediately be coined at the royal mints.[43] This meant that a coinage fee would be deducted from the metal, adding to the crown's receipts.

Some of the persons covered by the proclamation made their declarations on board Fernández de Santillán's flagship, but many others did not. Don Pedro Fernández Navarrete, the governor general of Guipúzcoa, then issued a second proclamation and had it cried through San Sebastián as well as Pasajes. A few dozen more persons responded, but most of them declared that they had brought no uncoined metal on the voyage. In other words, the royal proclamation did not elicit full compliance, to say the least, but the officials in charge did not press the matter further, simply closing the accounts on September 4, 1708. According to the official report dated a week later, the uncoined metal declared by its owners or commissioned agents totaled an unimpressive 2,706 marks and 2 ounces of uncoined silver, and 3,403 pesos, 6 reals, worth of gold.[44] The true amounts carried by the fleet must have been far higher, though presumably far less than the 80 million pesos estimated by some. Whatever the true amount brought into Spain, private persons with treasure were reluctant to turn it over to the royal mints. Given the crown's pressing need for funds, they must have feared that it would be heavily taxed, perhaps even confiscated.

Despite the urgency of the European war, the royal bureaucracy did not forget needs in the Indies. In late November the Junta de Guerra de Indias urged the king to strengthen Cartagena's defenses. The councilors argued that although Don Joséph Zúñiga y de la Cerda, the current governor, had asked the crown for various kinds of help, he had omitted the most important element: "the need to have two frigates that would patrol the coasts, and the indispensable creation of two companies of dragoons (each of fifty men) to make it impossible for the enemy to land troops." The subcommittee also urged the king to fund repairs to the city walls of Cartagena against the inevitability of flooding in that tropical climate.[45]

Back in Cartagena, Almirante Gobernador Villanueva was less concerned with the danger of flooding than with the imminent need to repair his ships and pay his officers and men. In that endeavor he ran into strong opposition from Don José López Molero. On June 30, 1708, eight of the fleet's officers had supervised the moving of funds collected for the avería tax, plus vouchers and promissory notes for money still owing, to a safe in López Molero's lodgings. The total came to 128,000 reals, just under half in gold and the rest in silver, a total far lower than what was needed. By virtue of the powers of his office, Villanueva could draw on that sum for the three customary areas of expenditure for a Spanish military fleet: general accounts *(veeduría general);* captaincy *(capitanía general),* to pay the salaries of the officers and men; and provisioning *(proveeduría general),* for careening and repairs. López Molero refused to release any of the money in his care, however. Perhaps in retaliation, Villanueva refused to release the funds on the *San Joaquín* that belonged to private merchants, outraged that they had brought back profits from Portobelo, while the naval escort protecting them had suffered a terrible blow.

To break the stalemate, on August 18 Villanueva issued a decree ordering the liquidation of the assets held by López Molero so that the fleet's outstanding debts could be paid. He also had other royal officials in Cartagena certify that his demands were justified. On August 19 Villanueva appointed a more cooperative paymaster for the fleet, Joséph Rodríguez de Vidal. López Molero remained master of silver on the *San Joaquín,* though his relations with Villanueva were frosty at best. By late November Villanueva had spent 28,275 pesos. By mid-December he had spent another 14,000 pesos, bringing the total spent since his arrival in Cartagena to 42,275 pesos.[46] Of that amount, nearly half had gone for repairs to the fleet, especially to the *San Joaquín.*

Don Pedro García de Asarta oversaw those repairs as the vessel's captain of sea and war. As he reported in a letter dated July 31, 1708, to Bernardo de Tinajero, fiscal of the Council of the Indies, in addition to "the irremediable loss of the capitana and gobierno of these galleons, and of the urca belonging to Captain Don Francisco Fernández Nieto," the galleon *Nuestra Señora de la Almudena* had been dropped from the fleet once it reached Cartagena for being too rotten ("podrido") for service. García de Asarta sent Tinajero a complete diary of the work done to the ship up to July 31, when he put his report on the same Vizcayan patache that carried Villanueva's reports of the battle to Spain.[47]

Villanueva's new paymaster duly accounted for all of the payments for ship repairs from August 19 to December 18, including wages for carpenters, caulkers, and other craftsmen, plus the sailors, gunners, and infantrymen who served as porters and loaders of food and equipment while the ships were in port. Food represented a major expense for any fleet, and the costs mounted quickly when a ship was idle in a faraway port and most of the men had nothing better to do than collect their rations. In addition to flour, beef, pork, and other comestibles, Rodríguez's accounts registered shipments of wood, Dutch and French sail-cloth, tar, barrel staves, masts, flagpoles, and many other items needed for the repairs and refitting.[48]

In the meantime, Villanueva's relations with the local merchant community in Cartagena reached a critical point. On November 9, fed up with what they called "the violent treatment with which they see themselves oppressed by the said almirante gobernador," the merchants held a meeting to formulate a protest against his refusal to release their funds. The next day they met again at the request of Governor Zúñiga in the lodgings that Villanueva had rented in Cartagena. In addition to the merchants' representatives, several officers in the fleet attended the meeting: the captains Don Pedro García de Asarta and Don Manuel Antonio Alemán; Don Joseph Fermín de Larragoiti y Aris, general overseer and accountant for the crown *(veedor general y contador);* Don Miguel Rodríguez Vidal, supply master *(proveedor general);* the licenciado Don Alonso de la Cueva Ponce de León, general auditor *(auditor general)* for the crown; and the pilot major for the fleet, Antonio de Ojeda. In their testimony the ill-considered and ill-timed decision for the fleet to leave Portobelo came up again. According to many, Villanueva bore the blame for that decision, and he could not escape it.

Of the twelve men voting, nine voted that Villanueva should release the merchants' funds. He refused to accept the vote, however, arguing that because of the losses in battle and the dire state of the fleet, he was doing what was in the best interests of the king's service. Villanueva based his authority on a royal decree that had arrived with the Vizcayan dispatch boat the previous summer, and he said he would not relent unless he received a direct order from General Ducasse. Because everyone assumed that Ducasse and the New Spain Fleet had left Havana long before, the Cartagena merchants considered Villanueva's reasoning cynical and self-serving. In fact, the fleet had left Havana at the same time that the Vizcayan dispatch boat left Cartagena, at the end of the first week in August.[49] The net result was that Villanueva did as he thought best in Cartagena, with no higher authority to oppose him. What he thought best was to refurbish the fleet so that he could deliver the king's treasure.

The English heard about the wrangling from a high-ranking Spanish prisoner held in Port Royal, Don Joseph de Castillo Blanco, who told them that Villanueva felt so disaffected that he might be induced to come over to the anti-Bourbon side in the war. As a result, Wager, who had been promoted to rear admiral, and Governor Handasyd wrote to Villanueva that they had heard that he was suspected of wrongdoing and had "refused to let the merchants have their money ashoar that required it [and that] you have an inclination to come over with the ship you are in, and the effects in her to Jamaica; we send this to assure you that if you do resolve to come over and declare for King Charles the Third, the lawfull king of Spain," King Charles would provide a proper reward and an English military escort home.[50] Unless Villanueva was playing a highly duplicitous game, Castillo had misinterpreted the implications of his quarrels in Cartagena. The English offer to aid Villanueva's defection may even have strengthened his resolve to serve his Bourbon king.

We cannot know whether Villanueva thought in broader terms than his duty to the crown as a military man and a loyal subject, but the outcome of the war over the Bourbon succession would have profound implications in America as well as in Europe. If the Bourbons did not keep the throne of Spain, the empire would likely be broken up and parceled out among the members of the anti-Bourbon coalition. Not all of them had naval forces in the Americas, but those that did found it advantageous to cooperate against the Spanish and the French, in the hopes of gaining territories or commercial advantages that would result from a successful effort to oust Philip V from Spain and deal a blow to his grandfather Louis XIV.

No one knew this more clearly than the Marquis of Castelldosrius, the "viceroy, governor, and captain general of these kingdoms of Peru."[51] The viceroy's primary concern was how to make the viceregal government profitable again so that he could fund his administration and send surplus revenues to Spain. As we have seen, Castelldosrius realized very soon after arriving in Peru that the viceroyalty had been running a deficit for years, and he concluded that smuggling and tax evasion accounted for much of the shortfall. In October 1708 Castelldosrius issued a draconian set of rules designed to eliminate tax evasion in the payment of the royal fifth on silver and gold mined in Peru. Although the problem had existed for some time, Castelldosrius recognized that it had gotten worse in recent years. Many tax evaders simply bought smuggled merchandise with unregistered treasure in ports on both coasts of South America, leading to an "incomparable decay of royal revenues." Bad enough in peacetime, this "detestable fraud" during the ongoing war put both the monarchy and the empire at risk.[52]

The twenty-one numbered paragraphs in Castelldosrius's new rules forbade the private refining of metals and required that all metals be taxed before being transported anywhere except to a place where their owners could pay taxes and have the metal coined. Castelldosrius also required mine owners to keep precise and detailed records of all the precious metals extracted from their mines and mandated that all the account books be reviewed three times a year by inspectors with wide powers. Among their other duties, the inspectors were supposed to compare the amount of mercury used in their districts with the amount of silver registered. As mercury was the key ingredient in the process used to refine silver, the use of mercury would serve as a proxy for the amount of silver mined and refined in each district.

The penalties for malfeasance included heavy fines, jail terms, and exile, and the standard rewards for reporting irregularities were as appealing as the penalties were harsh. In addition to confiscated goods' being divided among the crown, the court, and the denouncer, slaves who denounced fraud were promised their freedom and Indians subject to tribute payments were promised exemption from such payments for the rest of their lives. If and when Castelldosrius's new rules went into effect, many wealthy residents of the viceroyalty, as well as residents aspiring to join their ranks, would have been hard hit.

Illicit trade constituted an even greater problem for the viceroy than tax evasion. As we have seen, the number of French vessels in the Mar del Sur increased during the war, and their captains expected to be able to sell goods in Peru as a more or less direct reward for helping the viceroyalty against the English. Pirates and privateers from England infested the coastline as well, as Castelldosrius complained, and they were generally impossible to find, let alone intercept, in the vastness of the region. In letters to Castelldosrius dated April 28 and May 17, 1708, the crown warned him that seven ships of fifty to sixty guns each had been armed by some English lords "to infest these seas . . . commanded by an Englishman named Dampierre."[53] The authorities in Madrid assumed that "Dampierre"—William Dampier—aimed to attack and occupy an island in the Southern Sea for use as a base, presumably the island of Juan Fernández, off the coast of Chile.

The warning letters did not reach Castelldosrius until March 17, 1709, however. By then the privateers had been raiding the coast of Peru for the better part of a year, adding to the efforts of other pirates and privateers who had arrived several years earlier. In May 1709 Woodes Rogers launched a major attack on Guayaquil with two well-armed ships and 450 men, inflicting serious damage on the city and its inhabitants. Rogers and his men took booty estimated at 23,000 pesos, as well as kidnapping and holding for ransom the son of the richest man in Panama.[54] By the time Viceroy Castelldosrius was able to put together a fleet of two local vessels and three visiting French vessels to send to Guayaquil, the marauders were long gone with their loot.

Spanish authorities could point to a few limited successes in dealing with the infestation. Three English pirate captains who had entered the Mar del Sur in 1704—Thomas Stradling, William Robert, and John Knowles—were eventually imprisoned in Callao, though they escaped briefly in a stolen canoe in January 1708 before being recaptured.[55] Others continued to elude Spanish authorities while raiding towns all along the Pacific coast. It is no wonder that the viceroy worried constantly about the need for defense and how to pay for it.

The merchant community of Lima, usually a source of generous donations to the defense effort, was ill disposed toward the viceroy as long as the illicit commerce continued. They accused Castelldosrius not only of sanctioning that commerce but of skimming profits from it for his own benefit. In a firestorm of opposition his enemies drew up a long list of charges that called into question his loyalty to the crown, his piety, his honesty, his attention to duty, and his commitment to the well-being of the citizenry. The government in Madrid took all of these charges quite seriously.[56] The denunciations flowed from many individuals whom Castelldosrius had alienated in his brief tenure in office; they were drawn up during the summer of 1708 and entrusted to the French ship *L'Aimable* when it left Callao for Europe on August 17.

Before *L'Aimable* sailed, however, Castelldosrius learned about the charges, further proof of the efficiency of the administrative network he had established in Peru. The viceroy knew that his best hope lay in sending proof of his innocence to his superiors in Madrid, timed to arrive along with the charges and to counteract them before they blackened his reputation. Via Captain Chabert on *L'Aimable,* Castelldosrius sent several sealed boxes of documents to his daughter Catalina, who was a lady-in-waiting to Queen María Luisa Gabriela of Savoy in Madrid. The documents provided proof of his innocence and presented his side of the story to the king, including his lament about the dismal state of finances in Peru and the economic decay in the area. Among other complaints, he noted that he could not find anyone to lend him money to carry on the crown's business,[57] which is hardly surprising, given that he had alienated some of the richest families in Peru.

In February 1709 Castelldosrius also sent his son Antonio an explanation of the plot, using as a courier a trusted cleric on his way to Mexico.[58] In vigorous and unguarded language he warned his son against several Spaniards who had become tools of the French in the illicit trade and railed against the calumny and ingratitude of those who had benefited from his patronage and then betrayed him. He also warned his son that he had learned that Captain Chabert, of *L'Aimable,* had turned against him. Castelldosrius's sense of helplessness and isolation permeates his letter. Most disheartening, he had come to doubt his royal patrons' commitment to the best interests of Peru. Noting that he had only forty soldiers to patrol hundreds of miles of coastline, Castelldosrius concluded that the only way to stop the illicit commerce was to prevent French ships from coming to the Southern Sea in the first place: "And thus the blame lies with he who permits and tolerates [the sailings] and not with this viceroy; . . . if those who being able to impede the traffic from Europe do not do it, it is a sign that the thing that is desired is the same as the thing that is censured."[59]

In other words, Castelldosrius suspected both Louis XIV of France and Philip V of Spain of playing a cynical game regarding the illicit commerce, leaving him trapped between duty and circumstance. Ironically, Castelldosrius had an unexpected ally in his fight against illicit commerce, namely, the English governor of Jamaica. Lamenting the depressed state of trade in the Caribbean during the war, Governor Handasyd wrote, "If there can be a method found out to prevent the French trading to Lima and the South Seas, trade here will soon be in a flourishing condition."[60] He knew as well as the viceroy that the method had to be applied in Europe.

Castelldosrius's quest for exoneration came at a very bad time. Full documentation of the disastrous losses suffered by the Tierra Firme Fleet on June 8 finally arrived in Madrid the second week of December, though unconfirmed reports had arrived somewhat earlier. The Council of the Indies met on December 11, reporting that it was "putting in the hand of Your Majesty the letters from the almirante of the galleons [Villanueva] and the captain of the almiranta [García de Asarta], with a diary of what happened with that armada and what occurred in Cartagena, where [the armada] remains."[61] Apart from the grievous loss of men who would never come home, the fresh infusion of revenues that the crown desperately needed to prosecute the war would not arrive any time soon. Half had gone down with the *San José,* and the other half remained in Cartagena with the remnant of the fleet.

Adding to the bad news arriving in Madrid, in mid-January 1709 the pope recognized the Habsburg pretender in Barcelona as the legitimate king of Spain. Soon thereafter Louis XIV withdrew his troops from the war and sought a separate peace, abandoning his grandson to his fate. In view of the formidable list of military and political forces arrayed against the Bourbon succession in Spain, Louis XIV acted prudently and in the best interests of France. In Spain, however, his withdrawal was seen as yet another example of French perfidy and prompted violent anti-French protests in Madrid. At the same time, Spaniards outside the Habsburg stronghold in Catalonia increased their loyalty to Philip V, the French Bourbon prince whom many had disdained earlier as a tool of Louis XIV.

Betrayed by the pope and by his own grandfather, Philip V would soon hear the accusation that the first Spaniard to salute him as king—the Marquis of Castelldosrius—had betrayed him as well. The ship *L'Aimable*, carrying the charges against Castelldosrius, reached Spain in the spring of 1709, having left Callao in mid-August of the previous year. Captain Chabert delayed delivering the boxes of exonerating evidence that Castelldosrius had sent to his daughter Catalina. Instead Chabert sent forward only the documents for the case against the viceroy, which began to move through the bureaucracy unchallenged. Seven months after *L'Aimable* arrived in Spain, Doña Catalina complained that she still had not received the consignment from her father, so that the Council of the Indies had little to weigh against the damning accusations against him.[62] It is not clear how the anti-French mood in Madrid might have affected the trajectory of Castelldosrius's case, but presumably it did not help. The viceroy's Frenchified ways and suspected loyalties formed a major part of his public image. That the charges against him centered on his supposed collusion with French interlopers into Spanish America only reinforced that image.

In late May 1709, on recommendation from the Council of the Indies, the king named a judge to examine the charges against Castelldosrius and also named a new viceroy, but that nominee was needed in New Spain instead. A few months later, Castelldosrius's daughter filed a petition asking for a full investigation of the charges against her father.[63] In her petition Doña Catalina summarized the contents of the papers she had finally received from Lima, but she was unable to stop the judicial process. In April 1710 the council recommended that the king remove Castelldosrius from office, although there would also be a full investigation of his tenure, as was customary. Before the king left Madrid on May 3 to confront the armies of the Habsburg pretender, he signed papers appointing a new viceroy for Peru.

Philip V's spirit and bravery on the battlefield won the loyalty of his Spanish subjects at all social levels, but the Bourbon cause in Spain looked worse by the day. Queen María Luisa reportedly suggested that they move the seat of the Spanish monarchy to Peru rather than ever concede defeat to the forces arrayed against them, and in the summer of 1710 that seemed more than a remote possibility. In the king's absence from Madrid, and with French troops already gone, the city lay open to attack. The army supporting the Habsburg pretender defeated the king's forces at Zaragoza, in Aragon, on August 20, and before month's end a British army had occupied Madrid. The British would remain there until December 3.[64] By then, however, Louis XIV had decided to reenter the fray, surprised and heartened by the strength of support for the Bourbon cause in Spain. Among other proofs of that support, a long list of Spanish noblemen signed a letter declaring their unshakable loyalty to Philip V that was delivered to Louis XIV at Versailles by the Duke of Alba. By the end of 1710, French officers had helped to reorganize the Bourbon army in Spain, which forced the British to withdraw from Madrid.[65]

Meanwhile, in this atmosphere of crisis and foreign occupation the case against Castelldosrius proceeded. No one in Madrid knew it yet, but fate had already removed the beleaguered viceroy from office. He died in Lima on April 24, 1710, mercifully unaware of his disgrace, at the relatively early age of fifty-nine. At least one contemporary believed that he died as a direct result of the strain caused by the accusations of malfeasance against him, noting that "the presumption remains that these voices cost the life of the Marquis of Castelldosrius."[66] Whether or not that was true, Castelldosrius served more than half his brief tenure as viceroy knowing that serious accusations about his personal and professional behavior had been sent to Madrid; that knowledge must have taken a toll on his general well-being.

Instead of dwelling on his misfortunes, however, Castelldosrius devoted his energies not only to official business but also to an ambitious program of cultural and religious activities in Lima. Less than a month after his enemies sent off the charges against him to the king, Castelldosrius organized a lavish spectacle of music and theater to honor the birth of Prince Luis in Madrid. He wrote the prelude and text himself and had it set to music by Roque Cheruti, the Milanese who directed the palace orchestra.[67] Castelldosrius also presided over regular intellectual gatherings and evening entertainments in which he introduced the literary, musical, and artistic tastes of Europe, especially France, to Lima. The viceroy's cultural program had an invigorating effect on the local cultural elite and earned him the praise and approval that he could not get from the merchant elite. The small circle of home-grown intellectuals who participated in his "academy" compiled two volumes of poetic and literary tributes to the viceroy after his death.[68] Although the academy did not survive him, Peruvian historians often cite Castelldosrius's cultural program as the defining feature of his term in office.

After Castelldosrius's death, the audiencia stepped in as a governing committee for the viceroyalty, just as it had done after Monclova's death. These arrangements followed standard practice. Nonetheless, it meant that the mercantile elite of Lima was in control of the government once again. The sealed orders that had accompanied Castelldosrius to Lima specified an order of succession for an interim viceroy, an appointment that fell to the aged bishop of Quito, the third on the list, because the two men listed above him had died. The bishop took over as interim viceroy on August 30, 1710. Despite his age and infirmities, he would act as viceroy until 1714.

On September 19, 1711, the bishop wrote a report on the previous year's income and expenses. A month later he wrote a revised report noting the lack of available funds and the near impossibility of collecting back taxes because of the lingering effects of the earthquake of 1687 and more recent reversals of fortune. In every particular his analysis echoed the lament that Castelldosrius wrote in 1707, at the start of his tenure. Before his death, Castelldosrius had begun another full accounting of income and expenses. The cost of outfitting the ships that he had sent to Guayaquil after the English privateer raid in May 1709 and other defensive missions dominated the list. The funds he had scraped together to pay for them came from salaries from vacant offices, income that the crown claimed from vacant encomiendas, half the salaries of his corregidores for one year, and a *donativo* (a more or less voluntary contribution) from local residents.[69] The bottom line, confirmed by the bishop of Quito in 1711, was that there was almost no cash on hand in the Viceroyalty of Peru.

The government in Madrid would not receive the bishop's report until 1713, and although they had read Castelldosrius's earlier accounting by then, the king and his ministers retained the bright hope that Peruvian wealth would solve their desperate need for cash if only they could tap into it. They thought they had found the solution in a series of royal decrees levying fees on officeholders in the viceroyalty: a 10 percent tax on salaries; the confiscation of all royal gifts *(mercedes);* and one-third of the value of most rents and offices alienated from the crown, all for 1711.[70] The tap that they devised, in other words, reached directly into the purses of royal officials.

Meanwhile in Cartagena, the remnant of the fleet that had brought Castelldosrius to the viceroyalty in 1706 still had not been able to return to Spain. Almirante Gobernador Villanueva, the ranking Spanish official as long as the fleet remained in port, continued his struggle with the local merchant community and various fleet officials over the use of funds.[71]

In August 1710 Villanueva wrote a full accounting of the monies he had spent, including private funds that had been entrusted to Don José López

Molero, the master of silver on the almiranta, whom Villanueva had ousted from the job of paymaster.[72] To pay for the needs of his fleet, Villanueva requisitioned sixteen boxes of silver that had been stored in the safe in López Molero's lodgings. Four of the boxes, which supposedly contained 3,000 pesos each, instead held only 2,999 pesos. It is not clear whether López Molero had extracted a peso from each box illegally or whether the missing pesos constituted a stewardship fee that he was entitled to deduct. He would have time and opportunity to tell his side of the story when and if the fleet returned to Madrid. In the meantime, Villanueva forced him to make good the shortfall.[73]

Officials on both sides of the Atlantic, from Madrid and Paris to Cartagena and Havana, worried about how to get the remnant of the 1706 fleet home safely. The best hope for achieving that aim lay in arranging for General Ducasse to escort the fleet from Cartagena. The political, financial, and logistical complexities surrounding Ducasse's escort squadron occupied a large swath of the Spanish bureaucracy for several years, beginning in 1708, as we have seen. With the French troop withdrawal in 1709, most of the earlier planning became moot for more than a year. It began again in earnest late in 1710. A royal decree in early November 1710 ordered General Ducasse to go to Cartagena once again with a squadron of three warships *(navíos de guerra)*. He left the French port of Brest in the spring of 1711.

In addition to documents establishing his authority as head of the operation, Ducasse also carried decrees announcing the special taxes on salaries and grants for 1711. Other decrees ordered royal officials in Cartagena to assist Ducasse in every way possible and to spend any available funds in the royal coffers there for his expenses in port and for the return voyage to Spain.[74] As soon as Ducasse dropped anchor in Cartagena, on June 4, he found himself in the middle of the disputes that had been simmering for several years. Most of the officials in Cartagena immediately obeyed the king's decrees. By contrast, Villanueva balked at returning the chests of silver that he had commandeered from López Molero in 1708; it took the personal intervention of Ducasse to gain Villanueva's compliance. Even then, López Molero would later complain that "of the thirty chests of silver [that Villanueva had confiscated from me], each containing 3,000 pesos, only twenty-three were recovered from Villanueva, and they did not all bear my mark."[75]

In Cartagena the taxes and "donations" levied on official salaries and incomes for 1711 were supposed to replenish funds already spent from the Portobelo treasure, but they fell far short of expectations. Governor Zúñiga, already engaged in a bureaucratic tussle with Villanueva over previous expenditures from private funds, continued to plead the case of the local citizenry. Asking the crown's pardon for the laughable sum that he had raised by the donativo from official salaries—1,302 pesos—he blamed the "miserable state of this poor city" and its salaried officials. He then recorded the contributions of each man with pitiable precision.[76] There was no time for further delay, however. Ducasse had his orders and intended to carry them out with a minimum of fuss. An English squadron was patrolling the area, just as it had done in 1708, and Governor Handasyd, in Jamaica, kept himself well informed about Spanish fleet movements. Even with Ducasse in charge, it would take considerable luck to get the remnant of the 1706 fleet home safely.

Several modern writers have published descriptions of the fleet's return, all of them mistaken in a variety of ways. What follows relies on the sworn and notarized testimonies of several witnesses, recorded in Spanish ports. Although, as we might expect, each witness had a unique perspective on the events, the phrasing in all the testimonies inspires confidence for its sober and neutral wording, perhaps influenced by the notaries. In any case, although the testimonies were subject to human weakness, they have the ring of truth.

Ducasse and his squadron did not arrive in Cartagena until June 4, 1711, and the ships were loaded as fast as possible thereafter so that they could leave Cartagena before the worst of the hurricane season. Ducasse sailed on the *San Miguel* as captain general of the squadron. The second ship in his command was the *Hercules*, and the third was the *Grifón*. Francisco de Quijano Ceballos, who represented the Tierra Firme Fleet as master of silver on the *Grifón* in Ducasse's squadron, sent a detailed account of the voyage to Spain.[77] After nightfall on August 5 the fleet left Boca Chica and sailed into the open sea. Besides the three ships in Ducasse's squadron, the fleet included Villanueva's *San Joaquín* and its dispatch ship; a vessel called only the "hulk of Honduras" and its dispatch ship; the *Espidea;* the *Estrella;* and several vessels that the writer identified only by their type and owner: the "hulk of Espeleta," which other witnesses said was called *Santiago;* the "fregata of Fajardo"; and a frigate that Ducasse had sold. The last-mentioned frigate may have served as the dispatch ship for Ducasse's squadron. Although it was a French vessel, it carried a Spanish flag on this occasion and was captained by a man referred to by another witness as Don Pedro Grillao, though this may have been a Hispanicized spelling of a French name.

Through a night of strong winds and seas the three ships in Ducasse's squadron were able to stay together, but morning found the almiranta *San Joaquín* and three other ships downwind and behind them at some distance. Their topsails were lowered, a sign that they were waiting for other ships to catch up, but Ducasse's squadron continued sailing north beyond Punta de Canoa. When they were near land at about 4:00 PM, they saw six sails to windward, five of them large, which they recognized as English warships. Ducasse's squadron then returned to Boca Chica, arriving there after nightfall on August 6. Over the next few days ships from the scattered fleet returned to Boca Chica, all with their masts and rigging severely damaged. The small frigate that Ducasse had sold off reported that the *San Joaquín* had been fighting with the enemy squadron, and the men on the frigate feared that it had been captured, along with the *Espidea*, because they had not heard artillery fire for some time after losing sight of the battle. The "hulk of Honduras" came in separately, but its crew knew nothing about the fate of the other ships. Finally, on the night of August 9, the small frigate of Fajardo arrived with the report that the enemy had indeed captured the almiranta *San Joaquín* and the *Espidea.* The next morning Ducasse and his squadron left Boca Chica again, but this time they sailed alone. They saw another damaged ship heading for Cartagena the next day (August 11)—either the dispatch ship of the Tierra Firme Fleet or the *Estrella*—but they did not turn around.

The English fleet that inflicted the damage, under Commodore Littleton, had obviously aimed its artillery to disable the Spanish ships, not sink them. The English had also let the smaller vessels escape, concentrating on capturing the almiranta *San Joaquín,* which had eluded Commodore Wager in 1708 and whose escape had cost two English captains their command. It was logical to assume that the remainder of the treasure would be carried in the *San Joaquín* when the fleet headed for home. That was standard practice for the Spaniards, and everyone knew it. This time the assumption was wrong. Ducasse and his squadron carried the treasure; the *San Joaquín* carried little more than her crew and its commander, Don Miguel Agustín de Villanueva.

Villanueva had earned a reputation as a skilled naval officer during his early career, but the loss of the *San José* and his inability to bring home the king's treasure had tarnished his name. In the years 1708–11 he had spent most of his time in unproductive disputes with officials in Cartagena. His future held little but reproach if and when he got back to Spain, and he must have known it. Villanueva may have hoped to salvage his reputation by engaging the English once again on the way home; if so, he was not disappointed. On August 7, 1711, he fought five English warships and finally surrendered after acquitting himself well and sustaining serious wounds.[78] The English remained unaware for some time that the *San Joaquín* carried little of value, conveying it to Jamaica in triumph before finding out the truth. Almirante Villanueva would die of his wounds in Port Royal, but he had the satisfaction of knowing that he had contributed to a greater goal. With the English squadron distracted and out of the way temporarily, Ducasse had no adversaries but wind and weather.

Continuing with Quijano Ceballos's testimony, after learning that the *San Joaquín* had been captured, Ducasse's squadron left Cartagena again the morning of August 10, as we have seen. The following day they sighted a ship whose topmasts had been shot away heading for Boca Chica. Because it had railings at the stern, they concluded that it was either the dispatch ship of the Tierra Firme galleons or the *Estrella.* Fighting strong winds and seas, Ducasse's squadron continued northeast toward Santa Marta. After rounding Punta de la Aguja, they headed north for Cabo de Tiburón, at the extreme western edge of Santo Domingo. Instead of going to Havana as expected, however, they sailed northeast between Santo Domingo and Cuba, via what is now known as the Windward Passage. On August 26 they stopped to rest at the French settlement of "Porto Pe" (Port-de-Paix), on the northeast coast of Santo Domingo, taking on water, supplies, and ballast. Presumably the ships had left Cartagena with light loads so that they could travel faster, but they needed proper ballasting to withstand the Atlantic.

The squadron resumed its voyage on September 7, sailing between the islands of Caicos and Mayaguana on the thirteenth with a favorable wind. Although they did not know it yet, the easy part of the voyage was behind them. Still heading northward, they sailed around the north side of Bermuda and continued on with favorable winds, reaching a latitude just short of 39° north.

Then at dawn on September 29, the day of San Miguel—the patron saint of Ducasse's ship—a powerful storm from the east-northeast hit the three ships, and the crews took down all but the mainsails to ride it out. Quijano Ceballos, on the *Grifón*, said that at about 10:00 AM the men on his ship saw one of the other ships, perhaps Ducasse's, upwind but thereafter could see no one. At about 4:30 PM the *Grifón* lost its bowsprit, foremast, and the main and mizzen topmasts, and the remaining masts were in rough shape. The rest of the day the *Grifón* was at the mercy of the storm, while the crew worked frantically to cobble together a serviceable rig. By the next day they had fashioned a bowsprit out of one of the remaining topmasts and managed to put it in place despite the storm. Once the wind died down, the crew used whatever they had on hand to fashion the rest of the rig. September had not ended well.

As Quijano Ceballos tells us, "In this manner we continued our voyage, with the anguish of not coming upon other ships and the fear of losing the foremast we had fashioned, because we had no others."[79] They set a course for Santa María, at the southern end of the Azores, to escape the strong winds and seas at higher latitudes, but the weather did not cooperate, and they were becalmed for a week. Then, with the ship at about 36° north, the wind came up from the southeast, blowing them back up to nearly 40° north. Because they had not seen any of the Azores, they assumed that they had passed through them without knowing exactly how. At last identifying the familiar landmark of Bocayna, on the island of Lanzarote in the Canaries, they set a course for Galicia, in northern Spain. Withstanding more strong contrary winds and high seas, they sailed on "until it pleased God to bring us safely to this port of Pontevedra on the 1st of November."[80]

When they arrived, they learned that the king had levied an additional tax of 12 percent on all the private treasure in the fleet, plus a forced loan of 150,000 pesos. The *Grifón,* as the smallest ship in Ducasse's squadron, carried the least valuables, but it was the first to arrive back in Spain and underwent a rigorous inspection and verification of the cargo and consignments that it carried.[81] In all, the ship carried 1,213,556 pesos subject to the new taxes, plus 42,260 pesos that officials in Cartagena had consigned to the House of Trade and the merchant consulado in Seville.

The two larger ships in Ducasse's squadron—the *San Miguel* and the *Hercules*—did not arrive in Spain until several months later. Although the merchants of Seville were anxious to receive their money, they were averse to unnecessary risks. The consulado wrote to Madrid on February 27, 1712, warning that a fleet of twelve English warships lay in wait near Cabo de Santa María and advising that Ducasse steer a course for Galicia or Vizcaya instead of Andalusia. Fortunately, Ducasse's squadron was already safe in Coruña by February 25, and the happy news reached Seville two weeks later.[82]

Accounting for the treasure carried by Ducasse's squadron and for the taxes levied on private remittances to pay for the squadron generated thousands of sheets of paperwork.[83] The master of silver on the *San Miguel,* López Molero, presumably did not yet know that his nemesis, Almirante Villanueva, had died in Jamaica. He did know, however, that the *San Joaquín* had been captured by the English and that he had arrived back in Spain before Villanueva. Making the most of the opportunity to tell his version of their dispute, as soon as the ship dropped anchor in Coruña López Molero wrote a lengthy report addressed to the Marquis of Risbourcq, who served as the governor and captain general of Galicia.

To paraphrase López Molero, immediately after General Ducasse's arrival in Cartagena de Indias on June 4, 1711, he had sent López Molero two dispatches from the king, both dated April 13, 1709, ordering Villanueva to return all the boxes of silver that he had commandeered. That having no effect, López Molero had taken the second dispatch to the governor of Cartagena, who also failed to gain compliance from Villanueva. Finally, López Molero had appealed to General Ducasse, who succeeded in extracting twenty-three of the thirty boxes of silver from Villanueva.[84] Villanueva had indicated as early as 1708 that he would obey no civilian authority in Cartagena, answering only to the king and to Ducasse, his military superior. It is somewhat surprising that he would not even obey a royal order delivered by civilian authorities. Royal documents were traditionally treated as if they were the king himself. In the end, López Molero recovered twenty-three boxes of silver and had to answer for their contents in his capacity as master of silver even though not all of the boxes bore his mark. In other words, some of the boxes that Villanueva handed over were not the same ones that he had confiscated from López Molero.

The patache of Honduras arrived in Sanlúcar de Barrameda at the same time that Ducasse's *San Miguel* and *Hercules* arrived in Coruña—the end of February 1712. All of the patache's cargo was registered and impounded under lock and key until taxes and ownership could be sorted out. When the funds and cargo consigned to merchants in southern Spain finally arrived from Galicia, they were taxed at a rate of 15.25 percent.[85] Don Joséph Salvador de Mimenza, the captain of the patache of Honduras, testified under oath about the circumstances of his voyage from Cartagena, filling in some of the blanks in testimony by the masters of silver on the *Grifón* and Ducasse's *San Miguel.*

Although he made no accusations, Mimenza's testimony provides a damning indictment of General Ducasse, who seems to have abandoned any pretense of escorting or protecting the convoy almost from the moment it left Cartagena. As other witnesses testified, the full convoy left Cartagena at night on August 5, 1711. By the next morning, Mimenza could see no other ship but the principal dispatch ship of the galleons, so they continued on together, and the next day they were joined by the hulk *Santiago,* owned and captained by Don Juan de Espeleta. The three ships then sailed on to Havana, the standard rendezvous point for Spanish fleets, entering the fortified port on September 1. There they waited for the rest of the convoy and the squadron of General Ducasse, who was supposed to escort them back to Spain. But Ducasse evidently had no intention of going to Havana or of carrying out his escort duties. As the master of silver on the *Grifón* had testified in Pontevedra a few months earlier, Ducasse took his squadron directly through the Windward Passage in the third week of August, going nowhere near Havana.

Mimenza and the men on the other two ships did not know they had been abandoned and continued to wait for Ducasse in Havana. The French frigate that had served as the dispatch ship for Ducasse's squadron soon arrived, flying its Spanish flag, under the command of Don Pedro Grillao. He brought the news that the English had captured the almiranta *San Joaquín* and the *Espidea* and that Ducasse's squadron had returned to Cartagena to take refuge for several days, departing again (on August 10). Grillao had stayed behind to finish repairs to his vessel. Having completed the repairs, he had left Cartagena for Havana, where he had arrived on September 17, evidently expecting Ducasse to be there waiting. Instead, he found only the three Spanish ships that had straggled in from Cartagena, abandoned by Ducasse.

The four ships waited for several more months before deciding to leave Havana on their own, which they did on December 13. No sooner had they left port for the Bahama Channel, however, than Grillao, in the French frigate, changed course and sailed away. The three Spanish ships continued in convoy for five days to the mouth of the channel. At 3:00 or 4:00 AM on the fifth day the *Espeleta*'s hulk fired three shots, indicating a ship in distress. Dawn confirmed the fears of Mimenza and his shipmates: the hulk had run aground at a place called Cabeza de los Mártires on Key Largo. The other two ships went to its aid. Sailing as close as they dared and sending their launches the rest of the way, they were able to rescue the crew of the hulk, twenty-six of whom came on board Mimenza's ship, with the rest boarding the patache of the galleons. They set fire to the wreck before sailing away. Before they made it through the channel the two ships were separated by a storm, and Mimenza did not see the patache again. According to later testimony, the patache ran aground across the Atlantic, on the Portuguese island of Faro, where the whole crew was taken prisoner.[86]

Mimenza's voyage was ultimately more successful, though hardly easy. The passage across the ocean took two months, during which Mimenza and his augmented crew battled winter storms and came close to starvation. Many of their provisions were ruined by incoming seawater during the early storms, and the twenty-six men he had picked up from the wrecked hulk put additional strains on the food and fresh water that remained. Mimenza considered it a "miraculous thing" that they made it safely to Sanlúcar, where they arrived at 9:00 AM on February 20, 1712.[87] Their survival may have been divinely inspired, but their predicament had resulted in large part from Ducasse's callous dereliction of duty.

López Molero's reckoning of the gold, silver, and other valuables carried for the king on Ducasse's *San Miguel* provides much more human drama than do most financial records, largely because of the trials he had undergone in the course of the voyage.[88] Since 1706 López Molero had served as master of silver on the almiranta and as paymaster for the whole armada, dismissed from the latter job by Villanueva in 1710. Because he held a royal appointment as master of silver, however, he remained attached to the almiranta until June 1711 and then followed the king's treasure on board Ducasse's *San Miguel* in the same capacity. In trying to safeguard that treasure he had locked horns with Casa Alegre, Villanueva, and Ducasse, one after another. In his March 1712 accounting in Coruña, López Molero did more than list the amounts he logged in and out, as he was required to do. He also complained at regular intervals about the violence, ill treatment, unauthorized demands for money, and personal indignities he had suffered in the king's name. At one point Villanueva had placed him under guard until he agreed to his demands. At another point he had had to take refuge in the Convent of La Merced in Cartagena, only to be pursued by Villanueva's men inside the convent and forced to give up his keys to the strongroom on board the almiranta.

López Molero's accounts help to explain why Ducasse's *San Miguel* and *Hercules* reached Spain months after the *Grifón*, the third ship in Ducasse's squadron. As we have seen, after the storm on September 29 scattered the three ships, the crew of the *Grifón*, with Quijano Ceballos on board as master of silver for the Tierra Firme Fleet, patched their ship back together and sailed it safely to Pontevedra, arriving on November 1. Ducasse might have been expected to do the same. Instead he turned around and took the *San Miguel* and the *Hercules* to the island of Martinica, in the Lesser Antilles, where the French had established a strong presence and where he had financial interests. There they spent the rest of the fall and early winter, not leaving for Spain until late January 1712.

López Molero makes no mention of Martinica in his prose version of the homebound voyage. In his accounts he merely enters expenses incurred in the Bahía de San Pedro (now St. Pierre) on January 13, 1712, and elsewhere he mentions expenses on Martinica.[89] Philip V of Spain may have considered Ducasse's services well worth the price, but he cannot have been pleased to learn why Ducasse took so long to bring home the treasure he needed for the war. The crews on the ships that Ducasse abandoned in Cartagena and again in Havana presumably took even harsher views. In short, Ducasse had behaved far more like the pirate and planter he had once been than the celebrated general he had become. From López Molero's reticence we can surmise that he did not want to be blamed for the sojourn on Martinica or for any of Ducasse's other failings.

López Molero spent considerable time in Coruña compiling the summary accounts that accompanied his official registers (see appendix 2). Like the other masters of silver in the fleet, López Molero created a register entry *(partida)* for each payment for the crown *(cargo)* loaded on the ship before each sailing; he also recorded the amounts paid out *(data)* at various times. He presumably created a similar set of accounts for private sums of money and other valuables entrusted to his care, and he kept both registers with him during the voyage. Keeping careful records ensured that he could hand over the money and other items to their rightful owners in Spain and file summary accounts and narrative reports with the government for the official portion. That was the essence of his job.

In accounts written in Portobelo on May 25, 1708, López Molero recorded shipments for the king that came under his stewardship as the fleet prepared to depart for Cartagena. Following standard practice in Spanish fleets, the *San Joaquín* would have carried exactly half the total, or as close to half as the masters of silver could arrange. The other half would have been loaded on the capitana *San José*, with Don Juan Martín de Isasi as her master of silver. Like López Molero, Isasi would have made an entry in his registers for every category of revenue and nonmonetary tribute entrusted to him for the crown. López Molero left no doubt that the king's treasure had been divided as equally as possible between the capitana *San José* and the almiranta *San Joaquín*. As he stated with regard to the miscellaneous revenues, he had received the amount listed—half the total—"as master [of silver] of the galleon almiranta, because the remaining half was lost on the capitana that sank on the coasts of Cartagena, of which the said Don Juan Martín de Isasi was master [of silver]."[90]

Before the Tierra Firme Fleet sailed to Portobelo for the fair, both masters of silver recorded many promissory notes that General Casa Alegre had written from 1706 to 1708, while the fleet remained in Cartagena. They also paid various bills—under protest—with monies on hand that were supposed to be used for other purposes. Once the fleet collected the king's revenues in Portobelo, they planned to restore the misused funds, pay other outstanding bills, and tidy up their books. As López Molero noted, he and Isasi "celebrated being able to reintegrate upon returning from Portobelo the various effects that have entered under our control as masters of silver, from the avería tax as well as from other sources."[91] But the *San José* never returned from Portobelo. When the ship sank on June 8, 1708, it took half the king's treasure, Don Juan Martín de Isasi, and all of his paperwork to the bottom of the sea. Three years after the battle that sank the *San José,* López Molero recorded various sums collected in Cartagena before Ducasse's squadron and the remnant of the fleet finally left Cartagena for Spain. Those sums, and what remained from the treasure loaded on the almiranta *San Joaquín* in Portobelo on May 25, 1708, arrived with Ducasse in Coruña early in 1712 on the *San Miguel.*

How much treasure sank with the *San José?* In the absence of Isasi's books it is difficult to know for sure. We do, however, have a precise accounting of the royal treasure registered on the *San Joaquín.* López Molero listed the principal elements of that treasure in numbered entries in his accounts (see appendix 2). In all, when she left Portobelo the *San Joaquín* carried 547,755.2 pesos for the crown—equal to some 4.4 million silver reals, using the standard equivalent of 8 reals to a peso. López Molero noted as well various small boxes and pouches of pearls and emeralds, which represented the royal fifth of those items, plus some uncoined gold and silver, but he did not place a monetary value on those items. This added an unknown but potentially substantial amount to the value of the king's treasure loaded in Portobelo. If we assume that the *San José* carried virtually the same amount of the king's treasure as the *San Joaquín,* the total for both ships was 1,095,510.4 pesos, or the equivalent of 8.8 million silver reals. Commodore Wager wrote to London on April 13, 1708, "It is said that the king's money is ready to be shipped off [from Portobelo] and that it amounts to eleven millions of pieces of eight."[92] Wager's sources thus estimated the Spanish king's treasure to be worth at least ten times its actual value, or perhaps they simply mistook reals for pesos. In any case, the legend of the *San José* had begun even before she sank.

Of the total funds entrusted to him for the crown, López Molero was able to hand over to the Marquis of Risbourcq in Coruña only 215,648.9 pesos, about 39 percent of the money loaded on the *San Joaquín* in Portobelo. The additional tribute payments in gold, pearls, and emeralds were not evaluated in the accounts. The dilemma facing López Molero in 1712 was how to explain why so little of the king's treasure reached Spain. López Molero's accounts describe in great detail when, where, and how the rest of the money had been spent. One after another, General Casa Alegre, Almirante Villanueva, and General Ducasse had forced López Molero and Isasi to record promissory notes and dip into the royal coffers to pay for the repair and provisioning of their ships, as we have seen. The handsome sum that Viceroy Castelldosrius sent down to Portobelo from Peru was reduced considerably to pay off those debts. More money flowed out during stops in Port-de-Paix and St. Pierre for the two ships from Ducasse's squadron that detoured to Martinica. The bottom line was that much of the king's treasure was spent before reaching Europe.

Once the incoming royal treasure and additional taxes on private shipments had been tallied and accounted for in Coruña, the Marquis of Risbourcq converted nearly all of it to gold doubloons, worth 60 reals each, and sent it to Madrid by overland couriers. By late June 1712 the equivalent of 1,148,883 pesos had arrived in the capital.[93] The Tierra Firme Fleet sent out in 1706 was supposed to fetch from Peru substantial royal revenues, accumulated for several years. Instead, when the remnant of the fleet returned in 1712 the crown received the equivalent of less than one year's income in the Viceroyalty of Peru, and that was only because the crown levied a heavy additional tax on the private shipments arriving in Coruña.[94] López Molero filed revised accounts in Madrid in late September 1712, at which point officials noted that "the irregularity of the voyage and the various expenses attached to the revenues" meant that the accounts were not yet complete. After various minor additions and corrections, they declared the accounts for the king's treasure concluded (*fenecido*) at the end of April 1717.[95]

The great unknown is how much private treasure in gold, silver, and other valuables the *San José* and the *San Joaquín* carried when they left Portobelo. Merchants, investors, landowners, and the other private citizens and public officials whose treasure was on board undoubtedly registered some of what they carried, and some of them may have registered all of it. Many of the merchants' sealed chests and boxes were exempt from inspection, however, as Villanueva noted in Cartagena. Those who did not enjoy exemptions can be assumed to have brought in at least some of their wealth unregistered and deliberately hidden to avoid paying taxes.

To combat this suspected fraud, the crown levied additional taxes on private shipments of treasure, but in attempting to collect those taxes royal officials ran into a major obstacle in the shape of López Molero, who would not turn over his registers. Though he presumably handed over private shipments to their owners or consignees once the *San Miguel* arrived in Coruña, he did not file "the letters of payment for the register entries of private individuals, either in the city of Portobelo or in the city of Cartagena, which he was obliged to conduct and bring to these Kingdoms of Spain." He must have kept records of the amounts entrusted to him, because their owners would have insisted upon it. At some point, however, he seems to have decided to withhold that information from the crown. It makes sense to conclude that the owners of private treasure, individually or together, had made it worth his while to do so. That part of the accounting was still pending in 1733, long after the war of succession had ended, when a newly appointed fiscal of the Council of the Indies tried to revive the investigation into López Molero's blatant breach of procedures.[96]

As for the private treasure that went down with the *San José*, Villanueva's estimate for the *San Joaquín* can serve as a plausible proxy. As we have seen, Villanueva thought that his ship carried "from 8 to 9 million" pesos' worth of private treasure when it left Portobelo;[97] it also carried the 775,805 pesos that represented half the revenues for the king.[98] Assuming that both royal revenues and private treasure had been divided as equally as possible between the two principal ships in the fleet, the *San José* presumably sank with from 9 million to 9.75 million pesos' worth of gold and silver coins, plus gold and silver objects and unworked metal, pearls, and gems.

In addition to the losses on the *San José*, the aftermath of the battle forced bureaucrats in Madrid to realize that the wealth of Peru was more legendary than real from the crown's standpoint. Private wealth related to Peru, however, could still rise to impressive heights for the merchant elite in Lima and the mining interests in Potosí, or at least that was the supposition in Madrid. The crown's inability to tap into that wealth because of tax evasion was a source of continual frustration and anger at court. Public officials who knew how to benefit from their offices had been making their fortunes in Peru for two centuries. For example, the Count of La Monclova, Castelldosrius's predecessor as viceroy of Peru, reportedly left an estate worth 14 million pesos,[99] more than twelve times what Ducasse brought back for the crown in 1712. The residencia that followed Monclova's term in office found nothing but praise for him among the leading citizens of Peru, no doubt because of his merits but perhaps also because he did not meddle excessively in their affairs.[100]

The inventory made after Castelldosrius's death in 1710 listed possessions with a total value close to 29,000 pesos, including jewels given to him by the kings of Portugal and France, other valuable goods, and six black slaves.[101] The income from Castelldosrius's estates in Catalonia was worth about 2,500 pesos a year, far less than the family needed to live, and his salary as viceroy had been about 60,000 pesos a year.[102] He had earned every peso of that salary, but he had also alienated much of the mercantile elite in the process. One reason for their wrath was presumably the close interest he took in their affairs and his forceful moves to reduce the shocking level of tax evasion for mining production.[103] His controversial but effective program of taxing illicit commerce added fuel to the fire.

The case fabricated against Castelldosrius by his enemies continued to grind on long after his death. His son, Antonio, had died fighting for Philip V at the battle of Zaragoza on August 20, 1710, leaving Antonio's sister, Catalina, to champion their father's honor. After the news of Castelldosrius's death reached Madrid, the standard investigation (residencia) of his term in office superseded the earlier inquiry based on the charges made against him and gaining added weight from them. As the residencia proceeded in Peru from 1712 to 1716, it became clear that Castelldosrius had supporters as well as enemies in the viceroyalty. The official outcome *(sentencia)* of the investigation, dated October 24, 1716, in Lima, exonerated Castelldosrius on all charges. The Audiencia of Lima duly certified and registered the result on November 3, 1717. On June 21, 1720, five large bundles of paperwork reached the desk of the fiscal of the Council of the Indies in Madrid. The government reviewed and confirmed the sentence on February 14, 1722, with full exoneration and praise for Castelldosrius.[104] By then, of course, he had been dead for nearly twelve years, and the war of succession had ended with the throne of Spain secured for the young man whom Castelldosrius had honored at Versailles as the first Bourbon king of Spain.

The bureaucratic consequences of the battle of Cartagena lasted long years afterward, as merchants, shipowners, naval commanders, and ordinary seamen and their families exercised their legal rights to compensation. Some of the most poignant claims emanated from the survivors of the *San José* and the families of the men who were lost when she sank, providing a rare glimpse into the hard lives of seafarers. In late November 1714, more than a year and a half after the war of succession ended, King Philip issued an edict calling on "all of the seamen and infantrymen who served in the most recent galleons under the command of the Count of Casa Alegre to appear in person or through representatives in the court [i.e., Madrid] to certify their identity and the amount of money owed for their service."[105] The edict, sent by the Council of the Indies to Seville, Cádiz, and other ports, gave the claimants two months to present their proofs in Madrid; if they failed to do so, they would forfeit all claims.

The situation was more complicated than the edict acknowledged, however. Don Francisco de Varas y Valdés, the official in charge of the inquiry in the southwest, wrote to Madrid on December 9 asking for a relaxation of the edict's

requirements in the interests of justice and compassion. His posting and proclamation of the edict in Cádiz and Puerto de Santa María had, he said,

> motivated various women to present themselves to me, some widows of those
> who were shipwrecked and drowned on the voyage, and others daughters of
> officials and gunners who experienced the same fate; and having notified them
> that they must remit their powers [of attorney in Madrid] to certify their iden-
> tities and the duration of the service of their husbands and fathers, [I realized
> that] the need and misery from which they suffer is so great that it is not pos-
> sible for them to do this; and feeling sympathy upon seeing such great difficulty,
> I find it necessary to present to the superior consideration of the Council [of the
> Indies] the possibility [of allowing] them to prove their identities in [Cádiz
> instead of in Madrid]. Otherwise they will be left without the consolation and
> relief that His Majesty deigned to give to the others who served on the occasion
> of the said Galleons.

Adding to the difficulty, some men who were owed wages could not present
their proofs in Madrid because they were serving on royal ships elsewhere.
Varas y Valdés mentioned two of the men by name. In 1714 Andrés Fajardo,
formerly the contramaestre on the almiranta *San Joaquín,* held that same post
on the royal ship *San Fernando,* stationed in Barcelona. And Gabriel Leonardo,
currently guardián on the *San Fernando,* had been a gunner on the gobierno
captured by the English in 1708. Varas y Valdés used them as examples of the
"many others who are currently found on [other ships stationed] along the Le-
vantine coasts, for which reason they cannot appear in [Madrid] during the assigned time; and since it is very appropriate to His Majesty's mercy to attend
to those who are currently in his service, these poor people should not be prej-
udiced by their absence." Varas y Valdés evidently expected the crown to grant
his request, because he had already collected documentation from the petitioners in Cádiz to send along with his letter. The Council of the Indies agreed
to all of his requests in a meeting on Christmas Day, 1714.

By early January 1715 the royal secretary had made a preliminary listing of
those who had filed declarations and proofs of their identities. The final version was drawn up in mid-May. Only 105 of the nearly 600 who died on the
San José were named on the final list, and almost half of them (47) had been
soldiers. Soldiers and their families tended to be identified with regiments and
other military units that retained an administrative identity, even though the
men serving in each unit changed over time. Perhaps their heirs learned about
the royal proclamation by way of the units in which their deceased relatives

had served. The rest of the men who died on the *San José*—sailors above all— also left heirs, but they may not have heard about the need to file a formal claim.

For the most part, the claimants represented people from society's lowest ranks, although the official records refer to all of them with the Spanish honorific *Don* or *Doña*. In earlier centuries, only those who enjoyed noble status would have been so honored, but over time the honorifics came to be used generally to indicate respect and respectability. As family members of those who had died serving the crown, they deserved that respect, but in life their husbands, sons, and brothers would not have been referred to as *Don* unless their birth or position merited such distinction. The highest-ranking petitioner, Doña Ana Altamirano, widow of the admiral Don Sebastián de Xijón, would have enjoyed the honorific regardless of her tragic circumstances. Her late husband had sailed on the *San José* as the captain of sea and war and the captain of the *maestranza*, the collectivity of workmen who carried out ship construction and repairs. Doña Ana lost not only her husband but also their son Pedro. He had no job title in the listing, and it is possible that he had embarked as his father's page, which was traditional for the young sons of distinguished fathers who went to sea.

The heirs of the chief pilot on the *San José*, Roque de Fuentes, also applied for benefits. Doña María González Barúa filed the paperwork as tutor and caretaker for Fuentes's younger sons, her nephews. If we can rely on common family relationships and naming practices for the early eighteenth century, her late sister had been Fuentes's wife and the mother of his sons. As we have seen, Fuentes started out as the chief pilot on the almiranta *San Joaquín*, where he clashed with Almirante Villanueva during the sortie to Gibraltar in 1704. He moved to the *San José* in August 1706 after the death of her first pilot, Captain Benito Alonso Barroso. Although the shift represented a promotion for Fuentes and relieved him of working with Villanueva, it turned out to have been a fatal assignment.

Widows accounted for 50 of the 105 claims filed for the men of the *San José*. One poor woman suffered the extreme ill fortune of losing three men in her family in the disaster. Doña Luisa Tomasa del Toro, of Puerto de Santa María, was married to Joseph Sánchez Quintos, who had served as the contramaestre on the *San José*. Her sons Salvador and Francisco Sánchez del Toro had served as gunners. Doña Luisa and another son, Don Diego Sánchez del Toro, an infantry lieutenant, filed the first batch of paperwork claiming the wages earned by her husband and sons on December 19th, 1708, right after the news of the disaster first reached Spain. In all, the crown owed the family 5,786 reals for the men's labor, a sizeable sum.

Doña Luisa must have been aware of the difficulties in collecting wages from the crown and perhaps hoped that an early petition would have a better chance of success. In the event, no one was paid until several years later, and Doña Luisa first had to file notarized proofs of her marriage to Joseph Sánchez Quintos and the baptisms of their legitimate sons Salvador and Francisco. Several witnesses also had to testify as to her identity and to the fact that neither of her sons had a wife or family, who might have better claims to their wages. She and her son Diego had the various documents drawn up in Cádiz, with dates that stretch from 1708 to the end of March 1716.

Besides Doña Luisa, thirty-seven mothers and two fathers filed petitions to collect the wages earned by sons who had died on the *San José*. Doña Polonia de Herrera was the mother of Doctor Don Antonio Augustín de Acosta, chaplain on the *San José*. The title *doctor* indicated that he held a university doctoral degree, presumably in theology or canon law, given his occupation. Don Antonio had begun the voyage in 1706 as chaplain on *Nuestra Señora de la Almudena*, which served as the dispatch ship of the fleet. He had moved to the *San José* in June 1707, a promotion that presumably made his mother proud. Another mother, Doña Mariana de Segovia, filed for benefits based on the service of her son Domingo Allen, a simple sailor. His surname suggests that father may have been a foreigner, perhaps one of the many Irish Catholics who found their way into the Spanish navy in those days. Other mothers and fathers had watched their sons go to sea as sailors, apprentices, and pages or as gunners, soldiers, and musketeers. Now they shared the same grief, though not necessarily the same fate.

One of the most heartrending stories came from Inés Garbanzo, whose brother Joseph, probably in his teens or early twenties, had been an apprentice seaman on the *San José*. Inés told the notary that she and her brother had been "orphaned of father and mother," suggesting that his death had left her quite alone to face an uncertain future. Whatever monies the crown might provide would be small compensation for her loss.

All but one of the petitioners claimed to have lost someone in the tragic sinking of the *San José*. The exception was Doña Sebastiana García, the wife of Bartolomé Ydalgo, an experienced soldier, who was paid a bonus each month because of his experience. His wife told the notary that he was "one of those who escaped during the battle" and was currently living in Cartagena de Indias. Whether or not her information was correct, Bartolomé had not come home, so she petitioned the crown for the wages owed to him. Only his death would give her the right to claim those wages, however. In the event, despite Doña Sebastiana's testimony, the documents recorded that her husband Bartolomé had died during the battle on June 8, 1708. Royal officials may have ascertained and recorded the truth of the matter, or they may simply have declared him legally dead so as to clear the way for his abandoned spouse to collect his wages.

In addition to the few survivors from the *San José* and the heirs of those who did not survive, thousands of men in the Tierra Firme Fleet of 1706 had experienced the "difficulties . . . in such an extended trip, as much in the encounters and battles that they had with the enemy, as in the imprisonment and loss of their property." The crown issued an order on January 8, 1715, that these men were to be paid one-third of what was owed them, presumably hoping to reach a conclusion in the matter of claims. The men were not so easily fobbed off, however. To collect the rest, they filed a collective petition in May that included men up and down the chain of command—"the captains, higher and lower officials, and other seamen and infantry who served on the galleons under the command of the general, Count of Casa Alegre."

The petitioners for the thousands of veterans of the fleet also included the heirs of men who had died while in service and who had already petitioned for payment without success. Choosing their moment carefully, the petitioners waited until the New Spain Fleet of Don Antonio Chaves was due to arrive and asked the crown to set aside funds from that fleet to pay the rest of their claims. According to their reckoning, 132,859 silver reals would cover the final two-thirds of the money owed to those who had filed claims.[106] That was a small fraction of the total unpaid wages for the veterans of the 1706 Tierra Firme Fleet. Official records indicate that the men on the *San José* alone had earned nearly 500,000 reals in wages up to June 8, 1708. They had collected less than 52,000 reals before the ship went down, with the rest still owed. Eight years later they had not yet been paid in full for their service, and it is not clear if they ever were.

Postscript

Three hundred years after the loss of the *San José* the historical record allows us to confront the legend about the ship and its cargo that has drifted into modern times. We began with Gabriel García Márquez's evocation of the shipwreck off Cartagena and my comment that virtually all of the details it contains are false. Let us look at the passage again with that comment in mind:

> Several times a year, fleets of galleons carrying the treasures of Potosí, Quito, and Veracruz gathered in the bay, and the city lived its years of glory. On Friday, June 8, 1708, at four o'clock in the afternoon, the galleon *San José* set sail for Cádiz with a cargo of precious stones and metals valued at five hundred billion *pesos* in the currency of the day; it was sunk by an English squadron at the entrance to the port, and two long centuries later it had not yet been salvaged. That treasure lying in its bed of coral, and the corpse of the commander floating sideways on the bridge, were evoked by historians as an emblem of the city drowned in memories.[1]

The harbor of Cartagena de Indias, as important as it was, did not host fleets of galleons several times a year, even in its heyday in the late sixteenth century. Instead, if all went well, once a year a squadron of galleons would escort a fleet of merchant vessels from Spain to Cartagena and elsewhere in Tierra Firme. Most of the merchandise brought to Cartagena would then be taken to Portobelo, in Panama. There, in a brief but intense fair, merchants would exchange silver and gold from the rich mines of the Viceroyalty of Peru for the goods brought from Europe. Representatives of the Spanish crown would collect taxes at the fair and also take charge of revenues brought from the Viceroyalty of Peru, which included most of South America in those days. After the Portobelo fair, the merchants would take the goods they had purchased back to Peru, and the Tierra Firme Fleet would return to Cartagena before sailing on to Havana on the first leg of its return to Spain. The New Spain Fleet would generally sail to Havana as well, coming from Veracruz on the Mexican coast. Together the two fleets would sail home from Havana. In other words, the Veracruz contingent did not visit Cartagena at all but followed its own circuit to and from Spain.

In the late seventeenth century the traditional rhythm of the fleets broke down, shattered by international warfare and financial uncertainty. When the *San José* left Spain for Cartagena in 1706, it was the flagship of the first fleet to Tierra Firme in a decade, and it remained in Cartagena for two years before a fair could be arranged in Portobelo. When that fair ended in late May 1708, the *San José* and its fleet left Portobelo for Cartagena. An English squadron had been patrolling the area for months, waiting for the Tierra Firme Fleet to make that journey and expecting it to be laden with money and other treasure from the Portobelo fair belonging to the Spanish crown and private parties. In the battle that took place on June 8 the *San José* sank at about 7:30 PM near the entrance to Cartagena's harbor. It is not clear whether English guns caused the catastrophic chain of events that sank the *San José;* that was surely not the intention of the English commander. Nonetheless, she sank, along with her officers and nearly all of her crew. The treasure she carried—mostly gold and silver, plus some pearls, gems, and other valuables—was probably worth somewhere in the neighborhood of 10 million pesos in the money of the time, not the half-billion García Márquez mentioned in his Spanish original ("medio millón de millones"), and certainly not 500 billion, which was the translator's error. Nonetheless, the gross exaggeration of the value of the *San José*'s cargo fits well with modern popular memories of her loss.

The *San José*'s fate, embellished by visions of her valuable cargo, has come down through the ages to lure treasure hunters. A well-publicized attempt to locate and claim the ship and her cargo was chronicled early in 1989 in a Sunday magazine called *West,* published by the *San José Mercury News* in California.[2] According to the article, a consortium of treasure hunters and investors spent $10–12 million in the late 1970s and early 1980s trying to find the wreck. Where she lies remains the subject of much speculation; it is certainly close to the city of Cartagena, though not at the entrance to the port. Trumping the claims of treasure hunters, the governments of Colombia and Spain have also claimed the wreck and continue to argue about it in the courts.

Many other governments are also interested in laws governing the salvage of lost state vessels. For example, the United States recently weighed in on the subject in a presidential statement of January 19, 2001:

Pursuant to the property clause of Article IV of the Constitution, the United States retains title indefinitely to its sunken State craft unless title has been abandoned or transferred in the manner Congress authorized or directed. The United States recognizes the rule of international law that title to foreign sunken State craft may be transferred or abandoned only in accordance with the law of the foreign flag State.

Further, the United States recognizes that title to a United States or foreign sunken State craft, wherever located, is not extinguished by passage of time, regardless of when such sunken State craft was lost at sea.[3]

In other words, the United States supports the notion that a sunken state warship remains the property of that state, regardless of where or when it sank, unless the state specifically relinquishes that right. Spain holds that same position in general and in the specific case of the *San José*, which sank nearly three hundred years ago. The government of Colombia disagrees, claiming territorial rights to shipwrecks off its coast. Only time will tell how the courts resolve the issue. In the interests of historic preservation, however, public authorities of some sort should retain control of the *San José* and all other historic shipwrecks so as to prevent their indiscriminate salvage by private parties.

The dramatic story of the *San José* remains peculiar in the annals of maritime history because popular memory preserved it, while serious history largely forgot about it. This book is an attempt to redress that imbalance and bring the *San José*, her officers, and her crew back to life—not only as a chapter in maritime history but as a memorial to an important vessel and the nearly six hundred men who died when she was lost. Whether or not the wreck of the *San José* is ever found, and whatever the value of her cargo, the men and the ship herself constitute the real historical treasure of the *San José*. Their lives and their deaths provide a glimpse into the Spanish world that bridged the Atlantic Ocean three centuries ago and helped to shape the modern global context for trade and international rivalry. The legacy of Spain's Atlantic world also shapes the present, in which popular memory and history continue their struggle for supremacy.

The Spanish and English Calendars in 1708

In the late sixteenth century, calculations commissioned by Pope Gregory XIII found that the Julian calendar had resulted in an accumulated error of ten days over the centuries. To correct this, the new, Gregorian calendar, instituted in 1582, designated October 5 as October 15 in that year.

Spain, France, Italy, Portugal, and Luxembourg immediately adopted the new calendar. The Holy Roman Empire and other states soon followed. England, however, retained the Julian calendar officially until 1752, and many English documents used it until 1800. We must therefore convert dates mentioned in English documents after October 4, 1582, to make them comparable to dates in the Gregorian calendar. The general rule is to add ten days to English dates from October 5, 1582, through February 2, 1700, and eleven days to English dates from February 2, 1700, through February 28, 1800.

For the purposes of the battle that sank the *San José* in 1708, the conversion is complicated because English ships' logs generally ran from noon to noon, and Spanish logs generally ran from dawn to dawn. To be sure that the standard conversion is accurate for discussions of the battle, it is necessary to find points of direct comparison between Spanish and English dates and days of the week. On the English side, Christopher Pearson, the master of the *Portland*, noted in his log that the Spanish galleons had left Portobelo on a Monday, and other English log entries used the same days of the week that Pearson used. Several Spanish witnesses also say that the galleons left Portobelo on a Monday, giving the date as May 28. In other words, both English and Spanish witnesses coincided in their designation of the days of the week, though they differed in how they numbered the days of the month. Several Spanish witnesses state that June 9, 1708, was a Saturday and that June 11 was a Monday. This would make the battle on June 8 fall on a Friday, although no Spanish report of the battle combines the date with the day of the week. English logs dated the battle Friday, May 28, 1708. These points of comparison verify that the standard conversion is accurate for discussions of the battle. I have therefore added eleven days to all of the dates mentioned in English documents, and to minimize confusion, I have indicated those changes in the text.

Treasure Registered on the San Joaquín in 1712

Account and sworn statement of Don José López Molero, master of silver on the almiranta
San Joaquín *and later on the capitana of the squadron of General Jean-Baptiste Ducasse.*
Excerpted from the accounts of José López Molero, dated 14 March 1712, Archivo General de
Indias, Seville, Contaduría, leg. 582, fols. 625–34. The full accounting appears on fols. 625–67.

Sums Received [*Cargo*] in Portobelo in April and May of 1708, and thereafter:

No. 1—Salaries—Firstly, I took charge of three hundred and twenty-six thousand, nine hundred and ninety-six *pesos escudos** and four reals of silver, for which I authorized an entry
in the register on the twelfth of April of 1708, in favor of His Majesty, from royal financial officials in the city of Portobelo, . . . pertaining to salaries for the ministers of the Royal
Council of the Indies, which I obligated myself to hand over to the President and Judges
of the House of Trade of the city of Seville. . . ;   326,996 pesos, 4 reals

No. 2—Income from the lodging house—Item: I took charge of ten thousand, six hundred
and one pesos escudos and one-half real of silver that the said royal officials handed over
to me on the said day [i.e., 12 April 1708], pertaining to the lodging house, to hand over to
the said House of Trade. . . ;   10,601 pesos, 1/2 real

No. 3—Royal Treasure—Item, I took charge of twenty-two thousand, one hundred and sixty-
one pesos escudos and six reals of silver that on the thirteenth of said month [April] and
year the said royal officials of Portobelo handed over to me pertaining to the royal treasure and remitted from the city of San Francisco de Quito to send to the said House of
Trade. . . ;   22,161 pesos, 6 reals

No. 4—Goods from deceased persons of Quito [who died without heirs]—Item, I took charge
of two thousand, five hundred and eighty-five pesos escudos and half a real of silver, which

*The *peso escudo de plata* mentioned in these accounts was equivalent to the *peso de a ocho reales*
(lit., piece of eight reals, or "piece of eight") at the time these accounts were written. The preliminary version (Archivio General de Indias, Seville, Contaduría, leg. 582, no. 1, fols. 1–7) listed the
amounts as pesos, whereas the full account listed them as pesos escudos. According to Lea, *History
of the Inquisition of Spain,* 1:561–62, "The peso, escudo de plata, or piece of 8 reales, was the leading coin, and in 1726 it was ordered that it, whether minted in the Indies or in Spain, should be current for 9½ reales, and, as this did not bring it to an equivalent with gold, in 1728 it was declared
equal to 10 reales." The full text of Lea is available in electronic form at http://libro.uca.edu/
lea1/append3.htm.

the said royal officials of Portobelo handed over to me on the said day, proceeding from the goods of deceased persons in the city of San Francisco de Quito, to hand over to the House of Trade...;   2,585 pesos, 1/2 real

No. 5—Goods from deceased persons in Lima [who died without heirs]—Item, I took charge of three thousand, eight hundred and forty-three pesos escudos and three reals of silver, which the said royal officials of Portobelo handed over to me on the said day, proceeding from the goods of deceased persons remitted from the city of Lima, to hand over to the said House of Trade...;   3,843 pesos, 3 reals

No. 6—Cruzada tax—Item, I took charge of thirty thousand, five hundred and sixty-one pesos escudos and one real of silver, which on the twenty-fourth of the said month and year the said royal officials of Portobelo handed over to me, pertaining to the receipts from the Holy Crusade tax, to hand over to the aforesaid House of Trade...;   30,561 pesos, 1 real

No. 7—Royal Treasure—Item, I took charge of one hundred and three thousand, seven hundred and eighty-four pesos escudos and five reals of silver that on the said day the same officials handed over to me, pertaining to the royal treasure, to hand over to the said House of Trade...;   103,784 pesos, 5 reals

No. 8—Fine from the merchants of Seville—Item, I took charge of thirty thousand pesos escudos of silver, which on the twenty-sixth of the said month of April of 1708 the aforesaid royal officials of Portobelo handed over to me via the hand of the deputies of the merchant community of Seville: Don Antonio Rodríguez Cortés, Don Juan Martín de Ysasi, and Don Francisco de Quijano Cevallos, which proceeded from the avería tax on the fine levied on "illicit commerce," to hand over to the aforesaid House of Trade...;

30,000 pesos

No. 9—5% levied on the salaries of officials in Tierra Firme—Item, I took charge of one thousand, nine hundred and thirty-two pesos escudos and seven and a half reals of silver, which on the fifth of May of the said year of 'seven hundred and eight the same royal officials of Portobelo handed over to me, pertaining to the five percent [tax levied] on the salaries of the realm of Tierra Firme, to hand over to the said House of Trade...;

1,932 pesos, 7½ reals

No. 10—From the merchant community of Peru—Item, I took charge of fifteen thousand, two hundred and eighty-eight pesos escudos, six reals and one-quarter, which is what remained in cash in my power from the fifty thousand pesos that on the fourteenth of the said month of May and the said year of seven hundred and eight the aforesaid royal officials of Portobelo handed over to me via the hand of the commissaries of the merchant community of Peru: Don Juan Estevan de Muñarriz and Don Joseph de Meneses; from which the Count of Casa Alegre, using his power and authority as Captain General of the city of Portobelo, entered into and took from my house with violence thirty-four thousand, seven hundred eleven pesos escudos, one real and three-quarters in silver, in closed boxes, of three thousand pesos each one, and the rest in cloth pouches [*talegos*], saying that was equal to the total authorized by royal decree for the careening in Spain that he had given to the galleon *San José*, the *capitana* under his authority, which action he carried out unreasonably upon the departure of the Armada in his command, without giving me any written receipt for my records for what he had done. All of which, as is publicly and well known, I testified to in the city of Cartagena de las Indias, before the Almirante Governador Don Miguel Agustín de Villanueva, and his auditor, General Don Alonso de la Cueva Ponce de León, and Juan de Castro Soria, Principal Scrivener of the said Armada of galleons; of which acts I have remitted an exact copy in testimony to His Majesty and the Royal Council of the Indies; by virtue of which the said fifty thousand pesos was reduced by the said thirty-four thousand, seven hundred and eleven pesos escudos, one real and three-quarters in silver, the remaining cash in my power being the sum mentioned at the start of this entry. . . ;   15,288 pesos, 6¼ reals

No. 11—Tribute of gold and pearls—Item, I took charge of different tribute payments of gold and pearls in the city of San Felipe de Portobelo that were given me by Don Joseph Gómez de los Helgueros, legal resident of Panama, so as to hand them over, by way of the hand of the President and Judicial officials of the House of Trade of Seville, to His Majesty (whom God preserve), according to the circumstances that are contained in the entry in the register that I authorized to those who remitted [them] to me. And because the remittance was in the aforesaid species, I left the value blank in the [credit and debit portions of the register]. . . ;   0

More items received, from the registry and declarations of Cartagena:

No. 12—Salaries and Lodging Houses—Item [July 28, 1711], I took charge of gold valued at seven hundred and forty-one pesos escudos and two reals of silver, which the royal financial officials of the city of Cartagena de las Indias handed over to me, pertaining to the salaries of ministers and [income from] the lodging house; as well as five hundred and ninety-eight pesos' worth of emeralds of second quality; one thousand and nine hundred pesos and four reals' worth of said emeralds of third quality; the one batch and the other being contained in a small sealed pouch marked with the number 1.

In addition, in a small box labeled number 2, eighty-six pesos and two reals of silver worth of emeralds of second quality; five hundred and twenty pesos and four reals' worth of emeralds of third quality, which come in a striped pouch of rough cloth, sealed; a small bar of silver and one hundred and seventy-three pesos and five reals' worth of gold dust, in a small pouch labeled number 3. And all has to be turned over to the current or future General Treasurer of the Royal and Supreme Council of the Indies, and taken together, the three items received are valued at seven hundred and forty-one pesos and two reals in money; and the rest of what was handed over of the said items received were not given a value and therefore were entered as a blank in the register. . . ;   741 pesos, 2 reals

No. 13—Gift from Santa Marta—Item [July 28, 1711], I took charge of two thousand, nine hundred and eighty-six pesos escudos and two reals of silver, which the said royal officials of Cartagena handed over to me, pertaining to the "gift" [*donativo*] of [the town of] Santa Marta, to hand over to the Treasurer of the Royal Council of the Indies, for which I [signed] three receipts of the same tenor. . . ;   2,986 pesos, 2 reals

No. 14—Taxes for the ministers of the Royal Council—Item [July 28, 1711], I took charge of three hundred and sixty-eight pesos escudos, four reals and three-quarters of silver that the same royal officials of Cartagena handed over to me, pertaining to the taxes of the Relator, the Scrivener of the Chamber, and the Fiscal Agent of the said Royal Council of the Indies, to hand over to the aforesaid treasurer, for which I signed three receipts of the same tenor. . . ;   368 pesos, 4¾ reals

No. 15—Salaries and Lodging House—Item [July 28, 1711], I took charge of fifteen thousand, one hundred and sixty-five pesos escudos, seven reals and one-quarter of silver that the aforesaid royal officials of Cartagena handed over to me, pertaining to salaries and income from lodging houses of the ministers of the Royal Council of the Indies, to hand over to their treasurer, for which I authorized three receipts of the same tenor. . . ;

15,165 pesos, 7¼ reals

No. 16—Confiscations and contraband—Item [July 28, 1711], I took charge of one thousand, eight hundred and fifteen pesos escudos and one-half real of silver that were handed over to me in cash by the same royal officials of Cartagena, and also a small bar and a small piece of gold [*oro de ley*] of nineteen carats and one grain, with one hundred and thirty-one *castellanos* in one small pouch numbered 3; all of it proceeding from confiscations and contraband, to hand over to the said treasurer of the Council of the Indies, for which I signed three receipts of the same tenor, pertaining only to the cash in reals, leaving blank the value of the [uncoined] gold. . . ;

1,815 pesos, ½ real

No. 17—10% of the salaries of the ministers—Item [July 28, 1711], I took charge of eight hundred and sixty-five pesos escudos and two reals of silver, which the aforesaid royal officials of Cartagena handed over to me, pertaining to the ten percent [tax on the] salaries of ministers, to hand over to the treasurer of the Council of the Indies, for which I signed three receipts of the same tenor. . . ;

865 pesos, 2 reals

No. 18—The fine from Spain—Item [July 28, 1711], I took charge of sixty-one thousand, eight hundred and seventy pesos escudos, one real and a half of silver that the said royal financial officials of Cartagena handed over to me, which was received from the deputies of the merchant community of Spain, proceeding from the contribution for the fine [*indulto*] of the galleons and fleet of Tierra Firme, under the command of the [Captain] General the Count of Casa Alegre, to hand over to the treasurer of the Royal Council of the Indies, for which I signed three receipts of the same tenor. . . ;

61,870 pesos, 1½ reals

No. 19—Gift [*donativo*] of the Archbishop and town council of Santa Fe—Item [July 24, 1711], I took charge of two thousand, seven hundred and thirty-four pesos escudos of silver that were handed over to me in the city of Cartagena de Indias by the Reverend Father Rector of the Company of Jesus, Francisco Javier y Opolo: of which one thousand, seven hundred and thirty-four pesos were remitted by the Most Illustrious Archbishop of Santa Fe, as a gift given to His Majesty; and the one thousand remaining pesos were remitted by the Venerable Dean and chapter of the holy church of the said city for the same purpose of a gift to His Majesty; consigned to the Prior and Consuls of the city of Seville, to hold pending orders of His Majesty, as is referred to in the entry in the register that I authorized on July 24, 1711, before Ignacio Sánchez de Mora, Public Scrivener and scrivener for the registers of the city of Cartagena.

2,734 pesos

No. 20—Avería tax from Santa Fe—Item, I took charge of two thousand, eight hundred and twenty-six pesos escudos, three reals and one-quarter of silver that the royal financial officials of the aforesaid city of Cartagena handed over to me, pertaining to the avería tax of the merchant community of Santa Fe, as stated in the register entry that I authorized on the 28th of July of the year 1711, before the aforesaid scrivener Ignacio Sánchez de Mora, to hand over to the President and Judges of the House of Trade in Seville. . . ;

2,826 pesos, 3¼ reals

No. 21—Gift from Mompox—Item, I took charge of two thousand pesos escudos of silver that
were also handed over to me by the aforesaid royal officials of Cartagena, proceeding from
the gift from Mompox, to hand over to the Prior and Consuls of the city of Seville, to hold
pending orders from His Majesty. . . ;   2,000 pesos

No. 22—Gift from the clergy of Cartagena—Item, I took charge of four hundred pesos escudos that I received from Doctor Don Lorenzo Gutiérrez de Figueroa, Maestre Escuela of
the holy cathedral of Cartagena, its Provisor, Vicar General, and Governor of its bishopric,
. . . proceeding from the gift collected from the ecclesiastics of the said city, by virtue of a
royal decree, to hand over to the President and Judges of the House of Trade of Seville, in
fulfillment of the orders that His Majesty gave them, as indicated in the entry in the register that I authorized on the 29th of the said month of July and the year of 1711, before
the aforesaid scrivener Ignacio Sánchez de Mora. . . ;   400 pesos

So that the twenty-two entries of items in my charge that have been described in detail here
total six hundred and thirty-nine thousand, five hundred and twenty-eight pesos escudos
and one real of silver, exclusive of what is contained in entry number 11, whose value is
left blank; [and] number 12 and 16, [which are] in other species that are not reals and which
are noted in their own species in the payouts for this account and sworn statement. . . ;

639,528 pesos, 1 real

Introduction

An earlier version of segments of this chapter previously appeared in Phillips, "Galleon *San José*."

1. García Márquez, *Love in the Time of Cholera,* 18. The sum of money mentioned in the English edition appears to be a mistranslation of the Spanish. The phrase "medio million de milloues de pesos" should be translated as "half a billion pesos," not "five hundred billion pesos."

2. See the Web site "Archivos Españoles en Red," sponsored by Spain's Ministry of Culture, http://aer.mcu.es. On some PC computer brands the Microsoft Web browser does not work with the search features inside the AER.

3. For example, Kamen, *War of Succession in Spain,* contains a thoroughly researched chapter, "The Wealth of the Indies," that deals in part with the treasure carried by the fleet for which the *San José* served as flagship.

One • The Last Galleons

An earlier version of segments of this chapter first appeared in Phillips, "Galleon *San José*"; and idem, "Galleons."

1. The Dutch used the word *Galjoen* to refer to the beakhead, a forward-thrusting projection below the bowsprit at the prow, but not for the ship type as a whole.

2. For more extensive discussion of the galleon and its evolution, see Phillips, "Galleons."

3. Scholars generally agree that the codo measured 557–75 millimeters, but they disagree about its precise dimensions. The definition used here is based on the *quarto de codo* depicted at the end of the regulations printed in 1618, which measured exactly 5.25 inches. AGM, Caja Fuerte, 134.

4. See the discussion of measurement and ship construction in Phillips, *Six Galleons,* 57–65. See also idem, "Spanish Ship Measurements Reconsidered."

5. "Ordenanzas expedidas por el Rey en Madrid a 21 de Diziembre de 1607, para la fábrica de los navíos de guerra y mercante, y para la orden que se había de observar en el arquea-

miento de los que se tomasen a particulares para servicio de las Armadas Reales," in Fernández Navarrete, *Colección*, vol. 23, pt. 1, doc. 47, p. 587.

6. Ibid.

7. The 1607 rules are published in Fernández Navarrete, *Colección*, vol. 23, pt. 1, doc. 47, pp. 575–93. An original printed version of the 1618 rules is in AGM, Caja Fuerte, 134.

8. Rubio Serrano, *Arquitectura de las naos y galeones*. The author analyzes most of the printed and manuscript treatises regarding ship design over a period of two centuries, and his work remains the definitive work on ship design from a theoretical perspective.

9. Ibid., 2:142.

10. AGM, Colección Vargas Ponce, XVII, doc. 262.

11. AGI, IG, leg. 2740, fols. 323–29.

12. Rubio Serrano, *Arquitectura de las naos y galeones*, 2:143–45.

13. AGI, IG, leg. 2740, fols. 368–72, 384–86, 426.

14. "Recopilación," AGM, MS 1690. Garrote's overview of the relative merits of Spanish and foreign shipbuilding come from the introduction, fols. 1r–11v. Twenty-four chapters then discuss various elements of ships and rigging (fols. 12r–62v), followed by a collection of illustrations.

15. Ibid., fols. 6r–11v.

16. Manera Regueyra, "La época de Felipe V y Fernando VI," 172.

17. *Antonio de Gaztañeta (1656–1728)*, 74.

18. AGI, IG, leg. 2740, fols. 130–33, 585–87.

19. See, e.g., Segovia Salas, "Hundimiento del 'San José,'" 22–23.

20. Phillips, *Six Galleons*, 23.

21. AGI, IG, leg. 2740, fol. 165r–v.

22. Ibid., fols. 474–77.

23. Gaztañeta, *Arte de fabricar reales*.

24. Gaztañeta, *Norte de la navegación*.

25. AGI, IG, leg. 2740, fols. 231–32.

26. Ibid., fols. 452v–497v, tracks the proposed measurements from Gaztañeta to subsequent deliberations on the north coast.

27. Ibid., fol. 475v. The full report of their meeting and the reasoning behind their adjustments to Gaztañeta's measures appear on fols. 474r–477v.

28. Ibid., fols. 478–80.

29. Ibid., fols. 508r–510v.

30. Packet of memoranda compiled by Antonio de Retana, the royal notary for matters of war in San Sebastián, in ibid., fols. 513–15.

31. Ibid., fols. 519v–521r.

32. Ibid., fols. 517–19.

33. Ibid., fols. 531–32, 517–19, 502–3, 513–15, 521–23.

34. Ibid., fols. 533r–v, 534v–543r.

35. Ibid., fols. 457v–467r, esp. fol. 459; 475v–477r; 508–9.

36. Ibid., fols. 550–51. The document was dated Madrid, 6 December 1697.

37. Ibid., fol. 552r–v.

38. Ibid., fols. 561r–562v, quotation from fol. 561v.

39. Ibid., fols. 555v–556v.

40. The various reports appear in ibid., fols. 554r–562v. Necolalde's report was dated 3 January 1698. Valladarías's report was dated 7 January 1697, but that must have been a slip of the pen. Both reports were addressed to Don Antonio de Ubilla y Medina, secretary of the Council of War in Madrid.

41. Ibid., fols. 565–68.

42. AGS, Guerra Antigua, leg. 3904.

43. Ibid.

44. AGI, IG, leg. 2740, fols. 261–70.

45. Ibid., fols. 578r–581v.

46. Black, "Love and Marriage in the Spanish Empire," 637.

47. My thanks to Javier de Solís, the current Count of Casa Alegre, for pointing out this fascinating possibility.

48. AGI, IG, leg. 2740, fols. 574–75, 600–630.

49. Ibid., fols. 430–1032. Documents related to the naval stores and munitions supplied by Hubrechtz take up much of the *legajo*.

50. Ibid., fols. 588–90.

51. Ibid., fols. 591–93, 595r–v, 594.

52. Callahan, *Honor, Commerce, and Industry*, 19, identifies Goyeneche as a royal treasurer and supplier to the navy. It appears that in this instance he acted as a private financier.

53. AGI, IG, leg. 2740, fol. 629.

54. Ibid., fols. 629r–643v, includes all the lists and Necolalde's cover letter.

55. Experienced ship carpenters earned 8 reals a day in 1702. Ibid., leg. 2560.

56. Ibid., leg. 2740, fols. 649–50.

57. Ibid.

Two • Commanders of the Fleet

1. For the family's complete genealogy, see Carraffa and Carraffa, *Diccionario heráldico y genealógico*, 83:58–63.

2. AHN, OM, catalog 13, p. 127, assigns him number 3019.

3. Domínguez Ortiz, *Golden Age of Spain*, 112–19.

4. Don Javier de Solís, the current Count of Casa Alegre, kindly provided information about Don José's family and early career from the family archive, including documentation for the year of his birth.

5. Document provided from the family archive by the current Count of Casa Alegre, Don Javier de Solís.

6. AGI, ESC, leg. 1166B.

7. AHN, OM, Expedientillos, no. 14148.

8. Ibid.

9. AGI, IG, leg. 2605. The 60,000 pesos, paid in coins of eight and four silver reals, was equivalent to 16,320,000 maravedis, at the rate of 272 maravedis per peso.

10. Ibid., documents from March through May 1681.

11. Unless otherwise noted, documents related to the careening are in AGI, IG, leg. 2605, dated November 1685–June 1686.

12. A copy of the 1674 instructions for captains general of Spanish fleets, including matters of precedence, appears in AGI, IG, leg. 2605.

13. Ibid., documents dated April–May 1687.

14. Unless otherwise noted, all documentation for the 1687–88 fleet is in AGI, IG, leg. 2605.

15. Two fine analytical studies of piracy are Ritchie, *Captain Kidd;* and Lane, *Pillaging the Empire.*

16. ". . . siendo el celo con que e solisitado cumplir con la obligazion en que me constituio la onrra que V. M. me hizo en la confianza desta flota mui ygual al esfuerzo con que me dedicare a conseguir que V.M. se de por servido de mi afecto y desvelo en que estare asta llegar a ponerme a los Rls Pies de V. M." AGI, IG, 2605, letter from Veracruz dated 22 September 1687.

17. I have found neither a reply to the secretary's note nor the diary itself.

18. AGI, IG, leg. 2605, letter of 21 September 1687, written aboard *Nuestra Señora de las Mercedes.*

19. Evidence from the inspection appears in AGI, ESC, legs. 1166A and 1166B. The final sentence is located in ibid., leg. 969.

20. This "second voyage as General of the Galleons" was scheduled to follow the voyage promised to Don Pedro Carrillo. AGI, IG, leg. 2607.

21. García Fuentes, *Comercio español,* 159–66. The book as a whole provides an exhaustive analysis of all the Indies fleets in the late seventeenth century.

22. Ibid., 163.

23. *Elenco de grandezas,* 751.

24. Walker, *Spanish Politics and Imperial Trade,* 23–24.

25. AGI, IG, leg. 2560. Don Javier de Solís, the current Count of Casa Alegre, generously provided me with his extensive notes and transcriptions from this legajo, which contains invaluable material about the early career of Don José Fernández de Santillán, the first Count of Casa Alegre, and his association with the *San José.* Solís's planned biography of the first count will provide a far more detailed discussion of his life and career than can be included here.

26. Ibid., documents from late May and early June 1702. Both sums were paid in *reales de plata antigua* (lit., reals of old silver), presumably to distinguish them from the coins devalued in 1680.

27. Hattendorf, *England in the War of the Spanish Succession,* 105–6.

28. AGI, IG, leg. 2560, Martín Pérez de Segura, president of the House of Trade, Sanlúcar de Barrameda, to King Philip, 27 August 1702.

29. AGI, IG, leg. 2560.

30. Ibid., Pérez de Segura to the king, 27 August 1702.

31. Ibid., Don José Fernández de Santillán, Cádiz, to Domingo López Calo de Mondragón, 10 September 1702.

32. Ibid., 17 and 25 September 1702.

33. Ibid., Don Francisco de San Millán y Ceballos, Cádiz, to Calo Mondragón, 1 October 1702.

34. Kamen, *War of Succession in Spain*, 180.

35. Ibid., 179–80.

36. AGI, IG, leg. 2560, documents from June and July 1703. Unless otherwise noted, information about the fleet's sojourn in Cádiz comes from these documents.

37. Ibid., documents from September 1703. Unless otherwise noted, information about the fleet's careening appears in letters and accounts from September–November 1703.

38. *Elenco de grandezas*, 203.

39. Detailed information about Admiral Rooke's fleet and armament can be found in BL, Addit. MSS 19029, fols. 90v–91v.

40. Hattendorf, *England in the War of the Spanish Succession*, 45, quoting the Lord Treasurer Godolphin to Richard Hill, 15 August 1704, BL, Addit. MSS 37529, fol. 57. Reports of the Council of War on board HMS *Royal Katherine*, 17 July 1704, come from BL, Addit. MSS 5440, fol. 197.

41. Hattendorf, *England in the War of the Spanish Succession*, 110.

42. AGI, CT, leg. 3216, 4170A.

43. Ibid., leg. 4170A.

44. AHN, OM, Expedientillos, no. 4295.

45. AGI, IG, leg. 2607, document dated Plasencia, 17 April 1704; AHN, OM, Expedientillos, no. 6381.

46. García Fuentes, *Comercio español*, 173.

47. In the sixteenth century, the patache de la Margarita was usually a small swift vessel, the common meaning of the word *patache*. Later, one of the eight galleons from the guard squadron of the Indies was periodically assigned the task of visiting the island of Margarita and patrolling the Venezuelan coast, leading to the confusing designation of a war galleon as a patache. AGI, IG, leg. 2607.

48. An escudo was worth 10 reals, 1 real less than a ducado.

49. Villanueva noted that he had prepared the *Begoña* so thoroughly that it was readied in a mere six days for Garrote's voyage, at a cost of less than 8,000 pesos. AGI, IG, leg. 2607, printed petition from 1704. Unless otherwise noted, documentation for Don Miguel Agustín de Villanueva's activities from 1700 to 1706 appears in that same legajo, which is unfoliated.

50. The council noted that each would cost 46,000 pesos to careen and outfit. Villanueva countered that all of the principal ships considered for the fleet would cost at least 40,000 pesos to careen and outfit, and a few would cost upwards of 50,000. Ibid.

51. AHN, OM, Expedientillos, no. 6381.

52. Ibid., no. 6380.

53. Veitia Linage, *Norte de la contratación*.

54. Unless otherwise noted, material related to Fuentes's complaint is from the document dated 5 February 1705 in AGI, IG, leg. 2607.

55. Unless otherwise noted, information about the career of Don Nicolás de la Rosa is from a printed document dated 23 March 1705 and inserted into ibid., leg. 2713.

56. Testimony about the incident appears in AGI, CT, leg. 132.

57. In the sixteenth century the word *bozal* would have denoted a newly arrived slave who did not yet know Castilian. By the early eighteenth century the meaning seems to have changed, as the witness obviously knew Castilian.

58. Printed document dated 23 March 1705 and inserted into AGI, IG, leg. 2713. Don Diego made his comments in a certification dated 8 December 1698.

59. Atienza y Navajas, *Nobiliario español,* 994.

Three • The Men of the San José

1. Unless otherwise noted, all documents related to the selection of a captain of sea and war for the *San José* are in AGI, IG, leg. 2607.

2. AGI, CD, leg. 578, crew lists compiled in 1716.

3. AGI, IG, leg. 2607, letter of 26 September 1705 from the Duke of Atrisco: "por no contener calidad ni condición alguna, sino haverseles conferido estos empleos lisa[mente] y llanam[ent]e."

4. A summary listing of the service records of the crew is located in AGI, CD, leg. 578. Documents for their service up to 1705 appear in AGI, CT, leg. 4927A.

5. Phillips, *Six Galleons,* tables on 238–40.

6. See ibid., 146–49, for a discussion of the infantry companies in the Armada de la Guardia in the seventeenth century.

7. See the discussion of relations between soldiers and sailors in Phillips, *Six Galleons,* chapter titled "Officers and Men," 119–51.

8. Unless otherwise noted, all information about the *San José*'s infantry regiment is from official accounts for the monies owned them, dated 12 January 1715 (AGI, IG, leg. 2719) and 19 October 1720 (AGI, CD, leg. 578).

9. For the social costs of seventeenth-century warfare in Spain, see White, "Los tercios en España."

10. The four men were Tomás Acevedo, Andrés Carmona, Pedro Garay, and Sebastián Guerrero.

11. See the tables of comparative pay scales in Phillips, *Six Galleons,* 237–40.

12. AGI, CT, leg. 3216.

13. A ducado was worth 11 reals, and an escudo was worth 10 reals. Both ducados and escudos were monies of account in the early eighteenth century. The actual wages were paid in silver or copper reals.

14. Phillips, *Six Galleons,* 140–41.

15. Documents listing the high officials of the fleet appear in AGI, CD, leg. 579B.

16. See Phillips, *Six Galleons,* 129–34, for the role and training of pilots. 17. AGI, IG, leg. 2560, document dated 15 March 1705.

18. AGI, CT, legs. 4159, 4162, 4165.

19. See Phillips, *Six Galleons,* 126–29, for the evolution of the master's role over time.

20. "Diálogo entre un vizcaíno y un montañés."

21. In the official scale of wages for the Armada of the Ocean Sea in 1633 a diver earned 66 reals per month, the same as a gunner or minor officer. Phillips, *Six Galleons,* 238.

22. See, e.g., Pérez-Mallaína Bueno, *Spain's Men of the Sea,* 57–59.

23. See ibid., 75–79, for discussion of the ages and duties of sailors, apprentices, and pages in the sixteenth century; and Phillips, *Six Galleons,* 140–44, for the same in the seventeenth

century. These patterns remained remarkably unchanged as long as large sailing ships dominated the world's oceans.

24. Pérez-Mallaína Bueno, *Spain's Men of the Sea*, 55–60.

25. According to Phillips, *Six Galleons*, 143, the number of apprentices was about three-fourths the number of sailors.

26. AGI, CT, leg. 4170A, document dated Cádiz, Dec. 7, 1705.

27. Ibid.

28. AGI, IG, leg. 2607.

Four • *A Tale of Two Viceroys, One Captain General, and a World at War*

1. Brading and Cross, "Colonial Silver Mining"; Garner, "Long-Term Silver Mining Trends"; Zulawski, "Wages, Ore Sharing, and Peasant Agriculture."

2. For collected articles on mining production in the Americas as a whole, see Bakewell, *Mines of Silver and Gold.*

3. See Espinoza Soriano, *Virreinato peruano;* and, for a later period, Descola, *Daily Life in Colonial Peru.*

4. Cook, *Numeración general.*

5. Frézier, *Voyage to the South Sea*, 218–19.

6. See Lane, *Pillaging the Empire;* and Haring, *Buccaneers in the West Indies.*

7. "Proclamation of putting this country in readyness and posture of defense against the attempts of an enemy," signed 7 July 1701 by Francis Nicholson, lieutenant governor of Virginia, Egerton Family Papers, record 2103, Huntington Library, San Marino, CA.

8. Buendia, *Parentación real.*

9. For the basic outlines of Melchor Portocarrero's career, see Carraffa and Carraffa, *Diccionario heráldico y genealógico*, 74:26–55. Artola, *Enciclopedia de historia de España*, 4:580–81, erroneously lists Portocarrero's birth year as 1636.

10. Hanke, *Virreyes españoles*, 154.

11. The review *(residencia)* of his tenure in New Spain appears in AGI, ESC, leg. 229C.

12. AGI, CT, leg. 5450, nos. 3–4 (1688).

13. Frézier, *Voyage to the South Sea*, 196.

14. Espinoza Soriano, *Virreinato peruano*, 157.

15. William Hacke, "A Wagoner of the South Sea: describing the sea coast from Acapulco to Albemarle Isle" manuscript in the National Maritime Museum, London. I used a microform copy in the Huntington Library.

16. Pérez-Mallaína Bueno and Torres Ramírez, *Armada del Mar del Sur*, 71–73.

17. Hanke, *Virreyes españoles*, 154.

18. See, e.g., Dedieu, "Procesos y redes."

19. See Suárez, *Comercio y fraude en el Perú colonial.*

20. Hanke, *Virreyes españoles*, 154. See also E. W. Dahlgren's classic *Relations commerciales.*

21. Lohmann Villena, *Historia marítima del Peru*, 4:239–40.

22. AGI, Lima, leg. 407, Monclova to the king, 8 October 1704. Unless otherwise noted, information about the corsairs comes from this source.

23. Lohmann Villena, *Historia marítima del Perú*, 4:239–40.

24. AGI, Lima, leg. 407, Monclova to the king, 8 October 1704.

25. Ibid.

26. Walker, *Spanish Politics and Imperial Trade*, 36–38, citing Scelle, *La traite negrière*, 2:147.

27. Carraffa and Carraffa, *Diccionario heráldico y genealógico*, 74:53–54.

28. Walker, *Spanish Politics and Imperial Trade*, 23–24.

29. Cespedes del Castillo, "Defensa militar del istmo de Panamá."

30. Céspedes del Castillo, *Lima y Buenos Aires*, 1.

31. Pérez-Mallaína Bueno and Torres Ramírez, *Armada del Mar del Sur*, 237.

32. Carraffa and Carraffa, *Diccionario heráldico y genealógico*, 64:134–37, 84:57–64; Atienza y Navajas, *Nobiliario español*, 586–87.

33. Ballesteros Gaibrois, introduction, 17–18.

34. For a good overview of Castelldosrius's life, see Castan i Ranch, "Nobleza y poder."

35. Ibid., 268.

36. The National Archive of Catalonia, in Barcelona, holds extensive documentation related to the family's estates and the personal histories of the titleholders. See the catalog *Inventari dels fons*.

37. This was the start of what is usually called the "War of the League of Augsburg," or the "Nine Years' War," which lasted from 1688 to 1697 and involved areas as dispersed as North America and India, as well as Europe.

38. Castan i Ranch, "Nobleza y poder," 269–72.

39. Dampier, *New Voyage round the World*, 30.

40. Palacios Preciado, *Trata de negros*, 7–19.

41. For the evolution of the city's defenses, see Segovia Salas, *Fortificaciones de Cartagena*. The best description of Cartagena and its environs in English from a military point of view is Harding, *Amphibious Warfare in the Eighteenth Century*, 93–95.

42. Pointis, *Monsieur de Pointi's Expedition to Cartagena*.

43. Ibid., 34–36.

44. Castan i Ranch, "Nobleza y poder," 268–69.

45. Saint-Simon, *Memoires*, 1:678–79.

46. Ibid., 1:762.

47. See Charles II of Spain, *Testamento de Carlos II*, esp. 45–77.

48. Saint-Simon, *Memoires*, 1:785–99.

49. Ibid., 1:800, 1206n1. Voltaire attributed the remark to Louis himself, and many historians have followed his lead.

50. Ibid., 1:814.

51. Ibid., 1:1193n, says simply, "He became viceroy of Peru and died very rich."

52. AGI, Lima, leg. 407.

53. AGI, ESC, leg. 548A, fols. 259r–260v.

54. Vargas Ugarte, *Historia general del Perú*, 74.

55. Walker, *Spanish Politics and Imperial Trade*, 45, citing Scelle, *La traite negrière*, 2:428; charges against Castelldosrius in 1709, in Saénz-Rico Urbino, "Acusaciones contra el virrey del Perú."

56. Dahlgren, *Relations commerciales;* Lohmann Villena, "Cuadernillo de noticias"; Moreyra y Paz Soldán, *Tribunal,* vol. 1; Castan i Ranch, "Nobleza y poder"; Saénz-Rico Urbino, "Acusaciones contra el virrey del Perú"; Villalobos, *Comercio y contrabando;* idem, *Comercio y la crisis colonial;* idem, "Contrabando francés en el Pacífico."

57. AGI, ESC, legs. 548A, 548B, 549A, 549B, 549C.

58. A detailed but negative discussion of Castelldosrius in Peru appears in Walker, *Spanish Politics and Imperial Trade,* 34–49.

59. AGI, CT, leg. 4170A.

60. Unless otherwise noted, all information and quotations regarding Castelldosrius's efforts to reach Portobelo are from AGI, Lima, leg. 407.

61. Letters to and from Casa Alegre are dated beginning in April 1706, as soon as the fleet arrived in Cartagena. Casa Alegre's principal letter to the king, running to twelve folios, is dated 15 May.

62. Moreyra y Paz Soldán, *Tribunal,* 1:39–41.

63. Ibid., 1:41–43.

64. Frézier, *Voyage to the South Sea,* 220–21.

65. Pérez Mallaína Bueno and Torres Ramírez, *Armada del Mar del Sur,* 23–24, citing AGI, Lima, leg. 89, Portocarrero to the king, 1 June 1690.

66. Quoted in Walker, *Spanish Politics and Imperial Trade,* 37.

67. AGI, ESC, leg. 548.

68. AGI, IG, leg. 2720, Castelldosrius to the king, 31 August 1707, translated and quoted in Walker, *Spanish Politics and Imperial Trade,* 40.

69. Pérez-Mallaína Bueno and Torres Ramírez, *Armada del Mar del Sur,* 159–71. See Moreyra y Paz Soldán, *Tribunal,* 1:98–190, for documents related to renegotiating the contract.

70. AGI, Lima, leg. 408, Castelldosrius to the king, 15 December 1707.

71. Walker, *Spanish Politics and Imperial Trade,* 41–42.

72. AGI, Lima, leg. 408, the king to Castelldosrius, 8 February 1710.

73. AGI, Lima, legs. 408, 409.

74. Dahlgren, *Relations commerciales,* 397–98 and 397n.

75. AGI, IG, leg. 432, L.46, fols. 14–43.

76. Ibid., fols. 48–80, contains copies of the order to Casa Alegre.

77. Ibid., fols. 89r–109v.

78. AGI, Santa Fe, leg. 322, no. 12, fols. 92–97, and no. 80, fols. 746r–749v.

79. AGI, ESC, leg. 969.

80. See copies of Casa Alegre's letters in AGI, IG, leg. 2610.

81. AGI, ESC, leg. 1179B.

82. AGI, CD, leg. 578. Unless otherwise noted, information about the men of the *San José* comes from this source.

83. AGI, IG, leg. 2607.

84. AGI, Lima, leg. 408, Castelldosrius to the king, 19 December 1707.

85. Ibid.

86. AGI, Lima, leg. 408; AGI, Santa Fe, leg. 293, fols. 866r–868v.

87. Pérez-Mallaína Bueno and Torres Ramírez, *Armada del Mar del Sur,* 161–66.

88. *Relación de las prevenciones.* See also Dahlgren, *Relations commerciales,* 416–19. Lohmann Villena, *Historia marítima del Perú,* 4:337, mentions that *L'Aimable* arrived in Peru in May 1708 but says nothing about its mission.

89. Alsedo y Herrera, *Aviso histórico,* 235.

90. Walker, *Spanish Politics and Imperial Trade,* 47–48.

Five • *The Last Voyage of the* San José

1. AGI, CT, leg. 2734. I am grateful to Eugene Lyon for directing my attention to this account.

2. Spanish documentation for the fleet appears in AGI, IG, legs. 2609 and 2610.

3. Burchett, *Complete History,* 707.

4. *London Gazette,* 2–5 August 1708, reporting on a dispatch from Jamaica dated 17 June 1708 in the English calendar (see appendix 1 for a discussion of the differing calendars used by Spain and England in the period).

5. Burchett, *Complete History,* 707.

6. Lorenzo Sanz, *Comercio de España con América,* 2:142–46.

7. Kamen, *War of Succession in Spain,* 181–82.

8. Pérez-Mallaína Bueno, *Política naval,* 48, citing AGI, IG, leg. 2637; PRO, *Calendar of State Papers, Colonial Series, America and West Indies, June 1708–1709,* 40.

9. Burchett, *Complete History,* 707.

10. English documents render this as *La Mieta,* as if it were the ship's name. See, e.g., PRO, *Calendar of State Papers, Colonial Series, America and West Indies, June 1708–1709,* 40.

11. *Dictionary of National Biography,* s.v. "Wager, Charles," provides the number of guns for the first three ships but none for the fire ship. A Frenchman who escaped from English captivity reported that the fire ship had thirty-four guns, at least while it was patrolling the coast. AGI, Santa Fe, leg. 293, fol. 902. The guns presumably would have been removed before the battle so that the fire ship could be used as a floating torch.

12. Zúñiga held the ranks of maestre del campo and general, and as governor he was the highest civilian official in Cartagena. He also served as captain general unless a fleet was in port, in which case its captain general took over his military functions.

13. AGI, Santa Fe, leg. 293, fol. 902, testimony of Don Pedro García de Asarta, the captain of sea and war on the almiranta (hereafter García de Asarta).

14. The Spanish witness used the word *balandra,* which meant a small vessel with one deck and one mast, usually translated as "sloop."

15. British Admiralty charts online, www.bluewaterweb.com/nauticalcharts/prodpages/b1278.htm; chart 1278 shows the area from Isla Fuerte to Cabo de Tiburón.

16. AGI, Santa Fe, leg. 293, fol. 902 (García de Asarta).

17. AGI, IG, leg. 2609, fols. 254r–255r, from the testimony of Don Laureano Ximénez Moreno (hereafter Ximénez).

18. Ibid., fols. 220v–221v.

19. AGI, Santa Fe, leg. 293, fols. 869r–873v, Don Francisco Medina (hereafter Medina), Cartagena, to Don Bernardo Tinajero de la Escalera (royal fiscal of the Council of the Indies

in Madrid), 22 July 1708. Unless otherwise noted, Medina's story of the battle and events leading up to it comes from this document.

20. AGI, IG, leg. 2609, fols. 134v–136r, testimony of Don Joséph Canis de Alzamora (hereafter Canis).

21. Ibid., fol. 222r–v, testimony of Don Pedro de Fuentes.

22. Ibid., fols. 222v–223r.

23. Ibid., fols. 232r–233r, testimony of Don Pedro de Medranda (hereafter Medranda). The quoted phrase was presumably taken as a flippant adaptation of the old refrain "Castile is broad, and many are its paths."

24. Ibid., fols. 224r–225v, testimony of Don Martín de Zamudio de las Infantas (hereafter Zamudio).

25. Ibid., leg. 2610, fols. 723v–724v (Zúñiga).

26. Ibid., leg. 2609, fol. 229v, testimony of Josép Alzamora Ursino (hereafter Alzamora).

27. Ibid., fol. 237v, testimony of Josép Múñoz de la Trinidad.

28. Ibid., fol. 239v, testimony of Don Francisco Serrano de Reina y Céspedes (hereafter Serrano). Nicto's vessel is generally identified as a merchant urca, or hulk. Serrano may have called it a navío, or warship, because it had been armed and manned for combat in 1708.

29. Ibid., fol. 250r–v, testimony of Esteban Trave (hereafter Trave).

30. AGI, Santa Fe, leg. 293, fol. 884. Governor Zúñiga summarized Villanueva's letter in AGI, IG, leg. 2610, fols. 704v–705v.

31. AGI, IG, leg. 2609, fols. 136r–137r (Canis).

32. Ibid., fol. 260r–v, testimony of Antonio Hernández Rom.

33. Ibid., fol. 250v (Trave).

34. Lieutenant James Thornton, on the English ship *Kingston*, 22 July 1708 (hereafter Thornton), said there were fourteen ships in all. PRO, ADM 1/5267. When necessary for clarity, the spelling, punctuation, and capitalization in the English log entries have been modernized. Burchett, *Complete History*, 705–6, noted other English testimony that the Spanish fleet included seventeen ships when it encountered the English.

35. AGI, IG, leg. 2609, fols. 233r–234v (Medranda).

36. See English reports of Spanish fleet movements, as well as English consultations in Port Royal, Jamaica, in BL, Addit. MSS 61583, fols. 73a–76b.

37. AGI, Santa Fe, leg. 293, fol. 902v (García de Asarta).

38. PRO, ADM 51/4294, log of Edward Windsor, captain of the *Portland* (hereafter Windsor), and ADM 52/257, log of Christopher Pearson, master of the *Portland* (hereafter Pearson), 9–20 May (Spanish calendar).

39. AGI, Santa Fe, leg. 293, fol. 903v (García de Asarta).

40. Ibid., fol. 904 (García de Asarta).

41. PRO, ADM 51/4294 (Windsor), log for 24 May (4 June).

42. PRO, ADM 51/4233, log of Timothy Bridge, captain of the *Kingston* (hereafter Bridge), for 23 May (3 June).

43. AGI, IG, leg. 2609, fols. 233r–234v (Medranda); AGI, Santa Fe, leg. 293, fol. 904r–v (García de Asarta).

44. AGI, IG, leg. 2609, fols. 251r (Trave) and 255v (Ximénez). Tesoro Island still bears that name in modern usage. I have not been able to identify the island that Spanish documents

called "Ziruelo" or "Ciruelo." It may be the modern island known as the Isla de la Rosa in the Islas del Rosario (Islas de Barú in eighteenth-century usage), but that is not clear.

45. Ibid., fol. 255v (Ximénez).

46. AGI, Santa Fe, leg. 293, fol. 870v (Medina).

47. AGI, IG, leg. 2609, fols. 233v–234r (Medranda).

48. Ibid.

49. AGI, Santa Fe, leg. 293, Don Miguel Agustín de Villanueva, Cartagena, to Don Bernardo Tinajero, 27 July 1708.

50. Ibid., fol. 870v (Medina).

51. AGI, IG, leg. 2609, fols. 137r–138r (Canis).

52. Ibid., fols. 256r–259v (Ximénez).

53. Burchett, *Complete History*, 705–6. Another official English source described the battle site as "between the Brew [presumably Isla de Barú] and Friends Islands [Islas de Barú]." PRO, *Calendar of State Papers, Colonial Series, America and West Indies, June 1708–1709*, 40. According to the same source, there were seventeen ships in the Spanish fleet. A detailed account of the battle appears in Segovia Salas, "Hundimiento del 'San José.'" Another account, well researched but fanciful, appears in Horner, *Treasure Galleons*, 167–77.

54. AGI, Santa Fe, leg. 293, fol. 904v.

55. PRO, ADM 51/4386, fols. 294v–295r, testimony of Caesar Brookes (hereafter Brookes).

56. In modern usage, the Islas de Barú are known as the Islas del Rosario.

57. Report from the *Kingston*, Thursday, 3 June 1708 (English calendar), BL, Addit. MSS 61643, fol. 146. I am grateful to John B. Hattendorf, Ernest J. King Professor of Maritime History and chairman of the Department of Maritime History, Naval War College, Newport, RI, for calling my attention to this source.

58. *London Gazette*, 2 August 1708, based on a dispatch from Jamaica dated 17 June (English calendar). Governor Handasyd, of Jamaica, used the same phrase for the location of the battle when he listed the Spanish ships involved. BL, Addit. MSS 61643, fol. 159.

59. AGI, IG, leg. 2609, fols. 256r–257r (Ximénez).

60. Ibid., fols. 138r–139r (Canis).

61. See, e.g., ibid., fol. 236v (Medranda).

62. The full testimony appears in AGI, IG, leg. 2610, fols. 999r–1073v.

63. Ibid., fol. 1061v.

64. Ibid., fol. 1062v.

65. Ibid., fols. 1062v–1063r.

66. AGI, Santa Fe, leg. 293, fols. 904v–905r.

67. PRO, ADM 52/161.

68. PRO, ADM 51/4294.

69. PRO, ADM 1/5267 (Thornton).

70. PRO, ADM 51/4386, fols. 294v–295r.

71. Burchett, *Complete History*, 706–8; Segovia Salas, "Hundimiento del 'San José,'" 22–23.

72. PRO, *Calendar of State Papers, Colonial Series, America and West Indies, June 1708–1709*, 39.

73. PRO, ADM 1/5267, testimony of Ralph Kelly, pilot on the *Kingston* (hereafter Kelly).

In the same set of documents, Lieutenant Thornton said that the *Kingston* "mett with some of the wreck of the Admiral's ship from off which took seven men before it was dark." The *Portland*'s master also noted the rescue in his log. ADM 52/257.

74. AGI, CD, leg. 578.

75. AGI, Santa Fe, leg. 293, fol. 905v.

76. AGI, IG, leg. 2609, fols. 256r–258r (Ximénez).

77. Ibid., fol. 139r–v (Canis).

78. AGI, Santa Fe, leg. 293, fols. 877a–882b, from Vega Florida's debriefing by Don Miguel Agustín de Villanueva in Cartagena several weeks later.

79. PRO, ADM 51/4386 (Brookes).

80. AGI, Santa Fe, leg. 293, fols. 877a–882b, from Vega Florida's debriefing by Villanueva.

81. The Cruisers and Convoys Act, of 31 March 1708, suspended private gain from prizes captured during the war, but the act's provisions evidently did not apply in the West Indies. See Owen, *War at Sea under Queen Anne*, app. F, pp. 284–85.

82. AGI, Santa Fe, leg. 293, fols. 874r–876v, Vega Florida to Don Bernardo Tinajero, 16 July 1708. Unless otherwise noted, Vega Florida's account of the battle comes from this document. A nearly identical letter to Tinajero, part of a packet compiled and dated 5 October 1709, appears in AGI, IG, leg. 2713.

83. AGI, IG, leg. 2609, fol. 227r–v (Zamudio). Zamudio seems to have misjudged the time and compressed the action somewhat, testifying that the *San José* vanished at seven, whereas most other witnesses said about half past seven, and some mentioned even later times.

84. PRO, ADM 51/4386, fol. 594v (Brookes).

85. AGI, Santa Fe, leg. 293, fol. 875.

86. AGI, IG, leg. 2609, fols. 234v–236r (Medranda).

87. Ibid., fol. 240v (Serrano).

88. AGI, Santa Fe, leg. 293, fol. 876, Vega Florida to Tinajero, 16 July 1708.

89. PRO, ADM 52/257 (Pearson).

90. PRO, ADM 52/161, log of Master John Taylor, of the *Expedition* (hereafter Taylor), for 29 May (English calendar).

91. Report dated Jamaica, 17 June 1708 (English calendar), in BL, Addit. MSS 61643, fol. 151.

92. PRO, ADM 52/161 (Taylor). The four ships seem to have been the patache, the small French frigate, the navío of Juan López de Dios, and—in the rear—Nieto's urca, which had followed them after the battle, mistaking the navío for the gobierno.

93. AGI, Santa Fe, leg. 293, fol. 880r–v, from Vega Florida's debriefing by Villanueva.

94. AGI, IG, leg. 2609, fols. 228r–v (Zamudio), 234v–237v (Medranda), 240v–241r (Serrano).

95. Ibid., fols. 236v–237r (Medranda).

96. Ibid., fols. 227v–228r (Zamudio).

97. AGI, Santa Fe, leg. 293, fols., 877a–882b, from Vega Florida's debriefing by Villanueva.

98. The following account of the urca's adventures comes from AGI, IG, leg. 2609, fols. 246v–249v (Canis), with supplementary information from fols. 258v–259r (Ximénez).

99. *London Gazette,* story dated Whitehall, 4 August 1708 (English calendar). The *Gazette* arguably received its information from the *Kingston*'s report that on June 1 (i.e., 12

June on the Spanish calendar) it had "chased one of their capitall galleons ashore on the Little Brew where the enemies burnt her." BL, Addit. MSS 61643, fol. 146.

100. PRO, ADM 52/202, log of Patrick Balnevis (hereafter Balnevis) for 2–13 June 1708 (English calendar).

101. See AGI, IG, leg. 2609, fol. 249r, for Canis's deposition. Don Pedro Punzentenas and Don Juan Bandale were the two noblemen who accompanied Captain Jorge to see the wreck.

102. AGI, Santa Fe, leg. 293, fols. 885v–886r, Villanueva to Tinajero, 22 July 1708, with a cover letter dated 27 July.

103. Ibid., fols. 886v–887r.

104. PRO, ADM 1/5267, testimony of Patrick Balnevis (hereafter Balnevis), punctuation and capitalization modernized for clarity.

105. PRO, ADM 1/5267 (Thornton).

106. PRO, ADM 52/257 (Pearson).

107. AGI, Santa Fe, leg. 293, fol. 887r.

108. Ibid., fol. 887r–v.

109. Ibid., fols. 887v–888r.

110. Ibid., fols. 888r–890r.

111. Ibid., fol. 905v.

112. Ibid.

113. Ibid., fol. 906r.

114. Ibid., fol. 906v.

115. Ibid., fol. 907r.

116. *London Gazette*, story dated Windsor, 2 August 1708, based on a dispatch from Jamaica dated 18 June (English calendar). The dispatch appears in BL, Addit. MSS 61643, fol. 151v.

117. AGI, CD, leg. 578.

Six • *After the Battle*

1. Postscript to *Flying Post*, no. 2088 (16 September 1708, English calendar), included in BL, Addit. MSS 61601, fol. 219.

2. Charnock, *Biographia navalis*, 2:444.

3. *London Gazette*, report dated Whitehall, 4 August 1708 (English calendar).

4. Burchett, *Complete History*, 707.

5. Bromley, *Corsairs and Navies*, 454 and notes.

6. *Calendar of State Papers Colonial Series, America and West Indies, June 1708–1709*, 38. Alsop, "British Intelligence," 115, notes that "authoritative news of Wager's 28 May 1708 victory over the Spanish fleet off Cartagena arrived at Whitehall on the following 16 September." The news had already been reported in the *London Gazette* for 2 August, however. All dates refer to the English calendar.

7. Report dated 18 June 1708 (English calendar), in BL, Addit. MSS 61643, fol. 151v.

8. PRO, ADM 52/161 (Taylor) and ADM 52/202 (Balnevis).

9. Charnock, *Biographia navalis*, 2:443.

10. PRO, ADM 51/4233 (Bridge).

11. Ibid.

12. PRO, ADM 1/5267 (Thornton).

13. PRO, ADM 1/5267 (Whitaker).

14. PRO, ADM 1/5267 (Kelly).

15. PRO, ADM 1/5267 (Balnevis).

16. PRO, ADM 1/5267, verdict of the court-martial of Captain Timothy Bridge, dated Port Royal, Jamaica, 22 July 1708.

17. PRO, ADM 51/4294 (Windsor).

18. PRO, ADM 1/5267 (Pearson).

19. PRO, ADM 1/5267, testimony of Ellis Brand, first lieutenant on the *Portland.*

20. Ibid., testimony of Emmanuel Rogers.

21. Ibid., sentence of Capt. Edward Windsor.

22. Thomas Handasyd, Jamaica, to the Earl of Sunderland, 2 August 1708 (English calendar), in BL, Addit. MSS 61643, fol. 160.

23. Charnock, *Biographia navalis,* 3:288–89.

24. PRO, ADM 1/5267 (Balnevis).

25. Baugh, "Sir Charles Wager." See also Charnock, *Biographia navalis,* 2:437–54, the source for most accounts of Wager's career.

26. Casa Alegre made the appointment in Cartagena de Indias on 6 June 1706, noting that López Molero would serve "without salary or ration, by virtue of royal ordinance." AGI, CD, leg. 579B.

27. Unless otherwise noted, discussion of Villanueva's report of 27 July 1708 comes from AGI, Santa Fe, leg. 293, fols. 892r–899v.

28. Burchett, *Complete History,* 707.

29. Ibid.

30. Thomas Handasyd to the Council of Trade and Plantations, Jamaica, 20 July (31 July) 1708, in PRO, *Calendar of State Papers, Colonial Series, America and West Indies, June 1708–1709,* 39.

31. *London Gazette,* report dated Windsor, 2 August 1708, based on a report from Jamaica dated 18 June (English calendar).

32. AGI, CT, leg. 3308.

33. AHN, Estado, leg. 2307.

34. Ibid.

35. *Relación de las prevenciones.*

36. AGI, ESC, leg. 1179B, contains Diego Fernández de Santillán's report on the New Spain Fleet.

37. AHN, Estado, leg. 2307, memorandum dated 16 August 1708.

38. Ibid., letters and memoranda dated May–November 1708.

39. Villanueva kept a detailed record of repairs to the *San Joaquín* and *Nuestra Señora del Carmen,* the principal dispatch vessel for the fleet. AGI, CD, leg. 583A, documents dated June and October 1708.

40. Bourne, *Queen Anne's Navy,* 170.

41. Charles Chaplin, Esq., Jamaica, letter of 17 June 1708 (English calendar), in BL, Addit. MSS 61643, fol. 152. Governor Handasyd reported to the Council of Trade and Plantations on

Wager's sickness as well but made no predictions about its effect on the fleet's strength. Ibid., fols. 149–50.

42. AGI, CT, leg. 2902B.

43. AHN, Estado, leg. 2307, official report dated 11 September 1708.

44. Ibid.

45. Ibid., memorandum dated 27 November 1708. On 1 December the memorandum was reviewed and signed by Joséph de Grimaldo, one of the king's principal advisers for foreign affairs.

46. AGI, IG, leg. 2611, fol. 752, Julio Xinés Pérez to Almirante Gobernador Villanueva, 27 July 1710.

47. AGI, Santa Fe, leg. 293, fols. 900a–901b.

48. AGI, IG, leg. 2711, fols. 752–55.

49. Ibid., leg. 2610, fol. 330r–v.

50. Letter and documents dated Jamaica, 21–22 November 1708 (English calendar), in BL, Addit. MSS 61585, fols. 65–68.

51. AGI, Lima, leg. 409, letter to the king, 15 July 1709.

52. "Instrucciones del Virrey del Peru, Marqués de Castelldosrrius para el cobro de los reales quintos de oro y plata, Lima, Oct. 17, 1708," manuscript in the Real Academia de la Historia, Madrid, Colección Mata Linares, 9-9-4, 1756. Unless otherwise noted, all discussion of the viceroy's new rules for paying the royal fifth come from this source.

53. AGI, Lima, leg. 409. The privateers were thought to have seven vessels, each armed with forty-four to sixty-four guns. See also AGI, IG, leg. 2610, fols. 651r–654v, for news of the vessels.

54. Pérez-Mallaína Bueno and Torres Ramírez, *Armada del Mar del Sur,* 317–18.

55. AGI, Lima, leg. 409, letter from Castelldosrius to the king, 20 January 1710.

56. Saénz-Rico Urbino, "Acusaciones contra el virrey del Perú," quotes at length from Castelldosrius's correspondence in the family archive in Barcelona, as well as from official documents. Lohmann Villena, "Cuadernillo de noticias," transcribes in full Castelldosrius's notebook about the charges against him and the men responsible for fabricating them. Unless otherwise noted, information about the charges and Castelldosrius's response to them comes from these two sources.

57. AGI, Lima, leg. 408, Castelldosrius to the king, 31 August 1708.

58. The cleric was general of the Bethlehemites, a new monastic order that ran the Santo Toribio Hospice for Incurables in Lima.

59. Saénz Rico Urbino, "Acusaciones contra el virrey del Perú," 124.

60. Handasyd to the Earl of Sunderland, 2 August 1708, in BL, Addit. MSS 61643, fol. 155.

61. AGI, CT, leg. 3308. See also, AGI, IG, leg. 2610, fol. 704, and AGI, Santa Fe, leg. 293, for documents mentioning the loss of the *San José.*

62. Saénz-Rico Urbino, "Acusaciones contra el virrey del Perú," 128.

63. AGI, Lima, leg. 482.

64. "Relación diaria de todo lo sucedido en Madrid, desde el dia 20 de Agosto hasta el 3 de diciembre de este año de 1710 en que S.M. entró en su Corte," Biblioteca Nacional, Madrid, MS 10.907.

65. See Martínez Shaw and Alfonso Mola, *Felipe V,* 69–78, for discussion of the war.

66. "Comercio ilícito en el Mar del Sur: Papeles del Archivo General de Indias," James Ford Bell Library, University of Minnesota, Minneapolis, Bell 1704 fAr, bk. 1, fols. 479v–480r. E. W. Dahlgren, the best-known historian of the illicit commerce in the Southern Sea, had two volumes of documents copied in longhand from the Archive of the Indies, in Seville, in 1914. These two volumes of documents are now at the Bell Library. The citation in use then was "Sevilla, Estante 153, Cajon 3, legajo 4"; the modern citation is AGI, IG, leg. 2720.

67. For Castelldosrius's cultural activities, see Lohmann Villena, "Tres catalanes;" Saénz-Rico Urbino, "Acusaciones contra el virrey del Perú," 126n17; and Revello de Torre, *Las veladas literarias*.

68. "Flor de academias que contiene las que se celebraron en el Real Palacio de esta Corte de Lima . . . ," Biblioteca Nacional, Madrid, MS 8722.

69. AGI, Lima, leg. 409, reports by the bishop of Quito, 19 September and 19 October 1711.

70. AGI, IG, leg. 432, L.46, fols. 191v–199v. The three royal decrees, addressed to Castelldosrius, were all dated 1 November 1711.

71. Many of these disputes are documented in ibid., legs. 2610 and 2611.

72. Ibid., leg. 2610 and leg. 2611, fols. 331–74.

73. Ibid., leg. 2611, fols. 700–802.

74. See, e.g., ibid., leg. 432, L.46, fols. 276v–279v, for Ducasse's authority in improving the defenses of Cartagena.

75. Ibid., leg. 2721, fols. 300r–301v.

76. Ibid., fols. 128–45.

77. Ibid., fols. 149r–150v.

78. Ibid., leg. 2719.

79. Ibid., leg. 2721, fol. 150r.

80. Ibid., fol. 150v.

81. Ibid., fols. 155–224, contains Quijano Ceballos's accounts for the *Grifón*.

82. Ibid., fols. 321–25, 342r–v.

83. AGI, IG, leg. 2721, contains much but by no means all of the documentation regarding Ducasse's 1711 squadron and the treasure it carried back to Spain. Much of it was written on official paper stamped for 1707, though the documents date from 1711 on—testimony to the irregular shipments of goods between Spain and Tierra Firme during the war.

84. Ibid., fol. 301r–v.

85. Ibid., fols. 374r–379v, 356r–363v. The full documentation continues on fols. 388–431.

86. AGI, CD, leg. 582.

87. AGI, IG, leg. 2721, fols. 391–93.

88. AGI, CD, leg. 582, fols. 625–67, contains the long version of López Molero's accounting of the income and expenses related to the king's treasure from 1708 to 1712. Fols. 1–7 provide a brief summary of the same accounts.

89. Ibid., fol. 651r–v.

90. Ibid., fols. 1–7, 625–67. The quotation comes from fol. 664.

91. AGI, IG, leg. 2721, fol. 648v.

92. Charles Wager to Josiah Burchett, 13 April 1708 (English calendar), in BL, Addit. MSS 61583, fol. 75a–b.

93. AGS, Dirección General del Tesoro, leg. 555.

94. AGI, CD, leg. 582, fols. 665–66. Income for the viceroyalty was about 1.5 million pesos per year; about 1700, expenses were running about 1.7 million pesos per year (see chapter 4).

95. AGS, Tribunal Mayor de Cuentas, leg. 1891.

96. AGI, CD, leg. 582, document dated Madrid, 5 March 1733.

97. AGI, Santa Fe, 293, fols. 892r–899v, Villanueva's report of 27 July 1708.

98. AGI, CT, leg. 2734. I am grateful to Eugene Lyon for directing my attention to this legajo. The full amount registered for the king in Portobelo was 1,551,609 pesos, 7 reals.

99. Dahlgren, *Relations commerciales,* 412–13.

100. AGI, ESC, leg. 546A. The full residencia of Monclova's administration fills four thick bundles, legs. 546A–B and 547A–B.

101. The inventory also included scientific instruments, more than five hundred books, many paintings, and four bundles of musical scores. Lohmann Villena, "Tres catalanes," 15. According to Louise Stein, a musicologist at the University of Michigan, many of the scores remained in Lima, and it is not clear how much, if any, of Castelldosrius's other collections were retained by the family. Personal conversation with Stein, April 2001, Santa Fe, NM.

102. Castan i Ranch, "Nobleza y poder," 271, gives all the figures for the viceroy's finances in libras, which I have assumed were Catalan libras, worth 10 silver reals (compared with the peso's value of 8 silver reals).

103. AGI, Lima, leg. 408, Castelldosrius to the king, 19 December 1707.

104. AGI, ESC, legs. 548A–B, 549A–C.

105. AGI, IG, leg. 2719. Unless otherwise noted, this is the source for discussion of the compensation claims related to the *San José*. The accounts for their wages are in AGI, CD, leg. 578, unless otherwise noted.

106. AGI, IG, leg. 2719, petition and accounts dated 17 May 1715.

Postscript

1. García Márquez, *Love in the Time of Cholera,* 18.

2. Schrieberg and Rodríguez, "Three Centuries of Greed."

3. "United States Policy for the Protection of Sunken Warships," press release by the Office of the Press Secretary, Washington, DC, 19 January 2001. John B. Hattendorf, Ernest J. King Professor of Maritime History and chairman of the Department of Maritime History at the Naval War College in Newport, RI, kindly provided the text of this press release.

Archival Sources

Archivo General de Indias, Seville
    Consulado
    Contaduría
    Contratación
    Escribanía
    Indiferente General
    Lima
    Panamá
    Santa Fe
Archivo General de Marina, Madrid (also known as the Museo Naval, Madrid)
Archive General de Simancas, Simancas (Valladolid)
    Dirección General del Tesoro
    Guerra Antigua (also known as Guerra y Marina)
    Tribunal Mayor de Cuentas
Archivo Histórico Nacional, Madrid
    Estado
    Ordenes Militares
Biblioteca Nacional, Madrid
Biblioteca del Palacio Real, Madrid
British Library, London
Huntington Library, San Marino, California
James Ford Bell Library, University of Minnesota, Minneapolis
John Carter Brown Library, Providence, Rhode Island
Public Record Office, London
    Admiralty
Real Academia de la Historia, Madrid

Printed Primary and Secondary Works

Alsedo y Herrera, Dionisio [1690–1777]. *Aviso histórico, político, geográphico, con las noticias mas particulares del Perú, Tierra Firme, Chile, y Nuevo Reyno de Granada.* Madrid, 1740.

———. *Memorial informativo... del consulado de la ciudad de los Reyes [Lima]... sobre diferentes puntos tocantes al estado de la real hacienda, comercio, etc.* no place, no date.

Alsop, J. D. "British Intelligence for the North Atlantic Theatre of the War of Spanish Succession." *Mariner's Mirror* 77 (May 1991): 113–18.

Antonio de Gaztañeta (1656–1728). San Sebastián: Museo Naval, 1992.

Antúnez y Acevedo, R. *Memorias históricas sobre la legislación y gobierno del comercio de los españoles en sus colonias en las Indias occidentales.* Madrid, 1797.

Artola, Miguel, ed. *Enciclopedia de historia de España.* 6 vols. Madrid: Alianza Editorial, 1991.

Atienza y Navajas, Julio de, barón de Cobos de Belchite. *Nobiliario español: Diccionario heráldico de apellidos españoles y de títulos nobiliarios.* 3rd ed., rev. Madrid: Aguilar, 1959.

Bakewell, Peter J., ed. *Mines of Silver and Gold in the Americas.* Brookfield, VT: Variorum, 1997.

Ballesteros Gaibrois, Manuel. Introduction to *Enseñat de villalonga: La vida de Cristoforo Colonne; una biografía documentada.* Valladolid: Casa Museo de Colón y Seminario Americanista de la Universidad, 1999.

Baugh, D. A. "Sir Charles Wager, 1666–1743." In *Precursors of Nelson: British Admirals of the Eighteenth Century,* edited by P. J. Le Fevre and Richard Harding, 100–126. London: Chatham, 2000.

Black, Charlene Villaseñor. "Love and Marriage in the Spanish Empire: Depictions of Holy Matrimony and Gender Discourses in the Seventeenth Century." *Sixteenth Century Journal* 32 (Fall 2001): 637–67.

Bourne, Ruth. *Queen Anne's Navy in the West Indies.* New Haven, CT: Yale University Press, 1939.

Brading, David, and Harry Cross. "Colonial Silver Mining: Mexico and Peru." *Hispanic American Historical Review* 52 (1972): 545–79.

Bromley, J. S. *Corsairs and Navies, 1660–1760.* London: Hambleton, 1987.

Buendia, José de, S.J. [1644–1727]. *Parentación real al soberano nombre e immortal memoria del Católico Rey de las Españas y Emperador de las Indias el sereníssimo señor don Carlos II: Funebre solemnidad y sumptuoso mausoleo....* Lima, 1701.

Burchett, Josiah. *A Complete History of the Most Remarkable Transactions at Sea, from the Earliest Accounts of Time to the Conclusion of the Last War with France.* London: J. Walthoe, 1720.

Burkholder, Mark A., and D. S. Chandler. *Biographical Dictionary of Audiencia Ministers in the Americas, 1687–1821.* Westport, CT: Greenwood, 1982.

———. *From Impotence to Authority: The Spanish Crown and the American Audiencias, 1687–1808.* Columbia: University of Missouri Press, 1977.

Callahan, William J. *Honor, Commerce, and Industry in Eighteenth-Century Spain.* Boston: Baker Library, Harvard Graduate School of Business Administration, 1972.

Castan i Ranch, Amelia. "Nobleza y poder en la Cataluña de la época moderna: Una aproximación biográfica al primer Marqués de Castelldosrius (1651–1710)." *Pedralbes: Revista d'Historia Moderna* (Barcelona) 13, no. 2 (1993): 263–72.

Céspedes del Castillo, Guillermo. *América Latina colonial hasta 1650.* México City: Secretaría de Educación Pública, 1976.

————. "La defensa militar del istmo de Panamá a fines del siglo XVII y comienzos del siglo XVIII." *Anuario de Estudios Americanos* 9 (1952): 235–75.

————. *Lima y Buenos Aires: Repercusiones económicas y políticas de la creación del Virreinato del Plata.* Madrid: Escuela de Estudios Hispano-Americanos de Sevilla, C.S.I.C., 1947.

Charles II of Spain. *Testamento de Carlos II.* Facsimile ed. Madrid: Editora Nacional, 1982.

Charnock, John [1756–1807]. *Biographia navalis, or, impartial memoirs of the lives and characters of officers of the navy of Great Britain, from the year 1660 to the present time: drawn from the most authentic sources, and disposed in a chronological arrangement.* 6 vols. London: printed for R. Faulder, 1794–98.

Cook, Noble David, ed. *Numeración general de todas las personas de ambos sexos, edades y calidades q[ue] se ha [h]echo en esta ciudad de Lima año de 1700.* Facsimile ed. Lima: COFIDE, 1985.

Dahlgren, E. W. *Les relations commerciales et maritimes entre la France et les côtes de l'Ocean Pacifique (commencement du XVIIIe siècle).* Vol. 1, *Le commerce de la Mer du Sud jusqu'à la Paix d'Utrecht.* Paris, 1909.

Dampier, William [1652–1715]. *A New Voyage Round the World: The Journal of an English Buccaneer.* 1657. Reprint, London: Hummingbird, 1998.

Dedieu, Jean-Pierre. "Procesos y redes: La historia de las instituciones administrativas de la época." In *La pluma, la mitra, y la espada: Estudios de historia institucional en la Edad Moderna,* by Juan Luis Castellano, Jean-Pierre Dedieu, and María Victoria López-Cordón. Madrid: Marcial Pons, Ediciones de Historia, S.A., 2000.

Descola, Jean. *Daily Life in Colonial Peru, 1710–1820.* Translated by Michael Heron. London: George Allen & Unwin, 1968.

"Diálogo entre un vizcaíno y un montañés." In *Disquisiciones náuticas,* edited by Cesáreo Fernández Duro, 6:191–92. 6 vols. Madrid: Sucesores de Rivadeneyra, 1876–81. A modern edition of the "Diálogo" with an excellent introduction by the editor, is *Diálogo entre un vizcaíno y un montañés sobre la fábrica de navíos,* edited by María Isabel Vicente Maroto, facsimile ed. Salamanca: Ediciones Universidad de Salamanca, 1998.

Dickinson, W. Calvin, and Eloise R. Hitchcock. *The War of the Spanish Succession, 1702–1713: A Selected Bibliography.* Westport, CT: Greenwood, 1996.

Domínguez Ortiz, Antonio. *The Golden Age of Spain, 1516–1659.* Translated by James Casey. New York: Basic Books, 1971.

Elenco de grandezas y títulos nobiliarios españoles. Madrid: Ediciones de la Revista Hidalguía, 1988.

Espinoza Soriano, Waldemar. *Virreinato peruano: Vida cotidiana, instituciones y cultura.* Lima: Biblioteca Nacional del Perú, 1997.

Fernández Navarrete, Martín, comp. *Colección de documentos y manuscritos compilados.* Edited by Julio Guillén Tato. 32 vols. Nendeln, Lichtenstein: Kraus-Thompson Organization, 1971.

Frey, Linda, and Marsha Frey, eds. *The Treaties of the War of the Spanish Succession: An Historical and Critical Dictionary.* Westport, CT: Greenwood, 1995.

Frézier, Amédée-François. *A Voyage to the South Sea and along the coasts of Chili and Peru in the years 1712, 1713, and 1714.* London, 1717.

García Carraffa, Alberto, and Arturo García Carraffa. *Diccionario heráldico y genealógico de apellidos españoles y americanos.* 88 vols. Madrid, 1920–68.

García Fuentes, Lutgardo. *El comercio español con América, 1650–1700.* Seville: Escuela de Estudios Hispano-Americanos, C.S.I.C., 1980.

García Márquez, Gabriel. *Love in the Time of Cholera.* Translated by Edith Grossman. New York: Knopf, 1988.

Garner, Richard L. "Long-Term Silver Mining Trends in Spanish America: A Comparative Analysis of Peru and Mexico." *American Historical Review* 93 (Oct. 1988): 898–935.

Gaztañeta, Antonio de [1656–1728]. *Arte de fabricar reales.* 1688. Facsimile edited by Francisco Fernández González, Cruz Apéstegui Cardenal, and Fernando Miguélez García. 2 vols. Barcelona: Lunwerg, 1992.

———. *Norte de la navegación hallado por el qvadrante de redivccion....* Seville: J. Francisco de Blas, 1692.

Hanke, Lewis, ed. *Los virreyes españoles en América durante el gobierno de la Casa de Austria. Peru.* Vol. 7. Biblioteca de autores españoles, vol. 286. Madrid: Ediciones Atlas, 1980.

Harding, R. H. *Amphibious Warfare in the Eighteenth Century: The British Expedition to the West Indies (1740–1742).* Woodbridge, Suffolk: Royal Historical Society, 1991.

Haring, C. H. *The Buccaneers in the West Indies in the XVII Century.* London: Methuen, 1910.

Hattendorf, John B. *England in the War of the Spanish Succession: A Study of the English View and Conduct of Grand Strategy, 1702–1712.* New York: Garland, 1987.

Horner, Dave. *The Treasure Galleons: Clues to Millions in Sunken Gold and Silver.* New York: Dodd, Mead, 1971.

Inventari dels fons: Marquesos de Castelldosrius, Castanyer, i "La España Industrial" de l'Arxiu Nacional de Catalunya. Edited by Josep Fernández i Trabal, Francesc Balada i Bosch, and Casimir Martí i Martí. Barcelona: Generalitat de Catalunya, Departament de Cultura, 1990.

Kamen, Henry. *The War of Succession in Spain, 1700–1715.* Bloomington: Indiana University Press, 1969.

Lane, Kris E. *Pillaging the Empire: Piracy in the Americas, 1500–1750.* Armonk, NY: M. E. Sharpe, 1998.

Lea, Henry Charles. *A History of the Inquisition of Spain.* 4 vols. New York: Macmillan, 1906–7.

Lohmann Villena, Guillermo. "El cuadernillo de noticias del virrey del Perú marqués de Castelldosrius (agosto 1708)." *Jahrbuch fur Geschichte von Staat, Wirtschaft und Gesellschaft Lateinamerikas* 1 (1964): 207–37.

———. *Historia marítima del Peru.* Vol. 4, *Siglos XVII y XVIII.* Lima: Editorial Ausonia, 1973.

———. "Tres catalanes, virreyes en el Perú." *Hidalguía,* 1962, 3–15.

Lorenzo Sanz, Eufemio. *Comercio de España con América en la época de Felipe II.* 2 vols. Valladolid: Diputación Provincial, 1980.

Manera Regueyra, Enrique. "La época de Felipe V y Fernando VI." In *El buque en la armada española*, by Enrique Manera Regueyra et al., 169–99. Madrid: Silex, 1981.

Martínez Shaw, Carlos, and Marina Alfonso Mola. *Felipe V.* Madrid: Arlanza Ediciones, 2001.

Moreyra y Paz Soldán, Manuel. *El tribunal del Consulado de Lima.* Vol. 1, *Cuaderno de Juntas, 1706–1720.* Lima: Instituto Histórico del Perú, 1956.

Norris, Gerald, ed. *The Buccaneer Explorer: William Dampier's Voyages.* London: Folio Society, 2005.

Owen, J. H. *War at Sea under Queen Anne, 1702–1708.* Cambridge: Cambridge University Press, 1938.

Palacios Preciado, Jorge. *La trata de negros por Cartagena de Indias.* Tunja: Universidad Pedagógica y Tecnológica de Colombia, 1973.

Pérez-Mallaína Bueno, Pablo E. *Política naval española en el Atlántico 1700–1715.* Seville: Escuela de Estudios Hispano-Americanos de Sevilla, C.S.I.C., 1982.

———. *Spain's Men of the Sea: The Daily Life of Crews on the Indies Fleets in the Sixteenth.* Translated by Carla Rahn Phillips. Baltimore: Johns Hopkins University Press, 1998. Originally published as *Los hombres del océano: Vida cotidiana de los tripulantes de las flotas de Indias, siglo XVI* (Seville: Servicio de Publicaciones de la Diputación de Sevilla, 1992).

Pérez-Mallaína Bueno, Pablo E., and Bibiano Torres Ramírez. *La Armada del Mar del Sur.* Seville: Escuela de Estudios Hispano-Americanos de Sevilla, C.S.I.C., 1987.

Phillips, Carla Rahn. "Galleons: Fast Sailing Ships of the Mediterranean and Atlantic, 1500–1650." In *Cogs, Caravels, and Galleons: The Sailing Ship, 1000–1650,* 98–114. London: Conway Maritime, 1994.

———. "The Galleon *San José,* Treasure Ship of the Spanish Indies." *Mariner's Mirror* 77 (Nov. 1991): 355–63.

———. *Six Galleons for the King of Spain: Imperial Defense in the Early Seventeenth Century.* Baltimore: Johns Hopkins University Press, 1986.

———. "Spanish Ship Measurements Reconsidered: The *Instrucción náutica* of Diego García de Palacio (1587)." *Mariner's Mirror* 87 (Aug. 1987): 293–96.

Pointis, Jean-Bernard-Louis Desjean, baron de [1645–1707]. *Monsieur de Pointi's Expedition to Cartagena; Being a Particular Relation. I. Of the Taking and Plundering of that City, by the French, in the Year 1697....* London, 1699. Originally published as *Relation de l'expedition de Carthagena* (Paris, 1697).

Relación de las prevenciones que el excellentíssimo señor marqués de Castell-Dos Rius mi señor virrey, governador, y capitán general de estos reynos, hizo para la defensa.... Lima, 1709. John Carter Brown Library, Providence, RI. Pamphlet sometimes attributed to Pedro de Peralta y Barnuevo.

Revello de Torre, José. *Las veladas literarias del virrey del Perú, Marqués de Castelldosrius (1709–1710).* Seville: Tip. Zarazuela, 1920.

Ritchie, Robert C. *Captain Kidd and the War against the Pirates.* Cambridge, MA: Harvard University Press, 1986.

Rubio Serrano, José Luis. *Arquitectura de las naos y galeones de las flotas de Indias.* Vol. 1, *1492–1590;* vol. 2, *1590–1690.* Málaga: Ediciones Seyer, 1991.

Saénz-Rico Urbino, Alfredo. "Las acusaciones contra el virrey del Perú marqués de Castelldosrius y sus noticias reservadas (febrero 1709)." *Boletín Americanista* (Barcelona) 20, no. 28 (1978): 119–35.

Saint-Simon, duc de. *Memoires du duc de Saint-Simon (1675–1755)*. Edited by Gonzague Truc. 7 vols. Paris: Editions Gallimard, 1956.

Scelle, G. *La traite negrière aux Indes de Castille*. 2 vols. Paris: L. Larose & L. Tenin, 1906.

Schrieberg, David, and Cecilia Rodríguez. "Three Centuries of Greed." *San José Mercury News, West Magazine*, 29 Jan. 1989.

Segovia Salas, Rodolfo. *Las fortificaciones de Cartagena de Indias: Estrategia e historia*. Bogotá: Carlos Valencia Editores, 1982.

———. "El hundimiento del 'San José' en junio de 1708." Inaugural lecture as a corresponding member of the Colombian Academy of History, Bogotá, 27 Nov. 1985.

Soulodre-La France, Renée. "Socially Not So Dead! Slave Identities in Bourbon Nueva Granada." *Colonial Latin American Review* 10 (June 2001): 87–103.

Suárez, Margarita. *Comercio y fraude en el Perú colonial: Las estrategias mercantiles de un banquero*. Lima: Instituto de Estudios Peruanos, 1995.

United Kingdom. Public Record Office. *Calendar of State Papers, Colonial Series, America and West Indies, June 1708–1709*. Edited by Cecil Headlam. 1922. Reprint, London: HMSO, 1964.

Vargas Ugarte, Rubén, S.J. *Historia general del Peru: Virreinato (1689–1776)*. Lima: Carlos Milla Batres, 1966.

Veitia Linage, Joseph de. *Norte de la contratación de las Indias Occidentales*. 2 vols. in 1. Seville: Juan Francisco de Blas, 1672.

Villalobos, R. S. *Comercio y contrabando en el Río de la Plata y Chile, 1700–1811*. Buenos Aires: Editorial Universitaria de Buenos Aires, 1965.

———. *El comercio y la crisis colonial: Un mito de la independencia*. Santiago: Universidad de Chile, 1968.

———. "Contrabando francés en el Pacífico, 1700–1724." *Revista de Historia de América* 51 (1961): 49–80.

Walker, Geoffrey J. *Spanish Politics and Imperial Trade, 1700–1789*. Bloomington: Indiana University Press, 1979.

White, Lorraine. "Los tercios en España: El combate." *Studia Histórica: Historia Moderna* (Universidad de Salamanca) 19 (1998): 141–67.

Zulawski, Ann. "Wages, Ore Sharing, and Peasant Agriculture: Labour in Oruro's Silver Mines, 1607–1720." *Hispanic American Historical Review* 67 (1987): 405–30.

Page numbers in italics denote tables.